About Island Press

Island Press, a nonprofit organization, publishes, markets, and distributes the most advanced thinking on the conservation of our natural resources—books about soil, land, water, forests, wildlife, and hazardous and toxic wastes. These books are practical tools used by public officials, business and industry leaders, natural resource managers, and concerned citizens working to solve both local and global resource problems.

Founded in 1978, Island Press reorganized in 1984 to meet the increasing demand for substantive books on all resource-related issues. Island Press publishes and distributes under its own imprint and offers these services to other nonprofit organizations.

Support for Island Press is provided by The Geraldine R. Dodge Foundation, The Energy Foundation, The Charles Engelhard Foundation, The Ford Foundation, Glen Eagles Foundation, The George Gund Foundation, William and Flora Hewlett Foundation, The John D. and Catherine T. MacArthur Foundation, The Andrew W. Mellon Foundation, The Joyce Mertz-Gilmore Foundation, The New-Land Foundation, The J. N. Pew, Jr., Charitable Trust, Alida Rockefeller, The Rockefeller Brothers Fund, The Rockefeller Foundation, The Tides Foundation, and individual donors.

About the Planning and Conservation League Foundation

The Planning and Conservation League Foundation works closely with the Planning and Conservation League to implement California's environmental policies and laws. Through research and public education, the foundation enables Californians to participate directly in protecting their environment. The foundation publishes handbooks for citizen action, assists decision makers in drafting effective policies, and produces action-oriented reports on statewide environmental needs. Foundation programs and publications help citizens manage the changes transforming California into the world's seventh-largest economy. The Planning and Conservation League Foundation gratefully acknowledges the support of the James Irvine Foundation in the preparation of this manuscript.

California's
Threatened
Environment

CALIFORNIA—SELECTED PLACE NAMES FROM *CALIFORNIA'S THREATENED ENVIRONMENT*

Redwood National Park

Humboldt Bay

Mount Shasta

Shasta Dam

Redding

COAST RANGE

SACRAMENTO VALLEY

Oroville Dam

Mendocino

Lake Tahoe

SIERRA NEVADA

Sacramento

Mount Diablo

San Francisco
San Mateo

Tracy

Mono Lake
Yosemite National Park

Friant Dam

Kings Canyon National Park

Santa Cruz

SAN JOAQUIN VALLEY

Monterey

Fresno

Mount Whitney

Sequoia National Park

Death Valley National Monument

COAST RANGE

Bakersfield

San Luis Obispo

Santa Barbara
Channel Islands

Mount Baldy

Los Angeles Long Beach

San Diego

Scale: ├──── 150 miles ────┤

California's Threatened Environment

RESTORING · THE DREAM

Edited by

TIM PALMER

Planning and Conservation League Foundation

ISLAND PRESS

Washington, D.C. ❑ *Covelo, California*

Graphics by Frank Espinoza and Janie McGuin, Drawing Board Studio, Sacramento, CA.

Grateful acknowledgment is made for permission to use Table 12-2, which appeared originally in Robert Cowles Letcher and Mary T. Sheil, "Source Separation and Citizen Recycling," in William D. Robinson, ed., *The Solid Waste Handbook* (New York: John Wiley and Sons, copyright © 1986). Reprinted by permission of John Wiley and Sons, Inc.

Library of Congress Cataloging-in-Publication Data

California's threatened environment: restoring the dream / edited by
Tim Palmer.
p.   cm.
Includes bibliographical references and index.
ISBN (cloth) 1-55963-173-2—ISBN (paper) 1-55963-172-4
(pbk.)
1. Pollution—California.   2. Land use—Environmental aspects—
California.   3. Ecology—California.   4. Environmental protection—
California.   I. Palmer, Tim.
TD181.C2C35   1993
333.7'16'09794—dc20   92-30944
                                                        CIP

Printed on recycled, acid-free paper

10   9   8   7   6   5   4   3   2

Contents

1. The Abundance and the Remains
   Tim Palmer   3

2. A Great Number of People
   Tim Palmer   19

3. The Atmosphere We Breathe
   Jane V. Hall   33

4. California Energy and Global Warming
   Chris Calwell   47

5. Transportation and the Environmental Costs of
   Auto Dependency   *Leif Erik Lange*   64

6. Water Supply: A New Era for a Scarce Resource
   Clyde Macdonald   80

7. The Quality of Water
   Alvin J. Greenberg   94

8. Troubled Shores: The Ocean, Bays, and Estuaries
   Barry Nelson   109

9. Land Use and Growth Management:
   The Transformation of Paradise   *Gary A. Patton*   127

10. Conserving the Land That Feeds Us
    Briggs Nisbet   139

11. The Forest: Fragmented Remnants of an Ecosystem
    Tim Palmer   154

12. Solid Waste: To Recycle or to Bury California
    William K. Shireman   170

13. Toxic Wastes: Proliferating Poisons
    Jody Sparks   182

14. Pesticides: In Our Food, Air, Water, Home,
    and Workplace   *Ralph Lightstone*   195

15. Parks and Recreation: Vital to a Way of Life
    Pete Dangermond   212

16. Wildlife and Endangered Species:
    In Precipitous Decline   *Sally W. Smith*   226

17. The Native California Landscape
    Tim Palmer   241

18. An Action Agenda for the Future
    Gerald H. Meral   258

Notes   271

Selected Environmental Organizations in California   291

Acknowledgments   295

Index   297

California's Threatened Environment

CHAPTER 1

The Abundance and the Remains

TIM PALMER

In Search of a Better View

The abundance of California's natural world and the life-giving qualities of its environment are why this land was settled and why many millions of people have come here. With the gold that was hauled away and the water that now runs short, the abundance has mostly disappeared, and the qualities that created California's reputation as a paradise on earth are stretched thin or reduced to wreckage. Yet the boom persists, and the dreams of fruitful fields, safe homes for our children, and strikingly beautiful landscapes persist as well, fed by the remains of a resounding spaciousness that our ancestors knew. It is this combination of what has been lost and what remains, of the threats and the dreams, that has led California to have the strongest environmental movement in America.

This book is about the strange juxtaposition of the environment,

---

Tim Palmer received a bachelor of science degree in landscape architecture and worked for eight years as a planner on a wide range of environmental and land use matters. He has been writing full time since 1980 and has had seven books published, including *The Sierra Nevada: A Mountain Journey; Endangered Rivers and the Conservation Movement*; and *The Snake River: Window to the West*.

the economic engine and the population explosion, the expectations of opposing forces, and the movement—intensely waged—to save the best of what is left of the original California and to make the state livable, desirable, and fulfilling for all its people.

The danger of learning a little about environmental problems is that the forces against a healthy California seem to be insensately overpowering. Our intent in this book is to push past the hopeless sense of loss that may come with an accurate appraisal of California's condition and to identify realistic possibilities for solving problems and retaining at least a semblance of the California that so many people know, remember, and love.

Beyond our own concerns, California is of interest—even if begrudgingly—to the rest of the country. One of the many clichés is its role as trendsetter. More important, the many-faceted front of environmental protection on these western shores articulates choices; we are a laboratory seething with experiments. We may have more problems than anyone else, but we have more people working on them, and those elsewhere can watch with interest and criticism—not necessarily with a willingness to follow but a willingness to learn.

The *1991–1992 Green Index* ranked California first among all states for its environmental policies but nineteenth for its environmental conditions. The state scored first for renewable energy but emerged abysmally in forty-ninth place for municipal solid waste generated and sustainable farming practices, and in forty-eighth place for violations of air quality standards.[1] Tragically, one of the lessons California provides best is what *not* to do. In this book, we will look at that and we will look beyond. We will see the imagination and the political savvy of those who seek a better California with the hope that others will go further and seek a better world.

It is certain that the coming years will bring unprecedented change, leaving environmental impoverishment in its wake. Some people subscribe to the theory that the future can be managed, controlled, designed, or manipulated to avoid environmental impacts, and while that may be partly true, ample evidence in the following chapters indicates that their hopeful view ignores history and current trends. To hope for improvement in the face of an extreme growth in the state's population—26 percent in ten years—might be credited to ignorance, denial, or deliberate conniving of vested interests. The environment cannot absorb 834,000 more people in 1990 and the population of another San Francisco *every year* and not feel the pain. The future has never looked worse for people dedicated to quality of life, broadly defined as health for all people and for the fundamental systems of life support—air, water, soil, and the whole community of creatures on earth.

Nine of the nation's twenty worst air quality regions are in California. The water quality of the Sacramento–San Joaquin Delta is threatened, though it is the source of domestic supply for 20 million people. More than 50,000 acres of farmland are lost to land development each year, and many more are ruined by nonsustainable irrigation practices. Every second, 1.5 tons of solid waste are generated. California uses 10 percent of all pesticides in the world, and doctors report nearly 3,000 cases of worker poisonings a year in the state. More than 1,200 species of animals and plants are of "special concern," many of them facing the threat of extinction. At the same time—and this is one of the centrally significant dynamics as California approaches its 150th year of statehood—the possibilities to act and institute change for environmental improvement may never be better.

One substantial problem with writing about 101,563,500 acres as intricate and varied as California is deciding where to stand for the finest view. To look at the environment of this 824-mile-long state is to look into a pulsating agglomeration of people—30 million of them—one of the more diverse collections of humans on earth. And, it is to look at a remarkable landscape, profoundly important not only in the context of the nation but of the world. To begin, four viewpoints may be helpful.

From Mount Baldy, overlooking the Los Angeles urban area, one can see out toward the sea—that wondrous gleaming edge of California defining both limits and extremes, attracting 80 percent of the state's population to a thirty-mile-wide belt of seismic real estate, running from Mexico to Oregon and fostering the most repeated cliché of the Golden State—the image of water, warmth, and a good, easy life. One can also see across the breadth and seaward slant of southern California's mountains to the human hive that constitutes the nation's second-largest urban region. This southernmost one-fifth of the state houses more than half its people. A mythic land of opportunity since early in the century, it remains so in spite of the worst air pollution in the nation, the sprawl of asphalt and suburbia that obliterated hills and farms, and

the dependence on thrombotic freeway arteries and on other regions' water, imported by destroying rivers and entire ecosystems
up to 600 miles away. To escape what is perceived by some to be a
California dream turned bad, people by the tens of thousands are
fleeing to the hills, the Central Valley, and the north; yet even more
tens of thousands are moving in from lands of lesser perceived
opportunity. As these newcomers have become a part of this state
and America, their needs and desires, their aspirations and disad-
vantages, must be addressed while the future of the land is addressed; they have come here and are now Californians. The social
experiment that is under way, not only in the valleys that fan out
beneath Mount Baldy but throughout the state, is one that will
frame the future and forge the fate of both society and ecosystem,
which, of course, become one in a broad and accurate perspective.

The view from Mount Whitney is quite different. The brilliant,
sublime grandeur of the 400-mile-long Sierra Nevada—one of the
truly great mountain ranges of the world—parades off in peaks,
canyons, forests, and glaciers. To the east lies the dramatic escarp-
ment, nearly a free fall to the Owens Valley, bathed in purple light
and streams of glittering snowmelt until diversions leave bone-dry
waterways. Beyond, the desert shimmers, an American Galapagos
of wildlife adaptation and a horizon-reaching playground to the
multimillions of southern California. Most of what can be seen from
Whitney is public land—part of the 49 percent of the state that
belongs to all the people, 45 percent of it to the taxpayers of the
whole nation. Both the Sierra and the desert remain vast and empty
by today's standards—healthy as modern ecosystems go, but that's
not saying much. Each is plagued by abuse.

Mount Diablo, rising over the Coast Range east of San Francisco,
offers a third view. From there one can observe the future unfolding
below. It is a curious mix. San Francisco Bay survives at a fraction of
its original size and quality, but like so much in life, it calls out and
draws people who never knew it when it was better. The larger Bay
Area, long a stronghold of enthusiasts of vibrant urban life, has
grown in many ways similar to the other three urban regions in the
United States—only three—that exceed its size. Growth does not
creep but gallops over ridges and up valleys and in all directions at
once. East of Diablo's looming summit rests the Central Valley,
kingpin of agricultural production in America, a new hot spot of
urban growth, fertile, flat, dusty, and sunny. Giant water projects

serving farms have converted the valley from a summertime grass-land and wintertime wetland where birds flocked and animals roamed as they do on Africa's Serengeti to an irrigated patchwork of cotton fields, rice paddies, vegetable rows, vineyards, orchards, and especially cattle forage. Beyond the heat waves that blur the urban growth, beyond the erosion, salinization, and poisoning of soil and water, and beyond the yellow sludge of atmosphere that is now human-made to the degree that it inhibits the growth of crops, the Sierra juts skyward in distant, celestial light, but is seldom seen from this distance anymore.

From the summit of Mount Shasta, once thought to be the highest mountain in the United States, the northland appears to be unlim-ited. The northern one-fifth of California is home to only 1.5 percent of its population. The Sierra and Central Valley fade off to the south, the Cascade peaks to the north. The rugged green washboards of the Klamath and Coast ranges recede like paper cutouts, one ridge beyond another, on and on to the west; in between are rivers burst-ing with life, and blanketing the mountains above the rivers are remnants of some of the world's greatest forests. A crowning glory of the Golden State, the redwoods of the North Coast are the tallest trees on earth and perhaps the finest example that, even in the north, the resources and qualities of California are not unlimited.

These are only four views of California; innumerable others have captured the imagination of America since 1849. Before and be-yond the fascination and vitality of the state's entertainment and defense industries, before its agribusiness empire and its cities, the natural environment attracted people's attention and made this land a magnet. Here in California lie more than 1,100 miles of coastline, 113 named mountain ranges, silent deserts, sodden for-ests, as well as our nation's largest agricultural industry and its most bustling tourist enterprise.

GRAPPLING WITH REALITY

California, the proverbial land of extremes, really is. Here are the oldest, the largest, and the tallest living things on earth. The Delta is the largest wetland on the West Coast. Lake Tahoe is America's largest mountain lake. The middle elevations of the Sierra were called the greatest conifer forest on earth by John Muir. Mount

Whitney is the highest point in forty-nine states, and Death Valley is the lowest in all fifty.

But the extremes and the extraordinary that exist today are only a token of what was, and much of the fraction that remains is under siege. The Central Valley wetlands were the finest on the Pacific Flyway for ducks and geese. The population of grizzly bears that foraged in places such as the San Francisco peninsula were probably more hale and hearty than any other group of the great bears. The population of American Indians was the densest, supported by the labor of gathering healthy food in an incomparably rich homeland. But little of that exists today.

Look, for example, at the official symbols of the state. The grizzly went extinct in the 1920s, before it was designated the official state animal. Logging has reduced old-growth stands of the state tree, the redwood, to 15 percent of their original range and much of that is unprotected and may be cut. The state bird, the California quail, does well but depends heavily on oak forests, which are in alarming decline with little regeneration of keystone species—the valley and blue oaks. The state fish, the golden trout, thrives in only a few streams in the southern Sierra, and the major one is now inundated by hordes of visitors served by an unnecessarily improved road to the backcountry. The state reptile, the endangered desert tortoise, is perhaps the best indicator species of the health of the desert and has declined in some areas by 80 percent in ten short years.

Splendor certainly remains and brings joy and wonder to Californians and visitors from all over the world, but in many places the splendor is only a remnant—effective as a tourist draw, which accounts for the state's largest industry, but woefully inadequate as an ecosystem to support the vibrant assemblage of life that was once California.

Many of the changes are obvious: urban hills are not only peppered with homes and carved with roads, but some are just plain gone, bulldozed into ravines to eliminate the double nuisance of hill and valley so that banal flats can accommodate shopping centers. But not all of the environment reflects a transformation as dramatic as asphalt, dams, and bombing ranges in the desert. Obscured from sight, a wholesale rearrangement of the ecology goes unnoticed but is all-important to this one-time Eden. The native grasses—virtually all of them—are gone because of cattle and exotic grass imports, and therefore gopher populations explode on the new exotic grasses. And, without predators to keep the gophers in check, many oak trees cannot grow past the seedling stage, and so, because of the cows, grasses, gophers, and lack of oaks, deer herds dwindle, mudslides are more plentiful without the latticework of oak roots, and groundwater is more scarce.

Lowlands, whose cultivated swirls or patchworks of crops may please the eye from the height of an airplane, once constituted the finest waterfowl habitat there was, and while one might see a duck now and then and conclude that California is a good place for them, waterfowl visit and live here in a tiny fraction of the numbers they used to.

Moving uphill to the conifer forests, stands of second growth sport healthy trees—sometimes—but grown in plantations like rows of soybeans wetted in herbicides, they cease to provide the diversity, sustenance, and shelter that are the very essence of a true forest.

Urban air lies in a haze that sometimes makes pretty sunsets, and people get acclimatized to the daytime dreariness; but ozone is killing pine trees in the Sierra, diminishing crops in the Central Valley, and leading to public health problems of epidemic proportions.

Rivers look clean and no longer smell like sewage, but most of the salmon are gone. In short, environmental quality has plummeted, sometimes in news-making of oil-spill scale but more often in incremental changes, unnoticed, such as the temperature of water in the proverbial frog pond that was warmed one degree each day so that the frogs, unaware, failed to jump out of the pond, then belatedly realized that they had waited too long and now *couldn't* jump.

It seems that the plunder of almost everything in California's natural world is up in the 80 percent or 90 percent bracket: Pacific Flyway wetlands, 96 percent gone; native grasslands, 99 percent gone; wilderness, 80 percent gone; riparian woodlands, 89 percent gone; salmon and steelhead, 90 percent to 100 percent gone; valley oaks, 98 percent gone; and all major rivers but one dammed at least once.[2] On the increase are people and cars. These kinds of statistics get tiresome but might be worth thinking about when one is confronted by the seductive, comfortable, and peace-making argument that we still need to compromise for environmental quality.

No one says that the development of California is not serving a purpose or that just about everybody here isn't enjoying at least some of the harvest of the economic machine. The state is home to more people than all the rest of the western United States, and its economy is larger than the economies of all but six nations. The needs and desires of its residents and the opportunities afforded them are real. But so much of what has happened to modern-day California seems to represent people's real needs gone berserk or, at least, gone shortsighted. Water that has been dammed and diverted goes to grow needed crops by family farmers, and that may well justify the subsidy and the trade-offs. But why can't we just leave it at that, instead of subsidizing waste and destruction? Is it wise public policy that huge quantities of water were developed with enormous taxpayer subsidies, destroying dozens of rivers and eco-systems, and that the subsidized water is used to grow crops such as cotton, which the government in many years pays farmers not to grow, and in the process produces toxic air and toxic drainage that causes new ducklings in national wildlife refuges to have such problems as one leg or no beak, and then, that the same water could flow on down to endanger the Delta, from which 20 million people drink, and could even threaten San Francisco Bay? We know all of this; yet this type of thing continues to go on. We are like arsonists striking matches to the environmental equivalent of our own homes of warmth and security, with only the vague realization that we will be living in the streets, as will our children and grand-children. How did we, as a society, get to this point?

Closer to home, perhaps, are myriad examples of freeways built at great public expense that tore out neighborhoods and led to more commuters, to further suburban sprawl, and thus to more cars and more freeways, with the resulting pollution that makes both Cali-fornians and the global climate sick. Flood-prone areas are devel-oped, displacing farms from the richest soil and exacerbating the need for expensive flood control levees or dams, which lend a sense of security and lead to more flood plain development, which, when a big enough storm comes, will be flooded anyway and require millions in disaster relief that common sense could have avoided. A lot of non-flood-prone land is available.

There is nothing particularly new about these observations. But if they're so familiar, why doesn't anything change? Why do we, as voters, as elected officials, and as a society continue to make short-sighted decisions regarding the environment? The California Envi-ronmental Quality Act states: "It is the policy of the state to . . .

ensure that the long-term protection of the environment shall be the guiding criterion in public decisions." With all respect to many organizations, individuals, and officials, we have made decisions for reform—a long list could be cited and would be more impressive than reforms made in any other state—but the list of continuing or worsening ailments is longer. The problems are growing faster than the solutions, and like the bucket-carrying brooms in *The Sorcerer's Apprentice*, they seem to multiply uncontrollably from the tools originally designed to make life easier.

SOCIAL EQUITY

Inherent in any discussion of the environment and the future is a raft of concerns regarding social equity. Does environmental protection limit the ability of disadvantaged people to improve their economic status? Does it conflict with human needs and with the ideal of opportunity for all? To the disenfranchised, the issue will not be the environment in its often-perceived though inaccurate sense of saving specimens of nature. The issue will be enfranchisement, including jobs, infrastructure improvements, basic services, and the health of the neighborhood and workplace.

But the poor suffer most from an inefficient and grossly polluting transportation system in which a person without a car can't hold down a job because of inadequate public transit. Polluted waters most afflict the people who live at the lower and urban ends of rivers or who depend on questionable supplies for drinking, rural or urban. The foulest pockets of air pollution and the dumping of toxic wastes take place in neighborhoods of people who are the least able to move away or gain control over their living places. Recreation and open space needs are felt severely in urban centers and among people who are not able to escape for a weekend at Mammoth, Monterey, or Mendocino. Farmworkers are emphatically on the front line of injury from improper pesticide use. The disadvantaged and the disenfranchised are the foremost victims of environmental abuse and may stand to gain the most by reform.

Beyond the public health and living space issues, some argue that endangered species, fish and wildlife, scenic rivers, and wilderness are elitist pursuits. Yet these are public resources, the enjoyment of them is often available for free, and they are more accessible to disadvantaged people than are many of the higher-touted fruits of our society—expensive cars or motorboats, for example. Additionally, "wild land" concerns have been eclipsed within the environmental movement itself by public health and global issues of life support, and furthermore, much environmental protection that may appear to deal with purely recreational or aesthetic pursuits is essential to other fundamental needs. Without sustained growth in forests, there will be fewer long-term jobs in rural logging communities, and housing costs will increase. Without watershed protection, water quality for cities and farms will be ruined and food costs will escalate. Without a rich and biologically diverse environment, entire ecosystems fall apart and lead to climatic changes, burdensome to all and threatening to life.

The three leading causes of death—heart disease, cancer, and stroke—are attributable at least in part to the environment of the victim. This relationship may be even more significant for people who have urgent problems with health care availability and insurance and who are unable to escape the toxins to which their neighborhoods are shackled.

Perhaps recognizing these linkages, the Latino districts of Los Angeles voted in 1990 in favor of the "Big Green" environmental measure, though it lost statewide. The Black Congressional Caucus in Washington, D.C., has one of the best environmental voting records.

One might argue that people's basic needs should be provided as a societal priority. Environmental goals need not conflict with this priority because it is often not the basic needs of food, shelter, health care, and education that cause the worst problems. While everyone must bear the burden of change from an exploitive and wasteful society to one that respects both the earth and human dignity, it is ironically the people who are the most able to change, to choose, to influence, and to reform who contribute most to the sapping of California's environmental wealth. Commuters who drive alone for dozens or even hundreds of miles a day dump carbon into the atmosphere at a far higher rate than people who ride buses because they don't own cars. Suburban housing that preempts the finest farmland is rarely bought by poor people.

The issue of subsidies falls in the midst of the social equity quandary. Taxpayer subsidies—nearly everyone's burden—permitted the damming of many rivers and the resulting extinction of various salmon runs; the building of freeways while ignoring public transit; the clear-cutting of national forests that often earns the government even less money than the government spends to sell the timber; and the grazing on public lands that returns less than it costs and, for a pittance of beef, destroys more wildlife habitat than any other single endeavor of humans in the West. These subsidies are paid by everybody who pays taxes, but too often the lion's share of benefits goes to an influential few who are adept at making their good fortune appear to be everyone's.

Looking to the future of California, the state's resources could be shared more equitably and the disenfranchised groups might partake more fully in the mainstream of society. But if everybody were to live the way the upper middle class now lives, environmental destruction would be exacerbated, much as if Third World countries were to consume as much energy per capita as Americans do—a scenario of global disaster far worse than even the current threat of global warming. It is inconceivable that our Third World neighbors or the underclass at home will take a dominant society seriously as it calls for environmental protection until it sees that particular society acting responsibly with the preponderance of wealth that it holds and controls. Rather than more people creating more consumption, waste, and pollution in pursuit of the materialistic American dream, people who have realized the goal of financial wealth could lower their standard of consumption—not to be confused with standard of living. For example, people who now drive to work could take improved public transit instead of everybody commuting in cars.

This short volume cannot adequately address social equity issues, except to suggest that such equity must be pursued and that people's impact on the environment may be one yardstick for measuring which changes are appropriate and which are not. Otherwise, the only social equity for anyone may be the ironic and tragic equity of environmental impoverishment for all.

This book explores what we must do to continue living in California and about what we might do for a land in which we not only survive and raise our children, but one that remains among the most beautiful, extraordinarily livable places on earth.

As Richard Reinhardt warned a decade ago, "We have no excuse for failing to recognize the probable results of today's decisions."

For the organization California Tomorrow, Reinhardt and others wrote *California 2000*, the closest thing the state has had to a plan for its future, given the absence of any identifiable document within state government. (An "Environmental Goals and Policy Report" is required by the state legislature every four years, but none has been produced since 1978, when the report consisted of an urban strategy.) California Tomorrow employed sophisticated research, public participation, and a consciousness that the future should be one of choice and quality, and produced a remarkable thesis of foresight in 1982. Few of its recommendations were embraced by state government, and even fewer were effectively put into action.

Influencing the future are population growth, diverse cultures, the marketplace, government actions, private investment of capital, research and technological development, education, and events such as earthquakes and droughts. This dynamic mix requires a better understanding of the physical environment and its problems. *California's Threatened Environment* strives to present basic facts, underlying causes, and proposals for the future.

From Mount Baldy to Mount Shasta, the view of California shows a land at once alluring and troubled. What is wrong with our care of the environment, and what have we done right? How much has been lost? Is there hope to correct chronic misuse? What is at stake if we do or if we don't? What can be saved? What can be recovered? What, really, are the chances of sustaining a California civilization that people desire? The questions are endless, and the authors of this book answer some of them in the seventeen chapters that follow.

We begin with a chapter on the driving force for environmental change—people. In 1990, 834,000 people were added to the state, and projections for the future are astonishing. The importance of this most neglected, yet most fundamental, environmental and social issue is undeniable when one considers the inevitability of the changes inherent in the most rapid population growth that California has ever known.

The next chapter is about air, few things being more basic than the atmosphere we breathe. No other area of the country suffers worse than California; 90 percent of its people live where pollution is a threat to health, compared to 40 percent for the nation. Energy production—which powers the engine of growth, economy, and lifestyle—is the primary cause of air pollution and is discussed in a chapter of its own. The chapter provides basic information and then focuses on perhaps the most massive environmental problem of the world—global warming—and how California contributes to it so catastrophically and how it can also lead the way toward solutions. Transportation, which consumes 41 percent of the state's energy, is discussed in the following chapter. There *are* alternatives to the main problem, which is the single-occupant automobile, and the transportation chapter focuses on them.

A chapter on water supply examines this vital substance and the politically charged matrix that determines who gets what. The myth of unlimited supply through more and more dams died an agonizing death during the past two decades. In its place must come a comparable commitment to efficiency, eminently possible because of purely physical and economic reasons, but also because the same engineers who brought us the world's largest plumbing system can turn their abundant talents to the economic and environmentally responsible use of that system. Assuming that water is wisely and equitably distributed, it is only as good as its quality, so the next chapter addresses such topics as the naivete of turning on the tap and expecting this life-giving substance to be clean. A chapter on California's coastal waters and the health of our oceans, bays, and estuaries follows, with an incisive survey of the thin, maritime edge that defines so much about the state.

A chapter on land use examines what is perhaps the most encompassing of issues affecting everything else, yet an issue essentially outside any public process that assesses the welfare of the state as a whole. Agriculture, a major aspect of land use, causes some of the thorniest environmental problems, and this vital industry must be a part of the environmental restoration of the state. The chapter on farmland clearly demonstrates that healthy agriculture and a healthy landscape are one and the same, that farming and environmental protection should be working partners in striving for a better California, and that maintaining and restoring good farmland for production of needed crops is high on the environmental agenda. Our forests, in myth, lore, and reality, symbolize our stewardship of the earth and are discussed in the next chapter. Whether we respect the forest as a community of life and take from it in a sustainable way, or treat it as another cash crop for short-term gain, says much about our regard for California and especially its public lands.

We cut forests and mine land at one end of the cycle of resource use, and at the other end we dump trash. Out of our forests, soils, and minerals we make solid waste, two tons per year per person. Just as the lack of new freeways could lead to mass transit, the lack of new landfills has led to recycling, one of the more hopeful areas of environmental reform. The next two chapters delve into toxic wastes and pesticides, which derive from economic purposes but result in one of the darker practices of humans on earth. Only one-tenth of Californian and U.S. hazardous wastes are disposed of without adverse effects on the environment. Far more insidious than many people think, this carcinogenic legacy constitutes a time bomb ticking in the midst of peaceful California communities.

The final set of chapters embraces the essence of the original conservation movement in America. Parks, recreation, and open space are inalienable from the notion of quality of life in the Golden State. Wildlife—including animals, fish, and plants—is perhaps the oldest environmental concern, and a mountain lion or dolphin holds the power to sway people when the most hideous scenario of toxic waste does not. Endangered species and the loss of natural diversity pose what many scientists regard as the foremost environmental problems of the next century, and California is called the epicenter of extinction in America. As Raymond Dasmann wrote in *The Destruction of California*, "If we create in California a world with no space left for wild animals, it will prove to be a world with little space for human freedom." Chapter 17 then views the native California landscape to see what remains of the allure and magic that our ancestors once found, and three features of imminent importance—deserts, oak woodlands, and rivers—are investigated. The final chapter offers a report on the political agenda that is essential if California, as we know it, is to survive.

All things being connected, the eighteen chapters cross paths frequently. If air pollution interests you, make sure you read the chapters on energy and transportation as well as the chapter on air quality. For water quality issues, see that chapter and the chapters on toxic wastes, pesticides, water supply, and coastal waters. For discussions of the natural environment, see the chapters concerning parks, land use, forests, and the native landscape.

We limited the book to coverage of classic environmental issues. It would have been interesting to add chapters on the growing proportion of minorities in the state and what environmental protection means specifically to them, on the economy and the environment, and on employment for a sustainable future. But space was limited if the book was to be economical, and our decision was to first produce a primer on the basics.

All of the book's authors are accomplished in their fields and bring a wealth of experience and insight to their chapters. The authors, who are private consultants, public interest specialists, academics, and government employees, used level-headed analysis and a calm perspective on the facts as they wrote these chapters. Their mission was primarily to describe California's condition to provide people with a basic understanding. Most chapters also offer some analysis, projections, and possibilities for reform. The final chapter includes a strong orientation toward the future.

To our knowledge, no one else in recent years has published a book that overviews the environment of California or of any other state. (Raymond Dasmann's *The Destruction of California*, written in 1966 and one of the finer books on California, offers an excellent historical perspective on the environment.) At the national level, the Council on Environmental Quality once prepared annual reports on the nationwide environment, but these were discontinued by the Reagan administration.

The summits of Mount Baldy, Whitney, and Diablo are revealing places from which to view California, and it is our hope that this book will provide another. Perhaps a mobilized society can sustain the dream of this land as a luxuriously livable home, not only in material wealth but in native qualities of air, water, and land. We should at least be aware of what is at stake, because the world will never know such a place again.

Looking out again across California from the snowy slopes of Mount Shasta, the harmony of the place is inspiring; yet, far from the smoking cities and crop-dusted farmlands, the verdant land stretching to distant horizons lies beneath a pall of yellow haze. The sickening air is not just a shroud over Los Angeles or Sacramento; it blankets the state and even beyond.

One needs no past affiliation with environmentalism to look across that sublime landscape submerged in yellow air and weep at the loss or shout in outrage that we could let this happen to such an enormous and magnificent place. That is an emotional response, but simply take the analytical response of the authors who wrote the chapters that follow and learn what is happening to the Golden State. Let this information be a warning and a call to all Californians that the innocence, ignorance, greed, and apathy that are allowing this beautiful, livable, beloved place to be needlessly ruined have got to stop.

CHAPTER 2

A Great Number of People

TIM PALMER

A RAPIDLY GROWING STATE

California, a fast-growing state for 150 years, is growing faster than it ever has in history. At two and a half times the national average, the growth rate here exceeds the long-term rate of any other industrialized region in the world. The 1980 population of 24 million grew to 30 million in 1990—a ten-year increase of 6 million, nearly the total state population in 1940. California's ten-year growth was greater than the population of each of forty-two separate states. In only ten years, there are one-fourth again as many people in what might be thought of as the island of California.

While the growth rate on a percentage basis has historically been high, the absolute numbers of new people now constitute a phenomenon. In one year—1990—the state grew by 834,000 people. The ten-year average growth was 619,000 per year, like adding a city of 52,000 each month.

The 1990 population was 57 percent white (it was 67 percent in 1980), 26 percent Latino, 9 percent Asian and Pacific islander, and 7 percent African American. People of color account for 43 percent of this ethnically rich population. The Asian population has more than doubled in the last ten years. The Latino population increased by 70 percent, which represents half of the state's total gain. These figures exclude undocumented workers and residents, whose numbers are unknown but estimated by the state at 1 million to 2 million.

Within the next ten to fifteen years, the combined minorities will become a majority.[1] By 2030, Latinos and whites may be equal in numbers, the balance swinging with great momentum toward the Latinos.[2]

The 1980 to 1990 rise in population through natural increase (births) accounts for 45 percent of the growth; migration from other countries, 37 percent; and migration from other states, 18 percent.[3] Some of the 18 percent, however, represents secondary settling of immigrants, mostly Southeast Asian refugees who enter America in another state and then move to California. In 1989, for example, 16,000 Southeast Asian refugees came from their countries of origin and 13,000 came from other states.

California's birth rate ranks among the three highest in the nation. The 620,000 births in 1990 broke the previous record by 51,000.

The significant population growth is no longer a result of people in other states moving to California. While 645,000 people moved in from other states in one year, 520,000 moved out, and the state's demographic research unit expected that out-migration to other states may *exceed* their in-migration after the year 2000. Then, more people living in California will see fit to abandon their state than other Americans will see fit to come.[4] That may mark the official end of a 150-year era of the Golden State as an alluring destination to the rest of the nation.

From a national perspective, California houses 12 percent of the people and holds fifty-two congressional seats—the largest delegation. The next-largest state, New York, has 10 million fewer people. One-quarter of the nation's growth was in California in the 1980s. It is one of the more urban states; 91 percent of its people live in cities.

Six of the state's ten fastest-growing counties on a percentage basis are in the Sierra Nevada foothills, much of their growth composed of white middle class and retired residents from the urban areas. Nevada County, for example, grew by 52 percent in ten years in that formerly picturesque, conifer landscape. Riverside and San Bernardino counties were high on the growth rate list and high in absolute numbers. Central Valley cities, southern California counties, and the San Francisco Bay Area were also high. Los Angeles

County added 156,000 new residents in 1990 alone, nearly enough to fill Bakersfield. (See Figures 2.1 and 2.2.)

THE EFFECTS OF UNLIMITED GROWTH

A population of 36 million is projected for the year 2000, growing to 39 million by 2005, or roughly a 6 million increase per decade.[5] In absolute numbers, this continues the 1980s level of runaway growth. The official state projections incorporate the conservative notion that the *rate* of growth will decrease to yield a steady growth of 6 million per decade in spite of the fact that the growth curve turned sharply upward in the late 1980s. Actual growth has leap-frogged ahead of past expectations; in 1983 the projected population for the year 2000 was 31 million, considered alarming, but the state reached that number in about half the expected time.

FIGURE 2.1
CALIFORNIA'S POPULATION 1900–1990
DEPARTMENT OF FINANCE PROJECTION TO 2005

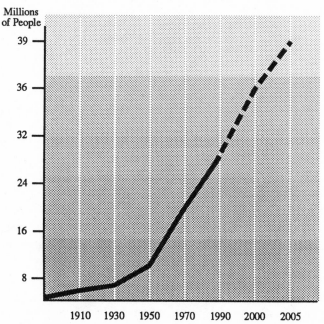

SOURCE: Department of Finance.

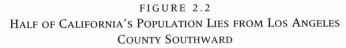

FIGURE 2.2
HALF OF CALIFORNIA'S POPULATION LIES FROM LOS ANGELES
COUNTY SOUTHWARD

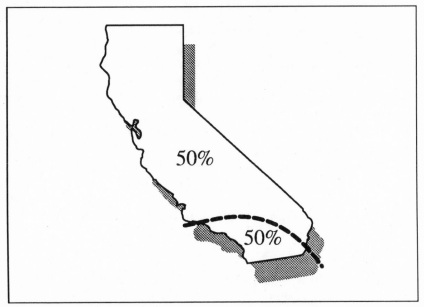

At the current growth rate of 26 percent per decade, California's population in 2020 would top 60 million—double the 1990 amount (see Figure 2.3).

The Sacramento area, long prized for its smaller-town atmosphere and livability, is expected to have the highest growth rate of any major urban area in the state and nation. Already experiencing a 34 percent boom in the 1980s, the area is expected to double in population between 1980 and 2000. In the 1990s, the San Diego area is expected to increase by 24 percent, the Los Angeles basin by 19 percent, and the San Francisco Bay Area by 17 percent.

The booming statewide population growth is due to higher birth rates, federal laws that permit substantially greater immigration than they did in previous years, and persistent economic strength, which, in the past, has scarcely been disrupted by minor and temporary slowdowns, though their effect on the poor and underemployed can be great.

The number of new illegal residents per year is estimated to be at least 100,000. About half a million people are apprehended and turned back at the border each year.

FIGURE 2.3
CALIFORNIA'S POPULATION GROWTH IF THE 26 PERCENT GAIN OF
1980–1990 WERE TO CONTINUE

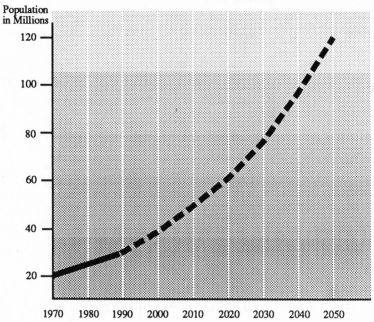

The effects of all this growth are extreme. Putting aside, for a moment, the environmental effects that much of this book documents, consider education. One of California's most insurmountable problems will be the 2 million additional students in its public school system, already straining because this big, seemingly prosperous state has one of the poorest-funded and lowest-scoring elementary and secondary school systems in the nation. The effects of massive population increase putting crowds of new students into schools while education capability is pathetically reduced will affect everything from prenatal health to aging to jobs and to crime, and could irrevocably set California into a sociological tailspin accompanied by the whole range of crowding and undereducation ailments. In other words, the future looks grim. People coming to California may realize they have their old problems *plus* a lack of education in an education-dependent society.

As new residents move into the older parts of cities, many long-time residents of those neighborhoods move out, making room for the newcomers and creating aggravated sprawl in distant suburbs, with resulting commuter gridlock and with fiscal crises in the older cities, which are drained of their tax bases and overcome with social-service needs. And from East Los Angeles to San Rafael, from Redding to Bakersfield, crime has increased as population has increased.

Demographers expect the population to grow much faster than available jobs. Workers face increasingly heavy competition as ample numbers of newcomers fill jobs.[6] The welfare system will be strained as much or more than the education system, and—in addition to becoming a political football—will be even more expensive.

Evidence mounts that seam-busting growth threatens economic prosperity in the short and long term. During the 1990 growth surge, only 17 percent of California households could afford to buy a median-price home. With unprecedented population growth, unemployment in early 1991 was 7.1 percent, higher than the national average, while the state budget deficit was at a panic level of $14 billion, causing per capita cuts in education that virtually guarantee a downward spiral. Affordable housing, public facilities, and social infrastructure all face crises directly attributable to the numbers of people to be served.

While the people who build in the suburbs, sprinkle their lawns until they flood the sidewalk, and commute many miles alone in their cars no doubt contribute more to the environmental ills of California than new immigrants who might settle in the crowded urban centers (see chapter 1), a transformation of the state and a precipitous environmental decline are also functions of so many people simply being here. Basic supplies of water, food, shelter, living space, and energy are needed by all. The environmentally costly flight of long-time residents to suburbs, distant cities, and rural areas is precipitated by increasingly crowded conditions elsewhere and by a desire to avoid changes in the older neighborhoods. And, in time, new residents who enter California society at the lower end of the economic scale fortunately move up that scale; in the process, their effects on the environment more closely match the poor example set by the dominant, white, consumptive culture.

Many problems are growing even faster than the population. The San Diego Association of Governments projected that auto traffic will double by 2005, and it is bad already. The number of miles driven in the South Coast air basin is expected to increase by two times that of the population—by over 60 percent by 2010. The San Francisco Bay Area population in the 1980s grew 1.2 percent per year while vehicle miles grew 4.2 percent, a driving frenzy typical of other urban areas, with no end in sight. The proliferating number of cars undercuts efforts to make them cleaner, and air quality will again worsen, undoing the hard-earned gains of the 1980s, which many people scarcely noticed anyway. By 2009, Californians are expected to use 30 percent more energy and produce 50 percent higher carbon dioxide emissions than they did in 1990. Urban congestion is compounded 15 percent per year, and by 2000, at the current rate of congestion, Los Angeles freeway drivers will average seventeen miles per hour,[7] a sprightly pace on a bicycle.

Fields of expensive new homes and condominiums and seemingly endless miles of commercial strip development convert farmland—and usually the finest soils—at up to 150,000 acres per decade, undercutting a key element in the economy and an important way of life, not to mention our source of food. If it isn't farmland that new development is consuming, it's wildlife habitat. Every year, new development eliminates 20,000 acres of oak woodlands—the third most valuable type of habitat. Wetlands and riparian zones are the only habitats more valuable, already reduced to token vestiges because of the urban, agricultural, and water supply systems that are fundamentally a cause and result of California's population growth.

Urban water use is expected to increase by more than 30 percent in twenty years; rationing—so hotly contested in the drought of 1991—will likely become a commonplace result of new growth.[8] The growing population's demands for water will result in more pressure to preempt more flows from farmlands, build more dams that destroy the scarce heritage of wild rivers that remain, and divert yet more water from rivers and the Delta at draconian environmental cost. Energy demands, after stabilizing through an era of conservation, will climb again, and while many needs can be met through renewable sources, the population growth of the state will impose endless pressures to continue or increase output from environmentally destructive oil, nuclear, and hydropower facilities.

None of this acknowledges the impacts of California growth on Colorado, where water is taken; on Idaho, Oregon, Washington, and British Columbia, where energy is taken from dams that exterminate landscapes and species and is used to justify destruction of the continent's ecosystems as far north as the Peace River; on Utah and Arizona, where coal is mined and burned while polluting half of the American Southwest; on Alaska and other areas where oil is drilled, piped, and shipped with consequences as great as the *Exxon Valdez*; and on all places to which our air pollution and toxic wastes overflow and go, including the Grand Canyon, where persistent smog is now blamed on the Los Angeles basin, more than 240 miles away. Then there is the overflow of Californians themselves. It is an understatement to say that people in Oregon and Washington are concerned about the effects of so many emigrating Californians—84,000 of them to those two states in 1990—who seek new communities that are not yet overcrowded.

If overpopulation is defined as exceeding the carrying capacity of the land by depleting resources at a nonsustainable rate and incapacitating the life systems that guarantee ecological balance and the supply of resources for the future, then California is surely overpopulated.

Some people who are knowledgeable about various aspects of California and its environment are hopeful that existing problems can be solved if we exercise unprecedented commitment, imagination, hard work, and money. But the existing problems are not the future problems. It is very difficult to find a nonvested expert in any environmental, educational, or social-service field who will call the needs of his or her specialty anything but hopeless given the current rate of growth.

Choosing a Future or Losing It

What will we see when we look across the California that grows by more than 2,000 people per day? Will it be devoid of the oak grove, the cool splashing river, the shaded pine forest, the golden hills? Indeed, with ozone, toxins, and acid fog, will California even be livable in a healthful sense?

With the current population explosion, one can talk about managed growth or quality growth, but the undeniable fact is that with the stress of so many more people, development will continue to sprawl like flood waters from broken dams out through the valleys to lap onto the slopes of the hills, farther and farther. Even the most idealized growth, which is about as likely as worldwide disarmament, will bring new demands on water, land, air, energy, transportation, wildness, and the whole inheritance of the natural environment.

In the early years of conservation and planning, perhaps before 1970, it seemed that people had a chance to mold a future of their choosing. A quality existence—maybe even better than the one we already had—seemed possible. But as Wendell Berry wrote, a profound change in the modern world is that the opportunity for a truly positive future may have passed us by. Now that Los Angeles suffers the poorest air in the nation, the big question is how do we prevent the San Joaquin Valley from becoming even worse? People fought for parks and wilderness, and a few were designated, but now we face the threats of global warming and acid rain, which could insidiously destroy our sequoia trees from afar. Even "simple" things—for example, to quit driving so much—seem difficult in the face of modern forces and of people's degree of willingness to change. In so many ways we have lost the choices of what we *want* to do and are backed into a corner: What *must* we do?

The success of environmental reforms in recent years shows that people *can* influence the outcome in this balancing act of using the state to ruin versus creating a sustainable future—the opportunity not just to survive but to live well. The legislature passed the California Environmental Quality Act. The coastal initiative ordered protection of the Pacific shore. Other initiatives—requiring votes of the people because the legislature and governor at the time refused to take action—imposed controls on pesticides and toxic wastes, made money available for public transit, and enabled communities to acquire open space.

Numerous reforms are noteworthy, helpful, save people's lives and money, and preserve a lot of habitat. But in the face of a population that would double in the next thirty years at the 1980s rate, the proudest accomplishments of the environmental movement may well be like rearranging the deck chairs on the Titanic.

If the current growth rate persists, California would hold 302 million people 100 years from now, more than currently reside in the nation. That rate, which would bind us to the crowded destiny of Japan, may change, but with no public policy on population growth, there's no telling what the change will be. With history as a guide and the finest futuristic thinking at our disposal, demographers conclude that breakneck growth will continue. We routinely speak of managing forests on a 100-year cycle. But as of July 1991, the longest-range projection the state has made of population—not involving management of any remote sort—was for fifteen years in the future.

The population question is often tangled with the question of providing for existing people in a socially equitable way. Our laws and government programs reflect a responsibility—at least in theory—for opportunities and fundamental goods and services being available to all. But here is a separate question: How many *additional* people is the society responsible for accommodating?

One organization working explicitly on the state population issue is Californians for Population Stabilization, which sponsors discussions with civic and organizational leaders, seeks to reduce immigration to a somewhat lower level, and promotes education on the benefits of a two-child family. Assuming limited success from this dedicated organization with a staff of three, the growth rate may not decline until the economy declines in a scenario of regional depression: businesses become unwilling to cope with congestion, poor air, expensive water, and high housing prices, and they leave the state. Rising social costs make it impossible for government to correct the root causes of economic decline, and the cycle continues.

The grimmest realization is that economic limits will impose other, related limits, already apparent in an early stage. Widespread poverty, failing health care and education, deteriorating public services and facilities, and public health epidemics grow in low-income areas and elsewhere. For a while, the upper class will fence and gate and insulate itself, but in a whirlpool of lowering expectations, most identifiable qualities of the state will be lost. The question is: Should population growth be limited now to save some of what remains, or should it be limited later, after little of value is left? Yet population is not even talked about in state policy discussions. Officials act as though growth-induced problems will fix themselves, but are awakening every day to find something else broken.

In the environmental movement of 1970 it was a common saying that "Whatever the issue, the issue is population." Interest in that universal subject was buried in the 1980s, intimidated by both the opinion that more people means more business and by the view that immigration should be opened and all people—not just American citizens—should be given the opportunity to reap the fruits of this generous land. But nations less developed and less educated than the state of California are addressing their population problems. In fact, most nations are. The government of Indonesia, for example, can see something that California cannot and has a "Small, Happy, Prosperous Family Program."

Most California officials who speak on the subject at all say that to influence population growth, even in the least authoritarian ways, is not an appropriate role of government. This argument has survived a deteriorating California and is retained even with projections of enormous growth while public facilities and services are faltering under present demands that often seem hopeless without even considering the far greater demands to come.

For no apparent reason, except perhaps to avoid the question, extreme population growth is seen by some as an all-or-nothing issue. At a July 31, 1991, hearing, Governor Pete Wilson stated, "Trying to simply deny growth—trying to haul up the ladder—has never really worked." At a Planning and Conservation League conference in 1991, Resources Secretary Douglas Wheeler recognized an annual population increase two times the size of Fresno or Sacramento and said, "There's not a lot we can do about that." As if there were a drawbridge, or as if anyone were even talking about one, Richard Sybert, director of the State Office of Planning and Research, said, "There's not a lot of sympathy in this administration for pulling up the drawbridge." These men are considered progressive relative to their predecessors. They sought answers on "growth management" while several bills under the same name called for regional planning and incentives to build new community infrastructure.

History clearly indicates that approaches toward "managed" growth have failed to stem the tide of environmental destruction statewide and have not alleviated long-term problems. Growth management in the political lexicon means to efficiently urbanize. But to make sure that the subdivider paves his streets and that water is waiting before the new condos go up is not so much growth management as real estate management. Even in the more progressive scenarios, new problems spring up in the same soil or pop out elsewhere. While per capita pollution, for example, may be less today from cars or sewage plants, the numbers of people and cars are so much greater that they outstrip the gains.

Do Californians want the kind of world we appear either committed or resigned to building? Will California be a better place with 60 million people in it? Why doesn't the state leadership address these questions? Working on the issue for twenty years, Judith Kunofsky pointed to three myths as reasons why population is not even discussed much: the false beliefs that the effects of slowing growth would be so harmful that the subject does not merit being raised, that extreme amounts of growth are inevitable, and that the means of slowing growth are too onerous. Fear of being the only person speaking out is yet another problem, not mythic but real.[9]

If 302 million people in the year 2092 is undesirable, or if a doubling of the population by 2020 does not lead to the California of choice, then when is the time to address the issue? When will it be any easier than now?

Because of California's dismal financial condition, with record state government deficits, the taboo of discussing immigration—though not population per se—was broken by Governor Pete Wilson in 1991. Citing the budget strains of a younger, less affluent population, the governor recounted that since 1985 a population increase of 18 percent was accompanied by a 23 percent increase in school enrollments, 31.5 percent increase in welfare, and 49 percent increase in Medi-Cal needs. Limiting concerns essentially to an influx of welfare recipients, he said in a November 18th *Time* interview, "We will have to minimize the magnetic effect of the generosity of this state."

The pervasive faith that people can solve the dilemmas of rapid growth needs to be tested by full knowledge of what in fact is happening to California. Perhaps it is time to map out a new vision of growth, one that recognizes quality as well as quantity, one that introduces a new era of sustainable resource use and growth based on meaningful labor rather than energy and resource consumption, one that recognizes that the growth of any healthy organism has limits, and one that restores values—many with sound social and economic worth—that have been lost.

Few people would argue that concerns of human rights and suffering, family reunification, equity, political asylum, and the simple desire of all people to live the best life possible should be ignored. People do argue, however, that all concerns should be weighed in an excruciating process against the reality of what is happening to California.

There is considerable interest in restraining the rate of growth. A *Time* poll (November 18, 1991) found that 66 percent of Californians believed too much population growth had occurred in their communities. Only 51 percent regarded California as "one of the best places to live," compared to 78 percent in 1985. A poll by the *San Francisco Chronicle* found that 61 percent of the people thought that, among all uses of water, new growth should be sacrificed first if supplies run short. A 1989 Field poll found that 58 percent of Californians believed that there had already been too much growth in their communities and 65 percent wanted new growth to be discouraged. That is greater than the plurality won by just about any elected official. A nationwide Roper poll found that 55 percent of Americans believed the United States has "major population problems." Another 32 percent believed that the country has "some population problems." Conducted before Congress increased immigration quotas, the 1990 poll found that 77 percent of the people believed immigration to the United States should not be increased; 74 percent of Hispanic Americans and 78 percent of African Americans believed immigration should not be increased.[10] "Slow growth" may be a major political movement just waiting to happen.

Specific approaches to limit new growth would appropriately evolve only through a public process, but a few items to be considered include more stringent immigration quotas and increased capability to stem the influx of illegal residents (these are federal responsibilities, but California and its congressional delegation wield considerable influence), increased private and public support for family planning services, and educational programs that stress alternatives to growth in population and development. A commission could be established to recommend effective, equitable, and popular solutions.

Lacking an official state approach to the problem of runaway population growth, local communities will become ever more entangled and divided. Landowners and businesses will likely continue to flee from older communities, taking the tax base and economic opportunities with them. Or, choosing to stay, the long-standing white population may throw up local barriers to newcomers, resulting in unfair discrimination and unnecessary hostility. Without state leadership and action, a troubled era could be in store for California in which individuals, groups, and neighbors are pitted against one another in the scramble for everything from jobs to space at the beach. Better alternatives may be available if state government takes some initiative in addressing the question of population growth.

As the Los Angeles area becomes more entangled in sprawl and gridlock, in foul air and crime, in its need for water, and in its floundering educational and health care systems, the San Francisco Bay Area and Central Valley cities are increasingly looking the same. The small foothills and coastal towns, once far from the undertow, are becoming like the urban areas that the small-town residents sought to escape only a few years ago. To the remotest outposts, the communities of California are becoming enmeshed in the acceleration of growth and its trailing impacts—social, educational, governmental, legal, fiscal, and environmental. Is this what today's Californians want for the rest of their lives and for future generations?

CHAPTER 3

The Atmosphere
We Breathe

Californians enjoy one of the most benign climates in the world.
Coupled with extraordinary natural beauty and continuing economic growth, the state is a magnet for people seeking the unique
combination of lifestyle and economic opportunity that California
represents. The pervasive and severe air pollution that plagues most
of the state's population is the dark side of this image. It is not just a
matter of image, though. Polluted air affects health, shortens lives,
reduces agricultural yields, damages our forest resources and ecosystems, and obscures many of the magnificent natural vistas that
define California in the eyes of many people.

In the entire United States, only one region—the South Coast
area surrounding and including Los Angeles—has air pollution
defined as "extreme" by an act of Congress. Virtually every one of
the 13 million people there directly experiences the harmful effects

Jane V. Hall has nearly a decade of experience with California's air pollution
challenges and views the problem from the unique perspective of someone who
has worked on related issues for environmental groups, regulatory agencies, and
the energy industry. She has conducted extensive research on the health and
economic impacts of air pollution and is a professor of economics at California
State University at Fullerton. She holds a doctorate from the Energy and Resources
Group at the University of California at Berkeley.

of air pollution.[1] Eight of the other nineteen worst air quality regions in the nation are in California also, including such apparently unlikely candidates as Fresno. The image of mountain ranges obscured by smog and children who cannot safely play out-of-doors is overtaking the image of a healthy, outdoors-oriented lifestyle.

Ironically, it is California's climate, terrain, and natural assets that encourage the lifestyle and economic development that inevitably produce hazardous air. In much of the state, smog is formed and captured in valleys hemmed in by mountains. The great number of sunny days provides the ultraviolet light necessary to cook the pollutants produced by our cars, homes, and industries, which are captured in these natural cauldrons and transformed into the witches' brew we breathe. The breezes that eventually clear out our valleys carry pollution to the national parks and forests, where it directly or indirectly reduces the vitality and beauty of our wild areas. Our ongoing love affair with the automobile and lifestyles based on the freedom it represents have proven intractable contributors to the problem. In 1987, residents of just the South Coast region drove more than 240 million miles. By 2010 this is projected to be nearly 390 million miles each year—an increase of more than 60 percent.[2] This phenomenon is not unique to this region and presents a challenge throughout the state.

The critical question is: How willing are we to accept responsibility for the air we share, and how can we act as a community to ensure its recovery and protection?

STATE OF THE AIR

The air that many Californians breathe is unhealthy. In the South Coast region, one or more federal health-based air quality standards were exceeded on 211 days in 1989. The ozone standard there was violated *three times* more often than in the next worst place in the United States, which is also in California. The South Coast region also suffers the most frequent violation of carbon monoxide standards (two and a half times the runner-up) and the highest average annual particulate concentrations in the nation. Bakersfield, not usually viewed as a smog front-runner, averages forty-four days a year when the ozone standard is not met—*160 percent more days than New York.*

Unhealthy air concerns Congress enough that the U.S. Environmental Protection Agency (EPA) is mandated to limit some pollutants to levels that protect the most sensitive among us, with a margin of safety for error. These are called "criteria pollutants" and include ozone, sulfur dioxide, lead, carbon monoxide (CO), nitrogen dioxide (NO_2), and particles less than ten microns in diameter (PM_{10}). The California Air Resources Board (ARB), convinced that the federal standards do not provide enough protection, set stricter limits for California. The effect on global warming of compounds we spew into the air is a separate, major issue and is covered in the following chapter.

THE AIR AS A HAZARD

Pollutants produce a large range of adverse effects on the human body, from minor aggravations such as eye irritation to shortened lives.

Ozone is the most pervasive pollutant in terms of frequency and severity of standard violations and in terms of numbers of people affected. A colorless gas, ground-level ozone is produced by nitrogen oxides and hydrocarbons reacting together in sunlight. In the upper atmosphere, ozone acts as an essential filter of harmful radiation. When humans are exposed to it in the lower atmosphere, an array of symptoms, including eye and throat irritation, coughing, chest tightness, and headache, can result. The more severe effects can restrict normal activities. Ozone also produces subtle effects on the lungs, especially in children.[3] Recent research suggests that people living in polluted areas for ten years or more suffer reduced lung capacity. Ozone exposure can also reduce resistance to some infections.[4]

The more subtle effects of ozone may well be the most serious but are also the most difficult to understand regarding long-term health implications. Autopsy results show that 75 percent of otherwise healthy young males who die in accidents or by homicide in Los Angeles suffer chronic lung inflammation. Nearly all of them have chronic bronchitis, yet this obvious lung impairment did not show up as an illness when they were alive.[5] We are undertaking an immense experiment with the lungs of millions of people as guinea pigs as we await the eventual manifestation of long-term impaired lung function.

Particulate has been recognized as a potentially severe hazard at least since the infamous London fog of 1952, when thousands died. Effects are serious enough to alter normal daily behavior, including loss of work days and school attendance. The weight of evidence has increased during the 1980s and 1990s that PM_{10} is emerging as a key public health threat and can cause premature death.

Carbon monoxide is a gas that reduces the body's ability to use oxygen efficiently, resulting in impaired concentration, increased reaction time, and elevated symptoms in asthmatics and people with impaired cardiovascular systems.

Federal nitrogen dioxide standards are violated nowhere except in the South Coast region. Nitrogen dioxide increases the body's susceptibility to other challenges, including viral infection, and can reduce lung function. Health-based air quality standards for lead and sulfur dioxide are met everywhere in California, so adverse impacts are not an immediate hazard.

Air quality standards for some criteria pollutants have been in place for nearly two decades. During that time we have learned that a complex array of other compounds released into the air is also potentially hazardous. The Air Resources Board has identified fourteen compounds as cancer-causing. From a list of 300 compounds listed as potentially toxic, the ARB restricted the use of seven. These chemicals are associated with reproductive risk (birth defects and infertility) and acute organ damage as well as cancer.

Direct adverse effects on health are not the only reasons that air pollution is a continuing problem for the state. Ecosystem impacts, sometimes subtle, are just now beginning to be understood. Recent studies show that surface waters in the Sierra Nevada have the lowest acid-neutralizing capacity of any group of lakes in the country. This capacity drops to zero during spring snowmelt and after summer storms, when acid from precipitation reaches these lakes and streams. Some zooplankton species that form a major part of the food chain for trout are lost.[6] Acid levels are most elevated in urban areas, however, where acid fog poses an unmeasured threat to health. Ozone, carried to the mountains from great distances, has damaged nearly 60 percent of the jeffrey and ponderosa pines in

Yosemite National Park and a quarter of the pines studied at Lake Tahoe, where all ozone health standards are met.[7]

Agriculture is one of the state's largest industries, producing $8 billion a year in the San Joaquin Valley alone.[8] Crops worth $200 million are lost annually to air pollution, and reduced production means consumers pay an additional $184 million at the checkout counter.[9] Harvests of key crops, including grapes, cotton, alfalfa, and tomatoes, are reduced 10 to 20 percent by air pollution.[10] The yield of oranges—an historic symbol of the promise of California— is reduced by 25 percent as a result of exposure to ozone in the San Joaquin Valley.[11]

Visual enjoyment of our environment also suffers because of air pollution. The awesome natural beauty of the mountains surrounding Los Angeles is often obscured. The majestic Sierra Nevada, often seen from Sacramento and Fresno just a generation ago, is seldom seen anymore. Even more remote areas, including Yosemite and Sequoia national parks, do not offer the pristine vistas people travel there to see. Visibility in Sequoia is often reduced to five miles.[12] In the words of the Old Testament, "Where there is no vision, the people perish."

THE UNFORTUNATE SCOPE OF THE PROBLEM

California has nine of the twenty worst air quality regions in the country. While many regions across the United States occasionally violate a standard, here it is a routine part of daily life. Some idea of the scope of the problem is evident from Table 3.1, showing how many hours a year the ozone standard is violated. California and the EPA both have ozone standards that are not to be exceeded more than one hour a year. (The state standard is violated more often because it is stricter.) In the South Coast area, there were nearly 2,000 violations of the state standard in 1988 occurring on more than 200 days a year and more than 1,200 violations of the federal standard on more than 175 days. A next-door neighbor, the Southeast Desert region, missed the state standard during nearly 1,600 hours on more than 180 days. There are four (of fourteen) air quality regions in California where standards are not violated and others where violations are infrequent, but the overall picture is one in which the majority of Californians are directly affected by air

TABLE 3.1
EXCEEDANCES OF HOURLY OZONE STANDARDS* IN 1988

| Air Quality Region | (# hours/# days) | |
	California	Federal
North Coast	0/0	0/0
San Francisco Bay	131/41	9/5
North Central Coast	5/4	0/0
South Central Coast	643/135	163/55
South Coast	1,962/216	1,242/178
San Diego	716/160	159/45
Northeast Plateau	0/0	0/0
Sacramento Valley	455/98	105/35
San Joaquin Valley	943/154	206/73
Great Basin	9/3	0/0
Southeast Desert	1,589/188	591/124
Mountain Counties	149/39	14/7
Lake County	0/0	0/0
Lake Tahoe	0/0	0/0

SOURCE: California Air Resources Board.

* Number of hours/days that the state or federal hourly ozone standard was exceeded in each region in 1988. One exceedance is allowed per year; all exceedances beyond that are violations of the standard.

pollution. In the South Central Coast area centered around Ventura, federal standards are violated on fifty-five days each year; in San Diego, forty-five days each year. Sacramento exceeds federal health standards for ozone on thirty-five days each year. Clearly discouraging is the trend in the San Joaquin Valley, with its rapid economic and population growth: the California standard was exceeded during nearly 1,000 hours on over 150 days.[13]

The picture drawn by these numbers shows that severe air quality problems are not limited to Los Angeles, or even to urban areas. The second-largest number of violations in the San Joaquin Valley is at Parlier, an agricultural center. In the South Central Coast area, Simi Valley, adjacent to the Los Angeles basin, exceeds federal standards on fifty-two days.

The extreme variation from one region to another—from healthy air with good visibility to nearly 2,000 violations a year—is not the result of any single factor. The North Coast has good air quality because of the climate (low temperatures, fewer days of sunshine and more of wind) but also benefits from the terrain (mountains don't capture and hold pollution) and the lack of development. The South Coast region is just the opposite: there are many days with strong inversions, weak winds, and sun that photochemically encourages ozone. When 13 million people and 8 million trucks, buses, and automobiles are added to this, extreme levels of ozone are no surprise. This confluence of terrain, human activity, and climate also explains why nearly all of the emergency episode days in California occur in the South Coast or the contiguous Southeast Desert region. In 1988 there were nearly eighty days during which the air was so foul that schools were advised to keep children indoors.

WHERE DOES IT COME FROM?

Carbon monoxide, nitrogen dioxide, lead, and sulfur dioxide are emitted directly from human activities, while ozone and PM_{10} are largely secondary pollutants, created in the atmosphere by conversion of other compounds. All of these are strongly linked to the extensive use of fossil fuels in transportation, the production of electric power, and industry. Carbon monoxide results directly from the combustion of fossil fuels, and 95 percent of it comes from automobiles, buses, and trucks. Nitrogen oxides (NO_x) are also emitted in large quantities from mobile sources—about 75 percent of total emissions in most areas of California. Nitrogen oxides are important not just because the South Coast does not meet the federal NO_2 standard, but also because they are a very significant precursor to both ozone and PM_{10} as well as a factor in acid rain and fog. Controlling this group of compounds is therefore critical in many ways to improving health, protecting agriculture, preventing ecosystem damage, and improving visibility.

For ozone to form in the atmosphere, several things must happen at once. Nitrogen oxides and sunlight must be present, and so must hydrocarbons, which assist the formation of ozone from NO_x. The hydrocarbons that sponsor creation of ozone are generated nearly equally by mobile sources such as cars, and by industry, the use of common household products such as hairspray and paints, and many small businesses such as the corner dry cleaner.

The picture that emerges here shows the growing relative role that vehicular pollution plays in this problem. Controls on industrial sources—refineries, power plants, cement plants, smelters, canneries, and so on—have become increasingly stringent over the past several decades. While new vehicles are far cleaner than those manufactured even ten years ago, the number of cars and trucks and the number of miles they are driven are increasing even faster than the population. In the South Coast, for example, population is projected to grow 30 percent between 1987 and 2010, and the number of vehicles will grow 31 percent, but the number of miles driven will increase by twice that, or by more than 60 percent.[14] This means that pollution per mile driven has to drop by 60 percent *just to stay even* with the 1987 pollution level. Since industrial pollution is decreasing while vehicular use increases, mobile sources quickly become a larger relative contributor to air quality problems. The benefits of pollution-reducing technology can easily be overwhelmed by our choices about where to live and work, about modes of travel, and about how many miles we drive. From 1987 to 2010, the average resident of the South Coast is expected to increase the number of miles traveled in a private vehicle each day by 25 percent.

Another source of pollution involves "area sources." This category includes emissions from small facilities such as dry cleaners, consumer product use, and some kinds of equipment. These are not minor sources when taken as a group, although any one taken alone seems unimportant. Reducing their contribution to smog will also mean some lifestyle changes, such as lighting barbecues without reactive lighter fluid and using household cleaners that are not so polluting.

In the Sacramento Valley, burning 400,000 acres of rice stubble after harvest produces as much particulate pollution as sixteen coal-burning power plants.[15] A 1991 law requires rice farmers to reduce burning by changing the way they clear the fields every growing season. The farmers are allowed to sell their "pollution rights" to other polluters.

There are undoubtedly many additional reductions that can be achieved from industrial sources. At least equally clear, the role of transportation and other lifestyle choices that we make are already important and will become more important as the state's population and economic activity increase.

PROSPECTS

California has until 2010 to meet federal health-based air quality standards as specified in the federal Clean Air Act of 1990. Under the California Clean Air Act there are additional performance tests to demonstrate that each region is undertaking enough regulatory and enforcement efforts to attain state and federal standards. The California act is unique in requiring that *per capita exposure* to carbon monoxide, nitrogen dioxide, and ozone be reduced by 25 percent in 1994, 40 percent in 1997, and 50 percent in 2000. This is crucial to improved health because even if pollution is gradually falling, population growth can produce an increase in the absolute number of ill effects. This means that pollution levels must fall fast enough to prevent any increased risk to health. The act also states that emissions must fall by 5 percent each year or to the maximum extent feasible. For the first time, explicit plans to meet state standards are required of regional agencies with oversight by the California Air Resources Board.

A key question is whether this can be accomplished and how, but the past offers some hope. Californians have made an enormous investment to reduce air pollution, and we are beginning to see the payoff: the highest ozone levels in Los Angeles are half those of the 1960s, and the amount of pollution the average person breathes has been cut in half over the past ten or so years. There are many indicators that the air is getting better. The average Californian now "produces" (directly and indirectly) about 200 pounds per year of smog-forming pollution (one-third less than during the 1980s), compared to a national average of 300 pounds.[16] This dramatic reduction is the result of tougher standards for cars and trucks and new controls on industry. A dramatic decline in standard violations in the San Francisco Bay Area as well as the South Coast also reflects this trend. It is clear that air quality would have been much worse if current measures had not been envisioned a decade or more ago and then implemented. It is also clear that the gains of the past are not enough for healthy air and not enough to keep up with growth.

THE AIR QUALITY MANAGEMENT PROCESS

Every state must satisfy the EPA that it has a workable plan that will lead to improved air quality and eventually to attainment of federal standards. This is the state implementation plan. In turn, the California Air Resources Board relies on each of the fourteen air quality control regions to produce a viable plan demonstrating how each will attain and maintain the federal and state standards. An immense information base is necessary to evaluate what present air quality is, which sources are contributing how much pollution and what kind, what emissions will be from all sources, how population will change, and how control technology will evolve. Even good data may not be very useful without adequate models to estimate and forecast the combined effect of emissions, weather, and human behavior. Scientific uncertainty presents a very real problem.

CHALLENGES

How good is the emissions inventory? The contributions of most sources are not measured directly but are estimated from other information. An inventory for toxic air compounds is in its infancy. One big challenge is determining how much vehicles pollute as they age and as control systems become less effective. Another challenge is obtaining a clearer picture of how much pollution people really breathe. This depends on knowing how much time people are out-of-doors, how much pollution gets into buildings from outside, and what people do in different places. Children are at greater risk than adults because they are more active and not physiologically mature.

The problems are daunting but not insurmountable. Aggressive research programs supported by all levels of government and the private sector fill in new parts of the puzzle nearly every day. This is evident in the regular review and revision of the pollution inventory, of the air quality standards, and in new programs to regulate air toxics.

The ultimate challenge is whether or not California has the political will to deal with the increasingly obvious fact that how and where we live and how we travel are fundamental to solving air quality problems. The plan to achieve healthy air in southern California depends on land use and transportation decisions by local government officials—supervisors and council members—who are often reluctant to initiate change. Regional and state programs cannot succeed without creative community involvement and cooperation, yet the structure for this has not evolved with the critical need for it.

A great deal of attention and analysis has been focused on the South Coast because, if the air can be cleaned there, so goes the logic, it can be cleaned anywhere. Progress already made in most of the state shows clearly that air quality can get—and has gotten—much better, even in the South Coast, both overall and for the average Californian. The question now is how to make further inroads in the face of rising population, the demand for increased economic opportunities, and the competing demands of other social needs such as education and medical care.

A key goal will be to reach accord among the myriad local governments that will have to take action to make air quality plans a reality. When explicit action is required at the city level, elected officials will look hard at proposals that will require their constituents to sacrifice convenience for cleaner air.

MEETING THE CHALLENGES

In the most heavily polluted areas of the state, we are at least twenty years away from reaching the goal of healthy air, and this assumes that there are no discoveries of new hazards or demonstrations that the present standards aren't tough enough to protect health or agriculture. There is a real risk that the region of the state with the most rapid population growth—the Central Valley—will have trouble staying even in pollution discharges, in part because air pollution was not viewed as a real problem there until recently, when the extent of violations became apparent and agricultural losses were estimated.

Additional pollution controls will reach closer to home. The slogan "Use A Barbecue, Go to Jail" appeared in Los Angeles in 1989, when limits on lighter fluids were first proposed. It was a gross exaggeration of the proposed regulation, but the point was made: individuals will have to change the way they live and work if the air is to be safe to breathe. No one knows how the public will respond. So far Californians are adapting, but reductions in individual choice are just starting.

Whether technology will develop as fast as it must for air quality goals to be met is a good question. Even though the ARB has adopted stringent new requirements for 1993 automobiles and trucks and the fuels that they use, the most polluted regions will require the introduction of zero-emission vehicles for the standards to be met. The only way to meet this standard now is with electric vehicles, which still face economic hurdles as well as technical ones, including range. (In one sense, "zero emission" is a misnomer since plants producing the electricity to run these vehicles will not be zero emitters.) Because of the incentive of tougher regulations, the promise of these vehicles is greater now than it was even five years ago.

PROGRESS BY CALIFORNIANS

In the South Coast, the issue for the next ten years could be simply hanging on to progress already made. This is because of growth and unforeseeable setbacks, the discovery of uncontrolled sources, or the failure of predicted technical breakthroughs to meet expectations. Ten years beyond that, the gradual replacement of dirtier, older vehicles with ultra-low-emitting new ones is expected to ensure progress toward attainment of air quality goals. During that time the need to maintain progress will become even more critical as an ever larger population suffers the health and economic damage caused by the air around us.

For the San Joaquin Valley the question is more difficult. A large but not yet measured part of the valley's problem is imported from other regions. Compounding this is the spillover of population and economic growth into the valley. Population is forecast to increase by more than 40 percent between 1991 and 2005, and it already increased by 20 percent between 1980 and 1990.

In the San Francisco Bay Area, attainment is very close for ozone, and the federal daily PM_{10} standard is already met. Air quality is far better than it was ten years ago. Still, the impact of growth cannot be ignored. For the South Central Coast, including Santa Barbara and Ventura, offshore oil development continues to pose a question. Local and state air pollution control agencies have no direct control over facilities in federal waters and must rely on the EPA to adopt regulations.

SUMMARY

A challenge common to all regions of the state is evaluating and facing the impact of continuing population and economic growth. The fact that people's use of automobiles is increasing twice as fast as the runaway rate of population growth is especially distressing, and Californians show little commitment to alternatives to the single-occupant car. The South Coast is the canary in the coal mine—if vehicular use cannot be addressed successfully, air quality goals simply cannot be met, and that could be a harbinger for most of the urban regions of the state. If mileage on private vehicles is not reduced, short-term improvements will be followed by certain erosion and a worsening of air quality as the population increases. In the face of a tough federal law, this would mean even tighter restrictions on industry and area sources with economic implications for the affected regions.

A similar set of difficult choices was presented by the state's fifth year of drought in 1991. California awakened to the fundamental limits inherent in the inefficient use of water, and parts of the state nearly ran out. The limit on air is more subtle; we can choose to live with a filthy atmosphere or not. But inefficient use of air—polluting it so badly that it is unhealthy to breathe—takes a toll in human health, reduces the productivity of the land, and destroys the beauty of the landscape.

Ultimately, we know enough to get on with the job of providing healthy air to California's residents. The timing of progress toward this goal is not entirely clear, even without political hurdles, because there are surprises ahead about the atmosphere, health, the pollution inventory, technology, and human behavior, including population change. We clearly know enough about all of these things to continue improving the air, if only the political will exists. This means dealing directly and constructively with growth, an issue that pervades life in California. If growth continues, as it surely will, all of us may have to live differently than we otherwise would have done. For cleaner air, a two-vehicle family may own one electric car. Taking the bus or sharing a ride may be necessary. Telecommuting will gain ground. Zoning may change to encourage density and discourage commuting. Energy conservation can make a vital contribution. The possibilities exist, but harnessing them will require concerted public will, citizen action, individual responsibility, incentives for innovation, and informed elected and appointed officials.

CHAPTER 4

California Energy and Global Warming

CHRIS CALWELL

With energy, as with many things, California is uniquely situated among the fifty states: it simultaneously possesses the nation's most energy-efficient economy, its largest renewables industry, its largest utility investors in efficiency, its most automobile-intensive transport system, its most polluted city, and its largest population. The state is a living, growing paradox, concealing within its 159,000 square miles the best and the worst—uneasy neighbors.

Where does our energy come from? Where does it go? What are the environmental effects of our energy use, and how can we mitigate them? What is the role of the state in addressing global environmental problems such as climate change? These questions, though not distinctive of California, have found within our borders solutions of unprecedented scale and imagination. In the face of

Chris Calwell is a research associate with the Natural Resources Defense Council, a national environmental organization with more than 170,000 members. The NRDC has played an active and continuous role in California and Pacific Northwest energy issues for more than a decade, helping to shape appliance and building standards, utility efficiency programs, and energy legislation. Mr. Calwell works principally on utility demand side management, global warming, and automotive fuel economy issues and is also an avid environmental photographer.

unrelenting population and economic growth, they stand to challenge us even further.

In 1972, the Rand Corporation issued a now-legendary report stating that California energy use was rising by roughly 6 percent a year (doubling every twelve years) and that, by 2000, we would need an enormous nuclear or coal plant every eight miles along the coast to meet the demand.[1] Suddenly, energy was important enough to be its own environmental issue. In 1974, the state legislature created the California Energy Commission to forecast power demand, site power plants, and foster technologies and policies to use energy more efficiently. The commission's reports have, over time, provided biennial analyses of fuels, energy development, electricity, emerging energy technologies, and conservation. But now a new emphasis is emerging—global warming. Its relationship to state energy policy is this chapter's principal focus.

Global warming is primarily an energy issue. Nearly 90 percent of California's energy comes from fossil fuels, which naturally contain carbon. When burned or leaked, they release carbon dioxide and other gases, which rise into the atmosphere. These chemicals, known as greenhouse gases, are exactly the right size and shape to allow sunlight through to strike the earth, but they trap in the heat that is released in the process. The simplest way to reduce the quantity of those gases is to use less energy or increase the share of our energy that comes from renewable, non-fossil-fuel sources.

Although individual consumers exert far more control over how much energy they use than where it comes from, they often find it difficult to obtain basic background on both. It is useful to begin, then, with a brief discussion of where the state's energy comes from and what we use it for.

SOURCES OF ENERGY

Five basic sources of energy are used in California.

Oil

Although California has made a concerted effort over the last decade to diversify its energy base and reduce its dependency on oil, it is obvious from Figure 4.1 that we have a long way to go. Roughly

FIGURE 4.1
SOURCES OF CALIFORNIA'S ENERGY, 1988

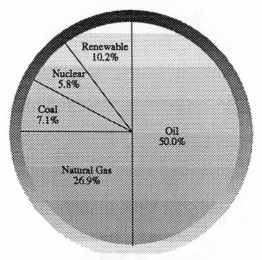

Renewable
10.2%

Nuclear
5.8%

Coal
7.1%

Oil
50.0%

Natural Gas
26.9%

SOURCE: California Energy Commission, Sacramento, 1989.

half of the oil is produced within our borders, much of it from heavy oil fields in the state's midsection that consume significant energy themselves in the extraction process. The remainder comes from Alaska, foreign countries, and wells off the coast.

Natural Gas

The California Energy Commission expects a 33 percent increase in state natural gas consumption over the next twenty years. Plentiful domestic supplies, relatively clean burning characteristics, and natural gas's potential to power vehicles are fueling a boom in pipeline construction and general demand. Currently, only 18 percent of the natural gas used by California is produced within our borders. The lion's share comes via pipeline from other states and countries.

Coal

The fact that no coal is mined within our borders and little is burned here conceals the extent to which we actually rely on the most polluting of all fossil fuels. Imported coal power from nearby states provides 17 percent of our electricity and 7 percent of our total energy. Three flows are involved: California rate-payer dollars flow to Utah and Arizona power plant operators, cheap electricity flows to California, and costly pollution wafts eastward. In spite of heroic efforts to revive its prospects with a costly "Clean Coal" program, coal appears to be following the path to gradual attrition already blazed by nuclear power.[2] Its carbon dioxide emissions are the highest of any major generating technology, and power plants face increasingly prohibitive pollution control and water acquisition costs.

Nuclear Power

Although California seemed headed toward an ever greater reliance on nuclear power in the 1970s, the last fifteen years have witnessed not only a cessation of new construction but a palpable reduction in nuclear capacity. After years of troubled start-and-stop operation, the Rancho Seco nuclear power plant was finally closed down at the ballot box by disgruntled Sacramento residents. No new nuclear plants are planned in the state, and Pacific Gas & Electric is recovering the steep construction costs of its Diablo Canyon plant only by operating it more efficiently than most plants in the nation.

Renewables

California's continuing reliance on oil and natural gas may be typical of other states, but its renewable and independent power industries are nothing short of extraordinary. California is abundantly blessed with renewable resources and a political climate that has nurtured them. As a result, we generate more electricity from wind, solar, and geothermal power than the other forty-nine states combined.[3] Wind power from a handful of sites around the state now meets more than 1 percent of our electricity demand. Geothermal power alone provided 8 percent of Pacific Gas & Electric's supply in 1990, nearly as much as hydropower. Biomass and co-generation plants represent two-thirds of the state's total nonutility generation. Our renewable resources provide enough electricity to meet the annual needs of 4.5 million people.[4]

Most Californians are aware of the tax credits that fostered the renewables industry during its troubled infancy, yet few have followed the story to its most recently written chapters. Today, most of the credits have lapsed, and only the leanest, most innovative companies remain. Their best new technologies are beating many fossil fuels in a fair economic fight. At a time when new coal generation costs nearly ten cents per kilowatt-hour, geothermal sites are providing it at six cents, and the best new wind turbines manage roughly five cents. Unfortunately, even at eight cents per kilowatt-hour, the solar thermal technology pioneered by Luz Solar is no longer profitable enough to keep them in business, even in the face of a state energy policy calling for half of all new generation over the next decade to come from renewables.

WHERE OUR ENERGY GOES

The individual uses of energy are divided into a number of small, specific parts (see Figure 4.2). The largest include cars and light trucks, non-auto transport, industry, and space and water heating. Each is dependent on a different mix of fuels and operates at different fractions of its maximum theoretical efficiency. As a result, it is difficult to correlate end uses specifically with environmental harm.

FIGURE 4.2
CALIFORNIA ENERGY CONSUMPTION, 1988

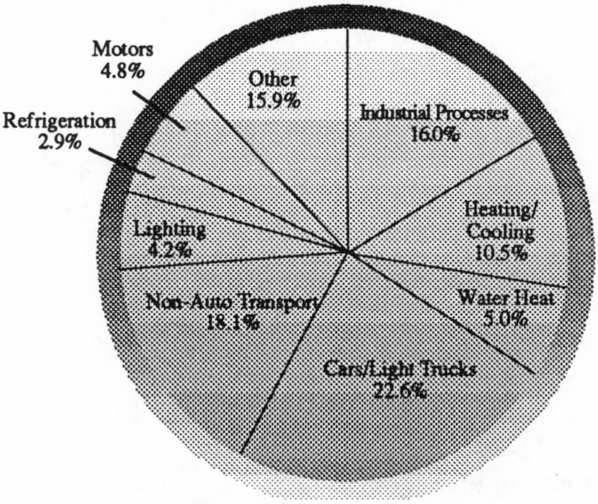

SOURCE: California Energy Commission, *Energy Efficiency Report* (Sacramento: California Energy Commission, October 1990).

But we can also simply compare energy use in the four main sectors of the economy. The numbers reinforce what we already know about the dominance of cars: transportation accounts for 41 percent, industry for 30 percent, residences for 17 percent, and businesses for 12 percent. Why is transportation so high? After years of ambitious and increasingly broad efficiency efforts aimed at buildings and appliances, only vehicles remain untouched by California's quest to cut energy waste. The mythically benevolent market hasn't helped much either—gasoline prices in real dollars are lower today than they've been in sixty years.

WHERE WE ARE NOW HEADED

A few figures from the official state energy forecasts tell the whole story. Between now and 2009, absent a radical shift in technology, behavior, or population growth, we can expect the following: 48 percent more households, 30 percent more total energy use, 21 to 32 percent more transportation fuel use, 33 percent more natural gas use, 50 percent more electricity use, and 50 percent higher carbon dioxide emissions. Furthermore, the same 90 percent of our total energy will still be coming from fossil fuels.[5] Nothing could argue more strongly for changing our current course.

Smog and Congestion

Few would challenge the assertion that smog is the state's most sinister, pervasive, environmental symptom of conspicuous energy consumption. Today, 80 percent of our local air pollution results from fossil fuel use, and fully 90 percent of the state's citizens live in areas with unhealthy air.[6] Conditions in many of the state's urban areas offer the perfect recipe for turning invisible emissions into extremely visible pollution: automobile-intensive development, booming economies, a sunny climate, and natural harbors rimmed by coastal mountains. Today, 75 percent of the state's population— 22 million people—cluster around bustling ports in our three largest urban areas: Los Angeles/Anaheim/Riverside, San Francisco/Oakland/San Jose, and San Diego.

In 1988, Californians drove 153 billion miles—three times the distance to Mars and roughly 75 percent farther than they drove fifteen years earlier. We used 14 billion gallons of fuel in 1988—more than a supertanker's worth of oil every day. California workers lose a total of 360 million hours of productive time each year because of congested roads, at a cost of $17 billion in wasted fuel and lost productivity. The California Energy Commission expects congestion to triple by the year 2000. Clearly, the road to automobility is leading us toward an increasingly *immobile* future.

Oil Spills

It is not difficult to identify the link between high oil usage and a high frequency of oil spills, even on the scale of a single state or city. The Los Angeles and Long Beach harbors alone move more than 9 billion gallons of petroleum products each year on about 1,000 tankers. They also annually experience roughly 500 oil spills of 1,000 to 10,000 gallons apiece. In the quest to keep oil cheap, we have allowed it to be moved on bigger and bigger tankers. The largest can require a half-hour and a few miles to come to a full stop, even with the engines running in reverse. Under those conditions, even attentive, experienced captains can get into accidents that cause oil spills.

This suggests to some that oil spills are, in aggregate, a statistical phenomenon and thus inevitable, but using more oil increases the likelihood of a spill.[7] Wherever spills occur, they wreak havoc with local ecosystems, leaving damage that lingers for years. The blame rests as much with companies that fail to equip their tankers with double hulls and sober captains as it does with a nation that blithely wastes oil in its cars, homes, and businesses.

Acid Deposition

Acidic chemicals can be transported and deposited in any number of forms, including rain, snow, fog, or directly as dust. The causal link between fossil fuel combustion and acid deposition is well understood. Most types of coal and oil contain some sulfur compounds, which, when burned and mixed with water vapor, form sulfuric acid. Likewise, most types of high-temperature combustion (including natural gas) cause molecular nitrogen (N_2) to split apart, combine with oxygen and water vapor from the air, and ultimately form nitric acid. When these acids reach streams and lakes, they can increase the acidity of the water to the point that many native species can no longer reproduce or survive. In the Northeast and Canada, more than 15,000 lakes have been severely damaged by pollutants originating in power plants, vehicles, and major industries such as smelters and refineries.[8]

Though California's own ecosystems have registered few effects as severe as those in the Northeast, many are nonetheless threatened. Currently, prevailing winds carry pollution from the Los Angeles basin to Arizona and Nevada, and likewise move the pollution from coal-fired power plants in which California utilities own a share farther to the east.[9]

LIKELY IMPACTS OF GLOBAL WARMING

Though other environmental problems are often more directly identified with California, this state has an undeniably significant stake in the stability of global climate.

1. Our agricultural sector is the nation's largest, producing $18 billion worth of food every year. Having evolved over the last century to be intimately dependent on a precarious supply of subsidized water from distant sources, agriculture is ill-suited to adapt to changing weather or to sustained drought.

2. Because all of California's largest cities are on its coast, the state remains extremely vulnerable to the effects of a rise in sea level. According to the EPA, an increase of 5.4 degrees Fahrenheit in global temperature would lead to a sea level rise of roughly three feet, enough to triple the flooded area of San Francisco Bay if levees are not improved, and to increase it by 30 percent if they are.[10] A 30 to 70 percent loss in coastal wetlands would normally accompany such a rise. Though many scientists believe that the EPA's estimate of sea level rise may be too high, the projected costs of protecting the state's costliest real estate from the sea would still be so enormous as to make all reasonable efforts to prevent global warming seem like bargains by comparison.[11]

3. California currently supports 250 threatened or endangered species and 700 species that may soon be added to those lists. Most have evolved slowly into specific climatic niches. Experts believe many would be unable to adapt or migrate quickly enough to survive significant warming, since an increase of 5.4 degrees Fahr-

enheit could move temperate land-based vegetation belts northward by roughly 200 miles. Even that comparison may understate the likely consequences, as Jessica Matthews has pointed out in the National Academy of Sciences report *Policy Implications of Greenhouse Warming*: "The fact that one can move with ease from Vermont to Miami has nothing to say about the consequences of Vermont acquiring Miami's climate." Forests in particular would face the twin threats of a greater incidence of forest fires and increased vulnerability to pests.

4. California's electricity grid shows a greater reliance on hydroelectricity than many other states. Global warming would likely change not only the magnitude of precipitation but also its timing. This could be especially threatening to the utilities that rely on hydroelectric dams for power and to the farmers who depend on them for water, since both uses count on a major fraction of annual precipitation being released slowly and late as snowmelt, rather than rapidly and early as spring rains. According to the California Energy Commission, a three-degree rise in temperature could reduce spring runoff by 33 percent, or 1.3 to 1.6 trillion gallons of water per year.[12] Such a change would simultaneously increase the risk of winter flooding and decrease the availability of water in the summer.

5. The state is already saddled with near-legendary levels of urban smog. Hot, sunny days not only cause such pollution to form faster, but they result in more use of air conditioning, which in turn increases local air pollution from power plants. Thus, global warming is projected to further aggravate an already tenacious smog problem and the human health effects that accompany it. According to the California Energy Commission, global warming could cause 2,000 additional Californians to die each summer from exacerbation of heart disease and strokes.[13]

THE RATIONALE FOR ACTION

Many people await further proof that global warming is already occurring before they are willing to invest in actions to prevent it. Yet these same people are willing to purchase fire insurance for their homes, simply to avoid bearing the financial risk of such an unlikely event. No one will sell a homeowner fire insurance once his or her house is aflame; likewise, the prospects of affordably reversing global warming once every scientist is convinced it is occurring are minimal.[14]

In any event, investing in insurance against global warming is a much more lucrative financial proposition than buying fire insurance. In 1988, U.S. property owners invested in $6.6 billion worth of fire insurance that paid out only $3.4 billion in loss claims. We lost nearly half our investment in one year. By contrast, the National Academy of Sciences concluded that investments in energy efficiency, renewable energy sources, and better forestry practices could reduce up to 40 percent of current U.S. greenhouse gas emissions, at a net savings of up to $100 billion in energy bills and non-greenhouse-gas pollution costs.[15]

Why should California act unilaterally to produce global cooling benefits that will predominantly accrue to other states and nations? The answers lie in the share California represents of the global problem and the financial lucre of developing the technology to achieve greenhouse gas reductions here first.

By itself, California possesses the world's seventh-largest economy and is the thirteenth-largest producer of carbon dioxide emissions. Not only do we make a global difference on our own, but we significantly increase the likelihood of timely federal action by acting here first. Indeed, California already has a proven record of strengthening federal standards on automotive emissions, appliance efficiency, and coastal protection by insisting on the right to more stringently regulate problems that are more severe here than nationally. As federal codes belatedly move to catch up, California has often taken the opportunity to further improve its own. The same can happen with global warming prevention, both nationally and internationally.

Though California has taken a leadership role in developing energy efficiency and renewable resources, it trails much of the industrialized world in its level of commitment to further action on global warming. Sweden, Germany, the Netherlands, the United Kingdom, Denmark, Norway, Belgium, France, Greece, Italy, Luxembourg, Portugal, New Zealand, and Japan have all set greenhouse gas reduction goals and demonstrated some level of commitment to attaining them. Likewise, a number of states, including Vermont, Oregon, and New York, are developing plans to reduce future carbon dioxide (CO_2) emissions significantly. For California's leaders, the question is not whether to lead, but whether to keep from falling behind.

TAKING ACTION

The California Energy Commission was recently charged by the state legislature with three new tasks: to assess the impacts that global warming would have on California, to estimate the state's contribution to the cause of global warming, and to recommend policies that would reduce that contribution. The commission has already produced final reports for each of the first two tasks and has released a draft document summarizing the findings of these reports.

In the interim, it makes sense to pursue with enthusiasm those policy options that save more than they cost, regardless of their value in reducing CO_2 emissions. In other words, if we do what needs to be done to fix the rest of the state's energy-related environmental problems, we will achieve substantial global warming prevention as well.

The Natural Resources Defense Council (NRDC) recently completed an analysis of the state's potential to do just that—achieve carbon emission reductions of 20 percent by 2000 and 40 percent by 2010 at net economic savings.[16] The NRDC found that current carbon emissions could be cut by more than half by 2010 through wider utilization of the best current technologies for using energy more efficiently and producing it more cleanly. Projected economic savings over twenty years would include more than $37 billion worth of energy saved. By avoiding damage otherwise caused by more troublesome pollutants, $50 billion would be saved.

As Table 4.1 suggests, some of the state's most promising options lie on the supply side. By preferring cleaner fuels for new power plants and vehicles, for example, we can gradually reduce per capita CO_2 emissions and fossil fuel consumption. One U.S. Department of Energy study revealed that California could generate locally or obtain from nearby states more renewable electricity in 2010 than it currently consumes from all sources, including natural gas, nuclear, coal, and oil.[17] Likewise, cogeneration—a type of

TABLE 4.1
EMISSION REDUCTION POTENTIAL FROM 1988 LEVELS

Source	Million Tons Carbon Saved/By Year	
	2000	2010
Automotive fuel efficiency	5.6	9.5
Reductions in miles/car	2.1	3.4
Alternative fuels for cars	1.6	3.4
Light trucks (all savings)	0.2	2.0
Aircraft efficiency	1.0	2.0
Railroad and ship efficiency	1.3	2.4
Total transportation	*11.8*	*22.7*
Residential electricity efficiency	2.0	3.6
Residential natural gas efficiency	5.1	9.9
Commercial buildings efficiency	−0.4	0.7
Industrial efficiency	2.7	3.8
Agricultural efficiency	0.5	1.0
Total nontransportation efficiency	*9.9*	*19.0*
Solar thermal electric	0.6	2.2
Photovoltaics	0.1	1.1
Wind power	0.3	2.5
Geothermal	0.2	0.9
Biomass, municipal solid waste, landfill gas	0.9	1.9
Hydropower	1.2	3.2
Total renewables	*3.3*	*11.8*
High-efficiency gas turbines	1.0	2.4
Cogeneration	5.6	8.6
Recycling	2.5	6.5
Rural carbon sequestering	5.0	10.0
Urban trees	0.2	0.4
*Grand Total**	*39.3*	*81.4*

SOURCE: Chris Calwell, Allen Edwards, Cliff Gladstein, and Lily Lee, *Clearing the Air: The Dollars and Sense of Proposition 128's Atmospheric Protection Provisions* (San Francisco: Natural Resources Defense Council, September 1990).

NOTE: These savings are expressed in the form of carbon rather than carbon dioxide. California's carbon emissions in 1988 were just over 145 million tons. Savings depicted can be realized from 1988 levels in spite of projected growth in energy consumption.

* Some savings are mutually exclusive; if all measures were employed, the total savings would be somewhat less than indicated.

power plant that produces both electricity and useful steam heat—can produce significant savings by displacing boilers that can produce only one or the other.

But bottom-line CO_2 savings result only if we can shut down a harmful, antiquated energy process when a new one is developed. At the moment, California's population is growing fast enough to double every thirty years. As a result, efforts to improve the environmental characteristics of new supply alone will at best slow the rate of growth in CO_2 emissions. To achieve absolute reductions, we must either minimize the environmental destructiveness of our existing sources of energy, or use them more productively. That causes us to turn our attention to the demand side, not with an emphasis on *conservation*, which implies sacrifice, but on *efficiency*, which connotes greater productivity.

In the utility sector, this has taken the form of dramatically expanded programs to help residential and commercial customers save energy. Energy efficiency investments in 1991 were more than double 1988 levels, and savings are projected to be three times higher. Two factors are responsible: a new focus on previously "lost" opportunities such as appliances and new buildings, and financial incentives that make good efficiency programs profitable to run.[18] Today, investor-owned utilities in California earn up to fifteen cents of profit for every dollar they save their customers on energy bills. Thanks to enthusiastic management support, efficiency investments have also risen dramatically at municipal utilities such as the Sacramento Municipal Utility District and the Los Angeles Department of Water and Power.

By demonstrating the viability of the most efficient technologies, the utilities are paving the way for future standards to require even more efficient homes, offices, and appliances. For the first time, the state is also creating a comprehensive inventory of its remaining opportunities to conserve energy. By continuing to strategically target those opportunities, we may actually be able to capture most of the cost-effective electricity and natural gas savings opportunities over the coming decades. As Table 4.1 indicates, the achievable carbon dioxide reductions from such savings are nearly as great as those found in the transportation sector.

California has also added its name to a growing number of states that are willing to impute an economic cost to the carbon dioxide emissions from new power plants. In the competitive bid process, this can often cause a cleaner power plant project to be chosen over a more polluting one. California has chosen a figure of seven dollars per ton, while both Massachusetts and Nevada assign a value of twenty-two dollars per ton to carbon dioxide emissions from new power plants.

With motor vehicles, a strategy embracing both the supply and demand sides is essential. Although it makes sense to increase the average fuel efficiency of the vehicle fleet, reduce the miles traveled per vehicle, and clean up the fuel, none of these options alone can deliver sufficient carbon dioxide savings. But together, the results are impressive. If, by 2010, we improved average fuel economy to 55 miles per gallon, reduced miles traveled per car by 20 percent, and reduced the carbon intensity of our fuel supply by 25 percent, we could achieve more than 16 million tons of annual carbon savings. Recent analysis of emerging fuel economy technologies reveals that it would be economically beneficial and technologically possible to raise the average fuel economy of new passenger automobiles to 46.5 miles per gallon (EPA rated) by the year 2000. These improvements would cost an average of fifty-one cents for every gallon of gasoline saved, with little change in the performance, ride, or interior room of the cars.[19]

While California lacks the legal authority to pass a standard requiring such fuel economy improvements, it does possess the means to offer economic incentives to achieve the same result. A simple system of fees and rebates linked to carbon dioxide and smog emissions of new cars would help to achieve that result by making gas guzzlers proportionally more expensive and gas "sippers" proportionally less expensive. The fees pay for the rebates and the costs of administering the program, leaving no net impact on the state budget. Such a bill is before the California legislature now; Massachusetts, Arizona, and the U.S. Senate are contemplating similar measures.

Likewise, policies to reduce dependence on the automobile are readily at hand, though federal leadership would increase their chance of success. They include greater attention to residential land use patterns, mass transit, ride-sharing, vanpooling, telecommuting, human-powered transportation, and high-speed rail projects. Funds to accelerate these programs were approved by the California electorate in three 1990 propositions, but the agencies in charge of apportioning the funds have largely committed them to additional freeway development. The prospects for change on the part of CalTrans and the California Transportation Commission through 1990 were particularly grim, since many of the agency decision makers had powerful financial and philosophical ties to automobile-oriented development. On October 10, 1990, the *San Francisco Bay Guardian* reported that of nine Transportation Commission members, five were real estate developers and development consultants, two had strong financial ties to the shopping mall industry, one owned a tire-manufacturing company, and one was president of a heavy-machinery supply company.

As Table 4.1 suggests, a number of other options, such as recycling and reforestation, offer substantial promise. The point is not to prejudge the most viable CO_2-reduction options, but rather to set in motion a process for selecting the best options on the merits of cost-effectiveness. Rather than require uniform percentage reductions in all sectors, for example, such a process would select the best bargains first, even if they fell principally in the transportation sector.

CONCLUSION

Nobody would deny that California has made substantial progress with its energy sector. Our utility conservation programs and renewables industry are the envy of many states. Improvements in state energy efficiency between 1973 and 1985 have already saved Californians $23 billion on their energy bills and prevented untold tons of air pollution.[20] Yet few states envy our dependence on the automobile, or the pollution it causes, or the costs it imposes. Few states envy our total energy bill; at $41 billion per year, it is the fourth largest in the world.

But we have the infrastructure in place to accomplish much. Our Energy Commission has repeatedly improved building and appliance standards to capture lucrative additional energy savings and improve comfort. Our Public Utilities Commission has fundamentally changed the rules of the utility business to allow conservation investments to compete on equal footing with new supply options. California utilities are now making a profit on efficiency investments and have no desire to get out of the business of saving energy. Pacific Gas & Electric has pledged to meet at least 75 percent of its anticipated load growth over the next decade from energy efficiency. Not to be outdone, Southern California Edison and the Los Angeles Department of Water and Power have committed themselves to absolute reductions of CO_2 emissions of 10 percent by 2000 and 20 percent by 2010.

By contrast, between 1974 and 1984, the nation's utilities were quite delighted to earn a steady rate of return on a half-trillion-dollar investment in new power plants and transmission lines that tended, if anything, to raise their customers' bills and pollute their air. Now, by allowing utilities to earn equally attractive returns on cost-effective efficiency investments, California has harnessed the profit motive to an environmentally desirable outcome—and lowered customers' bills in the process. This is not an isolated example; in most cases, clever regulation can permit the economic and environmental benefits of energy efficiency to work in tandem.

The decision by the state's regulators to weigh the environmental costs of new power plants also aligns economic and environmental forces sensibly. Clean air, good health, and a stable climate are valued in our society; either we choose to pay for them up front, through cleaner energy, or we hide them in more costly taxes, insurance, and litigation to pay for damages.

Obviously, energy savings do not occur without effort. If we can make the case that an environmentally sound future is also a fundamentally better, more financially attractive way of life, then much of the battle will be won. We are engaged in a struggle to improve the long-term health and stability of the state's economy. Buying more energy-efficient technologies will make us more productive and competitive; along the way, it should also help prevent a number of environmental problems for which we now pay billions. By their very nature, such investments involve initial costs, but they pay handsome dividends. These are savings that we can live with and, indeed, savings we may not be able to live without.

FURTHER INFORMATION

California Energy Commission, *Energy Efficiency Report* (Sacramento: California Energy Commission, October 1990).
California Energy Commission, *Global Climate Change: Potential Impacts and*

Policy Recommendations, draft (P400-90-003) (Sacramento: California Energy Commission, March 1991).

Chris Calwell, Allen Edwards, Cliff Gladstein and Lily Lee, *Clearing the Air: The Dollars and Sense of Proposition 128's Atmospheric Protection Provisions* (San Francisco: Natural Resources Defense Council, September 1990).

Ralph Cavanagh and Arthur Rosenfeld, "The Threat of Global Warming: Statehouse Effect Combats Greenhouse Effect," *Journal of State Government,* October/December 1990, 94–99.

National Academy of Sciences, *Policy Implications of Greenhouse Warming* (Washington, D.C.: National Academy Press, 1991).

Natural Resources Defense Council, *The Statehouse Effect: State Policies to Cool the Greenhouse* (Washington, D.C.: Natural Resources Defense Council, 1990).

CHAPTER 5

Transportation and the Environmental Costs of Auto Dependency

LEIF ERIK LANGE

They keep moving in, and they keep being born, and there are about 750,000 more of them each year. They need to go to work, they need to shop, and they need to take vacations, along with those of us already here. Californians, new and old, by the tens of millions, are making ever-increasing demands on the state's overworked and outmoded transportation system—a largely unimodal system consisting of freeways and local roads, conceived in another era, when the private automobile was king and when vanishing public transportation was considered symptomatic of progress rather than a reduction in consumer choice and convenience.

Today, looking forward to the California of tomorrow, which will

Leif Erik Lange holds a bachelor's degree in economics from the University of California at Berkeley and a doctorate in law from the University of California at Davis. He has been on the staff of the Assembly Transportation Committee of the California legislature since 1985. Previously, he was an attorney in private practice in Stockton and a transportation planner with the California Department of Transportation's Division of Mass Transportation in Sacramento.

need to accommodate and move 6 million more residents within ten years, it is easy to envision the worsening urban and suburban gridlock that will result when too many people drive alone wherever they go. Average speeds of nineteen miles per hour or less will soon be commonplace on many southern California freeways for extended periods of time, with commuters wasting thousands of hours of quality leisure and business time annually sitting in their cars, with freeways and suburban arterials congested for an increasing number of hours each day.[1]

At the same time, these slow-moving cars generate most of the air pollution problem that fouls our environment by burning huge quantities of fossil fuels. This demand for energy increases the pressures for oil drilling in environmentally fragile lands, such as California coastal waters, and requires increasing dependence on foreign sources, risking entanglement in conflicts far from our shores while adversely impacting our foreign trade balance, which would be in the black but for our oil imports.

Overuse of and overdependence on the automobile have made transportation one of the key environmental problems in contemporary California. The solutions are to reduce this overuse and overdependency through constructive changes in tax policy, to provide viable and more environmentally sound transportation alternatives, such as public transit and facilities for bicycles and pedestrians, and to implement corresponding changes in land use.

TRANSPORTATION: AN ENVIRONMENTAL ISSUE

Until recently it has not been universally accepted, even in the environmental community, that transportation problems are environmental concerns, along with such issues as saving the remaining old-growth forests, safely disposing of toxic wastes, and opposing the construction of more dams on wild and scenic rivers. Besides causing environmental deterioration where most people live, auto-generated air pollution is having major consequences on forests hours away from urban areas, as ozone damage to trees in the Sierra Nevada and elsewhere demonstrates.

Transportation does not differ substantially from other major environmental problems of our time. As with other issues, it is an environmental problem because it relates to the efficient use of scarce resources, living within our means, not wasting what we have, and thinking not only of today but also of the future.

THE STATE OF THE TRANSPORTATION ENVIRONMENT

California used to have a reasonable inventory of more environmentally sound transportation alternatives, such as the 1,200-mile Pacific Electric system of nonpolluting electric trains in southern California, dating from the 1920s. By the 1950s these systems seemed obsolete when compared with the many advantages of the automobile. Instead of updating and improving alternative transportation resources, policy makers allowed them to disappear, with many rail rights-of-way surrendered to accommodate the automobile.

Transportation policies at all levels of government have continuously favored investment in highways since the advent of the automobile, largely because roads were almost exclusively a public responsibility, while intercity railroads and urban transit systems were generally privately owned utilities. The government invested public money in the facilities it owned.

The development of the interstate freeway system and heavy investment in urban roads to accommodate increasing numbers of cars and trucks over the years has brought virtually all remaining passenger rail and urban transit services into the public domain as well, since private providers were unable to compete while faced with public highway spending and declining patronage.

However, public transportation has not fared nearly as well as the automobile in securing public investment to provide a good, competitive level of service necessary to help attract the discretionary user. In many cases, a vote of the electorate is required to provide a funding source for transit improvements, while road and freeway expansions are simply undertaken without a vote. Citizens have occasionally had to sue to stop improper diversion of limited transit funds to road purposes, particularly in rural areas.[2] Unlike Europe and Japan, there has been no investment in a high-speed intercity rail system, which could link northern and southern California cities.

California voters have supported a number of local transit tax measures, even though the votes occurred long after much transit service (and riders) had disappeared and virtual dependency on the auto had set in. The Bay Area Rapid Transit (BART) system had to rely almost exclusively on local financing at a time when neither the federal nor state governments acknowledged any role in transit.

Political support for public transit funding has always been weak compared with support for highway construction. One explanation may be that hardly any political leaders and policy makers are users of public transit, while they all most certainly drive cars. The political mood has recently begun to change, with more demonstrated support for balance in transportation spending, and support for transit and other alternatives to the auto becoming almost fashionable.

CALIFORNIA'S TRANSPORTATION INVENTORY

California today boasts 15,200 miles of state-owned highways, including 4,000 miles of interstate and other freeways, which carry a majority of all vehicular traffic. Counties maintain an additional 71,000 miles of public roads, and cities maintain 52,000 miles of streets.[3] The U.S. Forest Service oversees another 45,200 miles of roads in California. Competing for pavement space are 20 million drivers and 25 million registered vehicles, which are increasing by 300,000 annually. These vehicles consume more than 14 billion gallons of gasoline and diesel fuel and collectively travel 153 billion miles each year.[4]

Less glamorous is the human cost of a transportation system so dominated by the automobile: 5,400 persons are killed and 365,000 are injured each year on California roads and highways, with an accident occurring every fifty-six seconds. The last day without a traffic fatality in California was March 11, 1968.[5] The loss of life on all U.S. roads each year is roughly equivalent to American losses in the decade-long Vietnam War. In contrast, public transportation of all kinds (whether by transit bus, school bus, train, or commercial airliner) enjoys an enviable safety record.

California has seventy major local transit systems and a host of smaller ones, which between them carry more than 1.1 billion riders annually on buses, trains, and ferries.[6] Intercity rail service on a limited but growing network is operated by Amtrak, a government-owned corporation, with assistance from the California Department of Transportation, while intercity bus service remains in the private sector, with Greyhound and a few regional carriers.

Highway proponents frequently seek to portray the highway system as completely self-supporting from motorist-paid "user fees" while transit is accused of being a money-losing enterprise requiring subsidies. But according to the federal government, user fees cover only 65 percent of direct expenditures on highways at all levels of government, not even counting collateral expenditures on other government services related to highways (such as police and medical) or the costs of environmental impacts discussed below.[7] Just requiring the average motorist to pay for external air pollution and congestion costs caused by automobile operation would require a 50 percent increase in the cost of driving above the current level of thirty to forty cents per mile.[8]

Other transportation modes are also subsidized. The Federal Aviation Administration provides $2 billion annually in general tax support to the airlines to maintain the nation's air traffic control system, which is not covered by ticket taxes, and large trucks cause substantially more pavement damage than they pay in highway taxes.[9]

While most direct expenditures on the California state highway system are indeed covered by user fees such as fuel taxes and truck weight fees, user fees distributed to cities and counties cover less than one-third of direct local road costs, with cities, in particular, reaching heavily into their general funds to finance their road budgets.[10] Local governments receive no truck weight fees, even though the impact of large trucks on local roads is as severe in some cases as the impact on state highways. There are also many indirect auto subsidies, including property taxes forgone on extensive highway rights-of-way, policing and traffic control costs, medical expenses, and environmental cleanup costs.

Transportation infrastructure is expensive these days, particularly with high real estate costs. The last new freeway likely to be constructed in Los Angeles County, the Century Freeway, will end up costing more than $2 billion, or $150 million per mile, while the cost of reconstructing a major freeway interchange in California can exceed $300 million, as is the case with the 24/680 interchange in Walnut Creek. Where rights-of-way have not been reserved, the new freeway construction era is essentially at an end; the disruption of businesses and residences that would have to be relocated is too great even if funds can be made available.

Rail systems have a potential cost advantage given their relative efficient use of land compared to freeways, but this has not stopped transit planners from building gold-plated facilities such as the Los Angeles Metro Rail subway. At $4 billion for the initial 4.4-mile segment, Metro Rail is the nation's most expensive rail transit project. Fortunately, California rail planners have also demonstrated their ability to economize; San Diego's initial 16-mile light rail line cost only $80 million when completed in 1982, and Sacramento's 18-mile system opened in 1987 at a cost of $176 million. Both of these systems relied heavily on existing railroad rights of way and on proven, modestly priced European technology.

While local agencies can be quite effective in solving local transportation problems, the state has a better perspective for tackling multicounty or regional issues. However, fundamentally, California faces a leadership vacuum at the state level in the development of alternative transportation modes. The state Department of Transportation was found by a special state commission to have "an institutional bias toward highways which . . . [prevents] the department from aggressively pursuing cost-effective alternatives to highways, with less than one percent of its personnel dedicated to mass transit."[11] CalTrans also declines to spend 100 percent of the federal funding made available by Congress for bicycle programs, opting instead to build more roads with the money, and has abdicated to local agencies any role in commuter rail service that would alleviate traffic problems in corridors served by CalTrans freeways catering largely to the same local commuter traffic.

AUTO OVERDEPENDENCY AND CONGESTION IMPACTS

A well-designed mass transit system can accommodate crush loads and becomes more efficient the more it is used, while the automobile generally works best if there are few other drivers on the road. Since the perceived operating cost (gas, insurance, etc.) to a driver of using a road during peak usage hours is the same as using it in the middle of the night, there is no financial incentive to stay off the road when everyone else wants to drive. The result is congestion, which highway engineers attempt to avoid by building a facility large enough to accommodate peak demand, meaning the facility is overbuilt compared with demand at other hours. There also has been an emphasis on moving vehicles, rather than people, again catering to inefficiency and encouraging waste.

There is substantial evidence now that increasing highway capacity by building a new highway or even adding a lane to an existing highway frequently fails to accomplish its intended purpose—namely, reducing congestion, particularly in the long run and where population growth is occurring.[12] This is because the existence of congestion appears to have a deterrent effect, discouraging a certain number of trips. When capacity is increased, the deterrent to travel is eased, and people not only make more trips, but they also tend to make longer ones than before. Soon the additional highway capacity is fully occupied.

New capacity can also induce growth by providing access to previously undeveloped lands that were too far away to be within practical commuting distance of an urban area. The proposal to construct a toll road through the Delta region in Solano, Contra Costa, and Alameda counties is a good example of a project that threatens to convert farmlands and wetlands to development—development that is otherwise unlikely because of lack of access. Rather than serving to alleviate existing traffic problems, which is usually given as a justification for constructing them, these road projects may well compound congestion problems by adding other sources of auto-dependent commuters to existing roads elsewhere.

While development of transit alternatives can also encourage more overall travel and longer trips, those people taking such alternative transit are keeping their impact on the environment to a minimum.

AIR QUALITY IMPACTS

While polluting smokestack industries are a frequent target of the fight for cleaner air, the source of most air pollution today is the cumulative impact of millions of motor vehicles. In southern California, 64 percent of air pollution is attributed to mobile sources.[13] Each car is occupied, on the average, by only 1.13 persons.[14] The South Coast Air Quality Management District in Los Angeles estimates that air pollution imposes health, agricultural, and environmental costs of more than $7.4 billion annually in that air basin, or about $600 per resident.[15]

People who rely on other means of getting to work than the single-occupant car by using mass transit or a carpool markedly reduce their contribution to air pollution (see Figure 5.1). It is estimated that each person who leaves a car at home and commutes to work on public transit for a year will, on the average, avoid polluting the environment with 9.1 pounds of hydrocarbons, 62.5 pounds of carbon monoxide, and 4.9 pounds of nitrogen oxides, even if using a reasonably patronized diesel bus.[16] The reintroduction of electric-powered transit vehicles such as trolley buses and trains will improve transit's performance even more.

As with congestion, the key to reducing the automobile's impact on air quality is a reduction in vehicle miles traveled. That goal is difficult to achieve when motorists are continuously encouraged to drive by provision of added highway capacity, subsidized parking, and inadequate transit alternatives.

In the past, there were perceived to be air quality benefits from alleviating congestion through increased highway capacity, on the grounds that a vehicle in stop-and-go traffic polluted more than a faster-moving vehicle. However, when increased capacity encourages not only more trips but longer ones as well, air quality likely gets worse.[17] Worst of all is a scenario whereby the extra capacity fills with cars and stop-and-go traffic returns, only then there is more of it.

Much promise is held out for the development of so-called "clean fuels" such as methanol, natural gas, and electricity, which may someday become practical substitutes for gasoline. In addition to problems with implementation, some of these fuels have their own negative impacts on the environment, such as formaldehyde from methanol. While "clean fuels" may result in better air quality, they will not alleviate the highway congestion caused by too many single-occupant vehicles, nor will they provide improved transportation for the elderly, young, and poor.

FIGURE 5.1
AIR POLLUTION CAUSED BY VARIOUS MODES

EMISSIONS OF HYDROCARBONS*
(Estimated grams per passenger-mile for work trips)

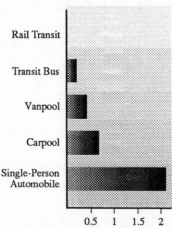

0.5   1   1.5   2

*Precursor of ozone, which irritates respiratory tract
and eyes, decreases the lungs' working ability, and
causes both cough and chest pains.

EMISSIONS OF NITROGEN OXIDES*
(Estimated grams per passenger-mile for work trips)

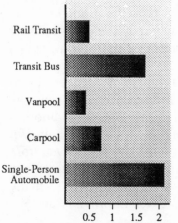

0.5   1   1.5   2

*Damages lung tissue. Also precursor of ozone, which
irritates respiratory tract and eyes, decreases the lungs'
working ability, and causes both cough and chest pains.

EMISSIONS OF CARBON MONOXIDE*
(Estimated grams per passenger-mile for work trips)

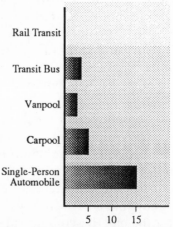

5   10   15

*Limits blood's ability to transport oxygen to
body tissues. Can cause dizziness, headaches,
impaired coordination, and death.

SOURCE: American Public Transit Association.

ENERGY OVERUSE IMPACTS

It is well established that the developed Western nations consume more than their share of resources of all kinds, relative to their population. The United States, however, is unique in overconsuming gasoline: with only 4 percent of the world's population, the United States consumes 40 percent of the world's gasoline.[18] The average gasoline consumption in U.S. cities is 4.5 times higher than in European cities.[19]

The low price of gasoline in the United States encourages the high per capita consumption of gasoline and discourages conservation. Today, the price of gasoline is lower in real terms than it was a generation ago (see Figure 5.2).[20] Federal "energy policies" consistently seem directed toward finding new resources rather than to promoting conservation. The gas price differential in most developed countries is because of hefty gasoline taxes, which not only promote efficient use of energy but also provide a source of revenues for mass transit. Gasoline taxes elsewhere tend to be consid-

FIGURE 5.2
CALIFORNIA GASOLINE PRICES ADJUSTED FOR INFLATION

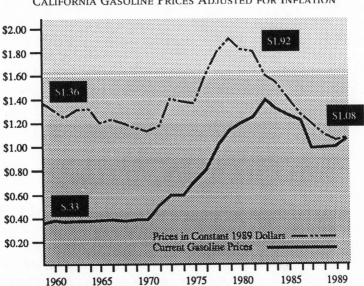

SOURCE: Senate Advisory Committee on Cost Control in State Government.

NOTE: Gasoline prices were $1.39 per gallon in 1960 when measured in 1989 dollars.

ered general revenues, rather than being locked up in a highway trust fund as has been the predisposition in the United States.

Since 1974, California gas tax revenues have been available in a limited manner for some mass transit purposes, and the federal government opened the door in 1982 by setting aside a "mass transit penny" from the federal gas tax and again in 1990 by earmarking portions of gas taxes for deficit reduction and mass transit. However, rather than leading to increased mass transit spending, the availability of trust fund revenues has led to a reduction in general fund spending on transit by the federal government.[21]

The overall level of the gas tax in California and the United States remains far too low to encourage any meaningful conservation. Political resistance to a tax diversion or even a tax increase for transportation purposes is strong, with interest groups protecting the unrealistically low gas price, frequently citing the interests of the poor, even though tax credits similar to California's income tax "renter's credit" could be devised to cushion this impact on poorer residents.[22]

Increasing the miles-per-gallon standard for motor vehicles is one approach toward conserving energy; it would tend to lead to the use of smaller, lighter vehicles. Faced with a choice between mileage standards and higher gas prices, the auto industry appears to prefer to limit the public's demand for gas guzzlers through higher gas taxes, which is more of a market-based approach than artificially restricting the supply of large vehicles coveted by the public when energy prices are low.

SUBSIDIZED PARKING IMPACTS

A corollary to low energy prices is a government policy that encourages subsidized parking, another element in the cost of owning and operating a car. Employers may provide subsidized parking tax-free to employees that is worth up to thousands of dollars annually and deduct that expense as a cost of doing business, but an employee who accepts an employer-provided transit pass must pay income tax if the benefit exceeds twenty-one dollars per month. A Los Angeles study showed that while Californians may love their cars,

24 percent fewer of them will drive to work alone if they have to pay for their own parking.[23]

Also contributing to the problem is the common zoning practice in many communities of requiring developers to provide a certain number of parking spaces per thousand square feet of development, creating an oversupply of "cheap" parking and making alternatives to driving less attractive. In the final analysis, this parking is not so cheap because it uses valuable land and increases the cost of developments, which developers pass along to consumers. Somewhere between a half and two-thirds of the land in urban areas is used for auto-related purposes, and the cost of constructing a single parking space can easily exceed $15,000.[24]

While inadequate attention to the funding of alternatives to the single-occupant auto has made California auto-dependent, low fuel and parking costs also play major roles in fostering this overdependency.[25]

UNDESIRABLE LAND USE IMPACTS

The development of low-density suburban sprawl is facilitated by low energy prices, and has a number of negative environmental impacts, including the evolution of a society virtually dependent on the automobile, usually with nothing within walking distance of residences located in single-purpose-zoned neighborhoods. Sprawl is difficult to serve with transit and makes virtual prisoners of anyone unlucky enough to exist there without a car, including the young and elderly. Lower-income job-seekers have a hard time getting to dispersed employment centers without a car, and even convicted drunk drivers are frequently issued restricted licenses by the courts rather than being totally separated from their cars.

Land use policies that enable and encourage sprawl also result in the decline of older, higher-density city centers, which are less able to accommodate suburban car owners because of higher parking costs. The downtowns compete with widely dispersed suburban employment centers, which are as difficult to serve with transit as are their residential counterparts. In addition, vast areas of open space and farmland face conversion to suburban sprawl, which has already made bedroom communities of San Joaquin/Stanislaus and

Riverside/San Bernardino counties and which threatens to march on to encompass available flatlands within one or two driving hours of the many urban areas.

Land-grabbing suburban development is not inevitable simply because of increasing population, as is demonstrated by the wide open spaces still remaining between cities in most of densely populated Europe. Even if it were deemed necessary to provide acre after acre of suburban tract homes, it is not necessary to do so in an environment of wide, high-speed arterial streets designed only with the automobile in mind and with few pleasant and safe sidewalks or bicycle paths.

With better coordination of land use and transportation planning, it should be possible to reduce the number of trips that are now taken in cars. Access to subdivisions for transit service could be facilitated rather than discouraged to enhance mobility for everyone. Moreover, California's weather is ideal for walking and bicycling to take care of minor errands, which incidentally could also contribute to the physical health of Californians more than sitting behind a steering wheel.

Progress toward a Better Transportation Environment

Not too many years ago, freeway alignments were routinely planned through parks because the government already owned the land and did not need to evict businesses and residents. Passage of the National Environmental Policy Act and the California Environmental Quality Act had a substantial impact in requiring road builders to be more environmentally considerate. Highways simply have to be better neighbors.

Perhaps the most promising recent development is a widespread recognition that our society has become too auto-oriented and that there is a need to pay more attention to alternatives—to provide a more balanced transportation system. Interestingly, this seems to be an arena where public opinion is ahead of the policy makers and political leadership, as reflected in a number of polls throughout the state showing substantially stronger public support for rail transit over more new highway construction. Election results in transportation sales tax elections also demonstrate that local tax measures with substantial transit funding components tend to fare better than highway-only measures.[26] Thanks to voter approval of two ballot measures, Los Angeles now dedicates a full 1 percent of sales tax revenues (generating $800 million annually) for transit and transit-related purposes, certainly a far cry from the 1960s and 1970s, when several transit tax measures were soundly defeated.

Yet, the transportation establishment tends to be conservative in outlook and finds it difficult to reallocate existing resources according to a more balanced formula—that is, favoring more investment in transit rather than in roads—and prefers to look for new revenues, difficult in an era when government faces constraints on its spending ability. There is also considerable debate about what constitutes balance; after all, moving money out of roads and into transit and other alternatives is difficult to justify when most people are still using roads.

The success of the new rail services that are the products of the 1970s and 1980s will only help the case for more investment in transit. Rail service caters to the middle-class rider with access to a car more so than does bus service and has a certain civic appeal to local leaders. Ridership is ahead of targets on new light rail lines in San Diego, Los Angeles, San Jose, and Sacramento, which is particularly encouraging since most lines serve low-density suburbs, largely relying on park-and-ride customers and feeder buses to adjoining neighborhoods.

The performance of Amtrak intercity rail lines between San Diego, Los Angeles, and Santa Barbara (which covers all direct operating costs from fares) and in the San Joaquin Valley is also exceptional for a segment of the transportation sector that was virtually abandoned in 1971 and now shows great promise for expansion to other corridors if the considerable institutional problems with private railroads can be worked out. Under state stewardship, the three daily round trips between Los Angeles and San Diego that carried 377,000 annual riders and covered only 36 percent of their direct costs from fares in 1975 had gradually expanded to eight daily round trips with 1.8 million annual passengers and a 104 percent fare box ratio by 1990.[27] State-level funding for transit and intercity rail service jumped with voter approval of rail bond measures in 1990.

California also took a big step by adopting ''flexible funding'' policies, which allow what were previously state highway resources to be reallocated to local roads and rail transit lines if local agencies wish to do so. The requirement for local agencies to implement congestion management programs also provides a basis for examining nontraditional ways to manage traffic demand. While few highway dollars have actually been shifted to transit since the legislation was adopted in 1989, the policy change is an important first step that will enable public officials to rethink traditional approaches in the future, in particular with corresponding changes at the federal level.

More challenging will be necessary adjustments in tax policy to end or at least reduce government interference in the transportation marketplace so heavily in favor of the automobile. Simply providing a better balanced mix of alternatives is important; but the economic return on transit investment would be much better (requiring fewer transit subsidies) if fewer auto subsidies and road capacity enhancements were provided, and the impact on the environment would be more beneficial. The reality, however, is that public sentiment for higher parking fees and $1-per-gallon gasoline tax increases is as weak as public sentiment for a better choice of transportation options is strong.

But everyone is for cleaner air, and stronger state and federal clean air laws will likely accelerate the need to implement more environmentally sound transportation policies. Predictions are that many urban road expansion proposals will face trouble in the years ahead as they run into conflict with air quality objectives.

MEETING FUTURE CHALLENGES

Changes in transportation policy take time. It now generally takes longer to construct a five-mile rail extension than it took to build the entire transcontinental railroad in the 1860s. Making a shift to a more pro-environmental transportation system will go up against ingrained societal attitudes, but that is not fundamentally different from convincing people to recycle beverage containers or to conserve water.

Californians *do* love their cars. But people are increasingly discovering that cars have their limits as population increases. The freedom and mobility that widespread ownership of cars made possible are increasingly being challenged, and Californians are recognizing that their transportation needs and the needs of the environment would be better served if more travel alternatives existed. More consumer choice and less dependency on a single mode sound attractive.

Reducing overdependency on the automobile does not mean that everyone must suddenly become a transit user. Many people can continue to use cars, with the emphasis on providing alternatives *some* of the time for those who can best take advantage of such choices.

A sound transportation environment in California must accommodate more people while maintaining quality of life and mobility. The planning for tomorrow's generations must start today.

CHAPTER 6

Water Supply: A New Era for a Scarce Resource

CLYDE MACDONALD

UNDERSTANDING WATER

Water is the cheapest salable commodity on the face of the earth. The federal government sells some agricultural water in California for about one cent for 1,000 gallons. Even dirt costs more. In our urban areas, fully treated drinking water costs about one cent for seven gallons.

Because water is incredibly cheap and conveniently piped to our farms, houses, and businesses, we use a lot of it—about 150 gallons per person per day in some urban areas. For a family of four, this urban use of water would fill 1,200 half-gallon milk cartons per day, weighing 4,500 pounds. When we say we need water, we need to understand how cheap water is and, really, how little we value it.

The subject of water is confusing, technical, financially complicated, and dripping with bloody regional disputes. But one fact

Clyde Macdonald received a bachelor's degree in engineering from the University of California at Davis, an M.B.A. from the University of California at Berkeley, and is a registered civil engineer. He has been on the staff of the California legislature for twenty-one years in various capacities, mostly dealing with water resources policy.

helps with understanding: in California, there is only enough developed water to irrigate or urbanize about one acre out of nine. And land without water isn't worth much. So, which land gets the water? And how much remains for the environment?

CURRENT WATER USE

In 1985, Californians used 40.4 million acre-feet of water, with an acre-foot equaling 326,000 gallons, or about one foot of water on a football field. Some of this water was used more than once; when we take out the multiple use, the "net" water use was 34 million acre-feet. Thirty-two million acre-feet were supplied by dependable, long-term water sources, and 2 million acre-feet were supplied by groundwater (well water) overdraft, which cannot continue in the long run. About two-thirds of the groundwater overdraft is in the agricultural San Joaquin Valley.[1]

Total net water use is about 80 percent agricultural, 16 percent urban, and 4 percent recreation, wildlife, and power generation (see Figure 6.1).[2] Of the 9 million acres of irrigated agricultural land, the largest uses are for cotton (1.5 million acres), irrigated pasture (1.0 million acres), alfalfa (1.0 million acres), and rice (0.5 million acres).[3]

Total water use is increasing at the lowest rate in our history, largely because agricultural water use stopped growing in about 1980 and began a slow decline. Almost all of the projected increase in water use is for California's urban areas, mostly to meet the needs of a population that is growing by about 750,000 people per year. Urban water needs are increasing about 64,000 acre-feet per year, which is about two-tenths of one percent of total water use per year.[4]

CURRENT WATER SUPPLY PROBLEMS

California's most critical water problem is how to meet the needs of a growing urban population. Compounding this problem, two existing urban water supplies will be reduced. First, in 1964, the U.S. Supreme Court ruled that the Metropolitan Water District of Southern California must give up 662,000 acre-feet of Colorado

FIGURE 6.1
HOW WATER IS USED IN CALIFORNIA

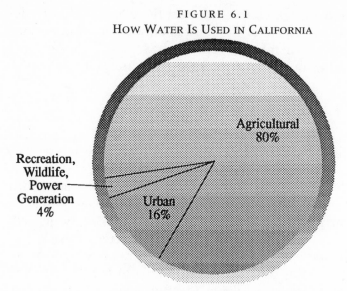

SOURCE: Department of Water Resources.

River water per year to Arizona when Arizona begins using its full share of the Colorado River, which is projected to occur in the 1990s. Second, because of a series of court decisions, Los Angeles is losing about 60,000 acre-feet of water per year that it had been diverting from the Mono Lake Basin.

The second most critical problem is the Delta, which is located in the middle of the Central Valley at the confluence of the Sacramento and San Joaquin rivers just before the combined rivers flow into San Francisco Bay (see Figure 6.2). The Delta's interconnected network of channels carries water north to south, supplying southern California, the greater San Jose area, eastern Contra Costa County, and the San Joaquin Valley. When the Delta lands were converted to agriculture 100 years ago, the lands were at sea level. Because of wind erosion and the oxidation of organics in the peat soil, the center of the Delta has been sinking about three inches per year and is now twenty to twenty-five feet below sea level and thirty to thirty-five feet below high tide. If the sinking isn't stopped, sooner or later the levees will fail, the central Delta will be permanently flooded, and more salt water will be able to flow into the Delta from San Francisco Bay. This would contaminate the 20 percent of the state's water that is now conveyed north to south through the Delta. In the short term, the fragile levees can be

FIGURE 6.2
CENTRAL VALLEY RIVERS AND SKETCH MAP OF THE DELTA

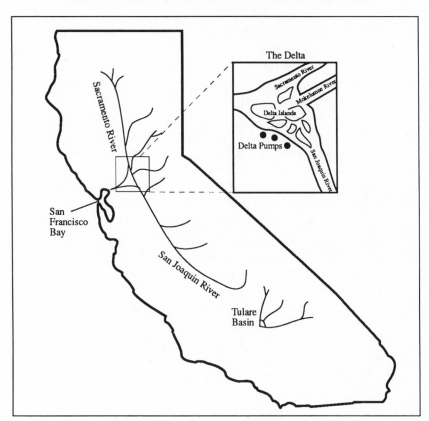

SOURCE: Assembly Office of Research.

strengthened. In the long term, the choices are to change land uses to stop the sinking or to build canals or pipes to convey water around the Delta, such as the Peripheral Canal would have done.

The third problem is drinking water quality. In the early 1990s the U.S. Environmental Protection Agency is expected to tighten its drinking water standard for trihalomethanes (THMs), which are suspected carcinogens. THMs are created when organic material reacts with halogens (chlorine, iodine, and bromine). Many of California's water systems may not meet the new standard. The choices will be to change treatment systems and/or to reduce the amount of organics and halogens in the source water supply. Because the Sacramento–San Joaquin Delta is such a large organic/

halogen source, construction of the controversial Peripheral Canal will be suggested again by some urban water agencies.

The fourth most critical problem is how to stop groundwater overdraft in the San Joaquin Valley, where some of the water supply was theoretically to be replaced by water imported from other areas. Expected amounts of imported water are not available because of cost and opposition from the other areas where the water would be obtained. Efforts to regulate groundwater overdraft have been attempted, but opposition to government involvement in managing groundwater has been intense.

The fifth critical problem is how to deal with salts accumulating in the soil and water on the west side of the San Joaquin Valley. These salts are brought in with the irrigation water and also leach out of the area's soils when the water is applied. Only a small part of the salts is carried away by the San Joaquin River; the rest accumulate in the soil and in shallow groundwater. Assuming no solution, about 1 million acres of agricultural lands will either go out of production or will have reduced agricultural productivity. The federal government constructed part of a drain to carry these salts to the Carquinez Straits—the waterway that connects the Delta with San Francisco Bay. Drain water was temporarily stored at Kesterson Reservoir and Wildlife Refuge. Later, the salts were found to contain toxics that caused hideous birth defects in waterfowl, and the drain was abandoned. The state and federal governments have not found a long-term solution.

PAST POLICIES

From 1850 to 1965, the water policy of the state was to establish institutions and laws to develop water and to construct dams and canals. More than 1,000 public water agencies were created: irrigation districts, municipal utility districts, reclamation districts, water storage districts, and one-of-a-kind entities such as the huge Metropolitan Water District of Southern California. In most cases, the agencies have been headed by boards of directors, either elected by voters or landowners who vote by the number of acres they own.

After gold mining declined, agriculture began a long period of dominance, and much of the state's available water was developed for irrigation. Today, agriculture uses 80 percent of the state's developed water, largely because farming was the first "big" economy in California.

At the turn of the century, the coastal cities began looking for water to satisfy their growing needs. The cities prevailed in conflicts with agricultural districts because of their growing urban power, economic and political. The cities typically entered into agreements with the affected agricultural areas, the exception being the Owens Valley, where Los Angeles simply used its economic power to gain what it felt it had to have. Elsewhere, city projects did not push agriculture out but coexisted with it.

In 1902, the most important water policy of all was established at the federal level: the decision to provide huge subsidies to agricultural water projects as a means to develop the agricultural economy of the West. Congress and the federal Bureau of Reclamation used a variety of methods to subsidize water: farmers didn't have to pay interest on the irrigation share of the capital costs; farmers who still couldn't afford the water were subsidized by the project's electrical users; "profitable" dams were used to subsidize the "unprofitable" dams; some dams, such as New Melones, were built without water contracts to repay the cost; and the government assumed all upfront costs, which meant that it took the financial risk if the project couldn't be completed, Auburn Dam being an example. Also, the bureau signed forty-year, fixed-rate repayment contracts, which meant that the government couldn't possibly collect enough money to pay back the federal treasury over the forty years because inflation would drive up the operating costs. Perhaps most importantly, the projects did not mitigate their environmental costs. With massive subsidies, federal dams and canals sprouted everywhere; the program was successful in promoting the development of the West. Towns grew, and people got jobs and paid taxes. For a long time these programs remained popular.

The largest Bureau of Reclamation project anywhere is the Central Valley Project, which consists of a series of major dams and canals, mostly serving the Central Valley. The principal dams are Shasta on the Sacramento River and Friant on the San Joaquin River. A large portion of the project's Sacramento River water is transported north to south across the Delta.

The State Water Project was authorized by the legislature in 1959 and was approved by 51 percent of the voters in 1960. Other than state's general fund bond financing, the project was not intended to contain external subsidies. To export 4 million acre-feet from north to south, the main features are Oroville Dam on the Feather River (north of Sacramento) and the California Aqueduct, which stretches from the Delta to southern California. By 1975, the dams and canals specified in the 1959 legislation were constructed, developing about 2.3 million acre-feet. Legislation approving the Peripheral Canal and new dams was passed in 1980 but defeated at the polls in 1982 following a referendum. Efforts to authorize an alternative Through-Delta Canal were abandoned in 1984.

IMPACT ON THE ENVIRONMENT

Water projects provided tremendous economic benefits to the state while ignoring environmental effects. In 1914, Congress authorized San Francisco to build O'Shaughnessy Dam, which flooded Yosemite Valley's sister canyon, Hetch Hetchy, within Yosemite National Park. This was probably one of the worst decisions, given today's perspective about the value of the excessively crowded Yosemite Valley. There are no good options to move the city's water and power facilities outside of the park.[5]

Los Angeles's diversion of Mono Lake Basin water was another environmentally damaging project, diverting the flow of the freshwater streams that nourish the saline lake, which has no outlet. With less inflow than evaporation, the lake began to shrink, creating a land bridge to an island used by California gulls for nesting. The major threat was that the lake would eventually become too salty to support the lake's brine shrimp, a critical food source for vast numbers of migrating birds. The problem has been approached on three fronts: court suits challenging the diversion of the tributary streams in violation of state law requiring the maintenance of fish below dams and diversions, court suits challenging the environmental impact on the brine shrimp and the migrating waterfowl, and bipartisan state legislation appropriating money for Los Angeles to develop an alternate water supply. Los Angeles has consistently lost in court. A final solution has not been reached, but the courts have made it clear that the lake should be protected.

Many of the best-known environmental damages were inflicted by the federal Bureau of Reclamation's Central Valley Project, an enormous project undertaken mostly before the environment became a high-profile issue. The major problems read like a who's who of water mismanagement in the West: Shasta Dam was constructed without the ability to control the temperature of the water released from the dam, making it difficult to protect downstream fisheries. Trinity Dam diverted 90 percent of the water of the Trinity River, and its world-class salmon runs were devastated. The Red Bluff Diversion Dam was built across the Sacramento River simply to lift water into a canal, creating a barrier to migrating salmon. Friant Dam diverted nearly all of the water of the San Joaquin River to canals, wiping out anadromous fisheries and a long stretch of river. The federal pumps in the south Delta pull in most of the San Joaquin River in most months, disrupting the migration path of fish and driving some species toward extinction. The Kesterson drainage and toxics problem was largely caused by federal water deliveries and inattention to the chemicals in the drainage water. Finally, New Melones Dam buried an incomparably beautiful canyon that provided the most-floated whitewater in the West.

After the State Water Project was built, almost all fisheries in the Delta declined, some dramatically. Striped bass have declined to less than 5 percent of their pre-1960 levels (see Figure 6.3). The winter-run salmon are now on the endangered species list. Delta smelt may be listed next. Contributing to these problems are industrial pollution, pesticides, dams, urban runoff, and introduced species that compete with indigenous wildlife.

THE FORCES CREATING POLICY CHANGES

From an economic perspective, the most significant fact forcing a change in water policies is that almost all of the good dam sites have been built upon. The remaining sites would require large, very expensive dams to create small reservoirs and small increases in water supplies. Another significant economic force for change is fiscal conservatism, which calls for lower taxes, fewer government programs, and fewer subsidies.

Another transition force has been the post–World War II expansion of the highway system, which opened mountainous areas to recreation. Along with other aspects of a changing California society, this helped create a constituency of fishermen, campers, hikers, rafters, wildlife groups, and others that favored protection, and the

FIGURE 6.3
INDEX OF NUMBER OF YOUNG STRIPED BASS

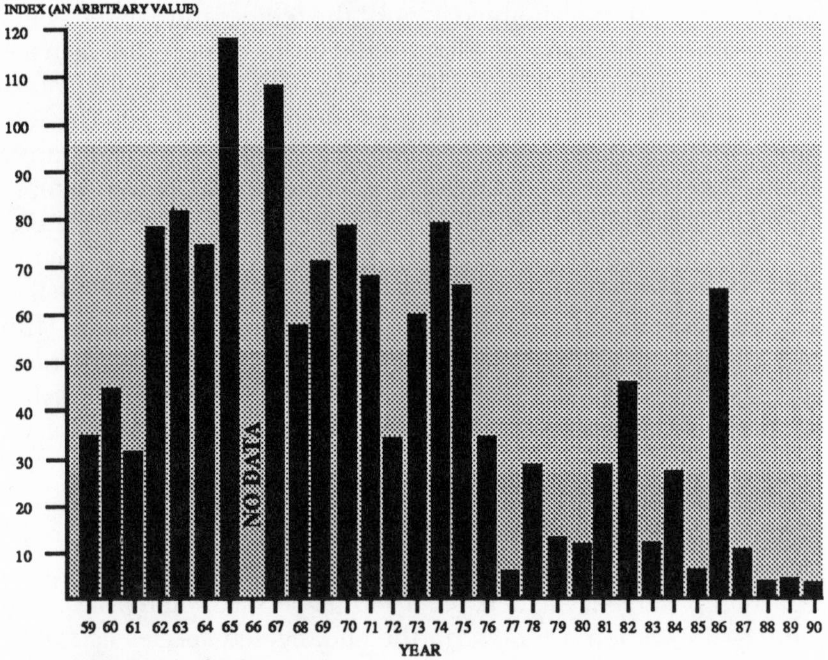

INDEX (AN ARBITRARY VALUE)

YEAR
SOURCE: Department of Fish and Game.

environmental movement grew, with concerns for ecosystems management, endangered species, and the many values that natural rivers provide.

The state and federal governments have provided better mechanisms to minimize environmental damages for new projects. State and federal environmental laws, such as the California Environmental Quality Act, the federal Environmental Quality Act, and the Endangered Species Act, have been aggressively used by fish, wildlife, and river enthusiasts to oppose environmentally damaging water projects.

A significant force for change has been the political activism of people in water surplus areas against export projects, such as the proposed Peripheral Canal, Through-Delta Canal, Mono Lake, and Owens Valley projects. In most of these cases, the activism did not occur with the first export, but with the second proposed export.

WATER POLITICS

Three basic problems repeatedly appear in the heated politics of water: the apparent goals of the different interest groups seem to be diametrically opposed, there is little trust among the parties, and the leaderships of the groups have little real authority to negotiate because their constituents are more entrenched than the leaders.

In fact, the major interest groups have many goals that are similar, although the reasons they have these goals may be different. The major interests support better protections for drinking water quality, more water conservation, more water reclamation, restoration of fisheries, and better protections for the environment. These similarities lend some hope that reasonable compromises can be reached.

NEW PROGRAMS

The inability to construct new dams has forced urban water districts to focus on conservation, reclamation, and desalination.

The main tools in water conservation are leak detection programs, ditch lining, landscape regulations, controls on automatic sprinklers, alternate-day lawn-watering regulations, water pricing, and multiple uses of water in industrial plants. In some areas, highly treated sewage water will be used to replace fresh water at golf courses, industrial plants, and at locations where fresh water is injected into the ground to prevent ocean water from invading freshwater aquifers. Reclamation of polluted groundwater by reverse osmosis is one option in southern California, where large groundwater basins contain salty and slightly polluted water. Conservation and reclamation have the potential of increasing urban water supplies by about 1.25 million acre-feet, which is almost 4 percent of total urban and agricultural use.

Along the coast, desalination of ocean water may assist in meeting water supplies where additional water is unattainable or costly. Since desalination is energy-intensive, the best locations will be near electrical generating plants, where the desalination plant can use waste heat.

Agricultural water conservation offers substantial opportunities to improve farm efficiency and output. More efficient water use increases crop yields, reduces fertilizer requirements, and lessens water pollution. One of many opportunities to save water in agriculture is to capture 650,000 acre-feet of drainage water that flows into unusable saline water bodies—the Salton Sea and groundwater on the west side of the San Joaquin Valley. The Metropolitan Water District and the Imperial Irrigation District have agreed to capture 100,000 acre-feet by lining leaky irrigation canals in the Imperial Valley.

A major policy change in recent years has been the state legislature's authorization of water transfers, which are the sales or leases of already developed water between willing sellers. For the most part, water transfers will be undertaken in drought periods, with water moving from low-valued agricultural uses to high-valued agricultural and urban uses, thereby protecting the state's economy. Proposed extensions of water transfers have caused a split between urban and agricultural districts that used to work together touting new dams. The urban areas are now beginning to see some of the agricultural areas as potential sources of water.

The principal advantage of transfers will be realized only when transfers are combined with conjunctive use, a management strategy of drawing more water from rivers in wet periods and more from groundwater in dry periods. The most likely operation will have an urban agency paying for conjunctive use facilities that will recharge the groundwater of an agricultural area in wet and normal years. In dry years, the stored water will be provided to the urban area, either directly or indirectly by exchange. In simple terms, the agricultural area will be "renting" its available groundwater space to the urban area without any impact on agricultural production and with a positive impact on the farm economy.

THE FUTURE

The most important characteristic of water policies in California is that, in the long term, they have proven to be flexible. Historically, water policy has changed to continue to supercharge California's economic engine, although change can be painful. For the future, the policy framework is likely to evolve in a number of directions.

There won't be any new, big water projects such as the Central Valley Project and the State Water Project.

Decisions to authorize water projects will shift back to the local level from the state and federal governments.

There will be very few new dams on streams. Auburn Dam will continue to be very difficult to build for economic, environmental, and political reasons. New reservoirs such as Los Banos Grandes and Los Vaqueros will be "off-stream," meaning that water will be pumped into essentially dry canyons during wet periods for later withdrawal.

Conservation, reclamation, and desalination will become much more common as we subsidize conservation and better management rather than dams. The old subsidies for dams and surplus crops will be attacked with greater ferocity because it will be inconsistent to subsidize conservation while continuing to encourage water use through water and crop subsidies.

Voluntary water transfers will reallocate water from low-valued uses to higher-valued uses during droughts. Conjunctive use programs will convert groundwater basins into storage reservoirs, which will have a positive impact on the farm economy.

Because central Delta agricultural lands will continue to sink as they have for 100 years, the Delta is doomed to permanent flooding or the lands will be converted to other uses.

The question of building the Peripheral Canal or something similar will be raised again because of drinking water quality issues, fishery problems, and concerns about the sinking of Delta lands.

Some irrigated farmlands on the west side of the San Joaquin Valley with the worst toxic drainage will go out of production because the owners cannot meet drainage standards. The water made available will be used to resolve the overdraft problems of other parts of the San Joaquin Valley and to supply urban areas. In the more distant future, the value of San Joaquin agricultural lands will require that a drain be constructed to San Francisco Bay or to the ocean to prevent these farmlands from going out of production because of excessive salt contamination. To protect the environment of the bay or ocean, the drains will be restricted to nontoxic runoff or the water will be treated.

The San Joaquin Valley will begin an internal struggle that will result in groundwater management programs to prevent the overdraft from getting worse and to avoid litigation over rights to groundwater.

Programs to correct the environmental damages of the past will become more popular.

CONCLUSION

The three groups that most influence California water development and management are irrigators, urban water agencies, and environmentalists. In the mid-1960s, when the environmental movement bloomed, the primary alliance was between irrigators and urban water agencies. The objections by environmentalists brought water development to a near stalemate for twenty-five years. The last time the state approved new water development was 1960, and the last large federal water development project was approved in 1968.

In the last decade the two groups forming the alliance have shifted, depending on the issue. Environmentalists and some large irrigators defeated the Peripheral Canal in 1982, bound curiously by opposite motives: the environmentalists thought the canal posed too great a threat to fisheries; the irrigators thought it was too constrained by environmental controls. In 1984 and 1986, the Through-Delta Plan was supported by irrigators, opposed by environmentalists, and stopped. In 1991, urban water agencies and environmentalists tried to enact legislation forcing irrigation districts to cooperate in transferring water from agricultural to urban uses, but their proposal was stalled by agricultural opposition.

The most hopeful sign came in 1991, when all three groups began negotiating to resolve the problems of Delta supply, water quality, water transfers, and environmental protections. Whether these negotiations will falter owing to the historic, serious differences between the parties remains to be seen.

Another roadblock could be fundamental differences about the future of the Central Valley Project, which are being considered by Congress. But the negotiations have proven to all three parties that they have more in common than they thought, and that the positions of the various parties are worthy of mutual respect. The outcome of these negotiations will produce either an historic agreement or simply another in the endless series of California water wars.

FURTHER INFORMATION

California Assembly Office of Research, *California 2000: Paradise or Peril* (Sacramento: California Assembly Office of Research, 1987).

California Department of Water Resources, *California Water, Looking to the Future, Bulletin 160–87* (Sacramento: California Department of Water Resources, 1987).

California Office of Planning and Research, *California Water Atlas* (Sacramento: California Office of Planning and Research, 1979).

Ernest A. Engelbert, ed., *Competition for California Water* (Berkeley: University of California Press, 1982).

Tim Palmer, *Endangered Rivers and the Conservation Movement* (Berkeley: University of California Press, 1986).

CHAPTER 7

The Quality of Water

ALVIN J. GREENBERG

The quality of water affects the very substance of our existence, the very health and well-being of our bodies. Concern over water quality abounds. When traveling to other countries, the admonition "Don't drink the water" is almost a given. Californians have come to rely on our water as being among the highest quality and best in the world. We depend on clean water for boating, fishing, swimming, irrigation, washing, cleaning, bathing, and, of course, drinking. Our water is a resource to be treasured, protected, and respected. There is probably no single act of faith more important or practiced more often by Californians than turning on the faucet and expecting clean, safe, high-quality water to flow from it.

The problem is that this single act of faith, along with the other acts of faith in fishing, swimming, and boating, may not be justified. Much of California's surface waters and groundwaters are contaminated with pesticides, herbicides, oil, grease, solvents, chemicals,

Alvin J. Greenberg received his doctorate in pharmaceutical/medicinal chemistry from the University of California in San Francisco. He is President of Risk Science Associates, a Corte Madera company providing consultation in toxic substance risk assessment, hazardous waste management, drinking water quality, and air quality matters. He has served on numerous county, regional, and state advisory committees, including the California Department of Water Resources 1982 Scientific Panel on Sacramento–San Joaquin Delta Drinking Water Supplies.

mining wastes, hazardous wastes, municipal discharges, industrial effluent, and runoff from cities, towns, and farms.

Take the massive Sacramento–San Joaquin Delta, home to thousands of waterfowl and thousands of fish, and the source of drinking water to 20 million Californians. The lower San Joaquin River, which flows into the Delta, was recently described by a scientist at the State Water Resources Control Board (SWRCB) as the "lower colon of California."

Note the fact that in 1984, more than 2,500 groundwater wells were so contaminated with pesticides that they could no longer be used as a source for human consumption. In a time of drought and extreme competition for dwindling available quantities of water, California can hardly afford to lose groundwater or surface water supplies because of contamination.

Something is being done to address the threat to water quality in California. The most important laws regarding water quality are the Porter-Cologne Water Quality Control Act—the basic California law for dealing with water quality problems—and the federal Clean Water Act.

The heart of the Porter-Cologne Act is the setting of waste discharge requirements. The state, usually through the regional water quality control boards (RWQCBs), imposes permit restrictions on discharges. The law also enables the state to act against pollution and regulate land disposal of wastes that might affect water quality. The federal Clean Water Act requires that water quality be enhanced and maintained. Together, these laws are the basis for establishing water quality objectives that address and limit pollution.

REGULATION OF WATER QUALITY

The goal of protecting water quality was advanced by the 1972 Federal Water Pollution Control Act, which had the noble but unrealistic goal of the elimination of the discharge of all pollutants into the nation's waters by 1985. The regulation addressed only a limited number of conventional and nonconventional pollutants and 129 specific toxic (priority) pollutants, while it had been estimated in the early 1970s that some 63,000 chemicals were already in commerce, with others coming into use at a rate of perhaps 1,000 per year.

The federal act and the Porter-Cologne Act have taken us toward that 1972 goal and partly assure that all waters are fishable, swimmable, and boatable. The purposes of the laws are to protect surface and groundwater quality from human-made pollution and to maintain the "beneficial uses" of water, which include not only public drinking supplies but irrigation, recreation, fisheries, and wildlife habitat.

The major requirement of these acts is the National Pollutant Discharge Elimination System (NPDES) standards for major discharges and standards to protect groundwater through state requirements. Industrial waste pretreatment programs are implemented by California under the Clean Water Act to control the discharge of toxic substances and thereby protect sewer systems, treatment plants, sludges, and receiving waters from toxic contamination. Where programs are approved, including California, the states have primary responsibility to apply and enforce the requirements of the Clean Water Act. Since 1987, the federal Clean Water Act has required each state to develop a nonpoint source program, and the SWRCB responded to this requirement.[1]

To address water quality degradation, California enacted additional legislation in the 1980s:

- Regulation of underground storage tanks (Sher, Cortese Bills) to prevent groundwater contamination.
- Regulation and cleanup of toxics pits to limit the use of surface impoundments for hazardous waste (Katz Bill AB 3566/3121).
- Regulation of hazardous solid waste disposal (Calderon Bill AB 3525/3374).
- Land disposal phaseout (Roberti Bill SB 1500), designed to protect groundwater by accelerating the transition from land disposal to hazardous waste treatment.
- Safe Drinking Water and Toxics Enforcement Act of 1986 (Proposition 65), to protect drinking water sources from toxic contamination by requiring the development of a list of chemicals known or suspected to cause cancer or reproductive damage and to prohibit their "knowing discharge" into drinking water sources.

Indiscriminate dumping of wastes in the waters of California is no longer tolerated, and it is clear that while much has been accomplished in the past to address water quality, much remains to be done. The history of water quality demonstrates that the bureaucracy of regulation moves slowly in a rapidly advancing society.

SURFACE WATER QUALITY

Surface water quality in California is one of the most important environmental criteria from not only a public health perspective but a quality of life and environmental perspective as well. Water can be impacted by a number of "point" sources of pollutants, such as industrial and municipal discharges regulated by an NPDES permit. The vast majority of point discharges are in compliance, and those that are not are generally subject to actions by the regional water boards.

"Nonpoint" sources of pollution are from widespread areas and include excessive or poorly timed applications of pesticides and fertilizers, agricultural drainage, septic systems, urban runoff, and acid mine drainage. These are harder to control than point sources and are now the major cause of water pollution in California. In one study of urban runoff, 200 toxic organic compounds and metals were detected in storm sewer waters.

Other nonpoint sources include channel erosion, sedimentation due to construction and land development, hydrologic modification, physical habitat alteration, and dredging. Even increased sedimentation (total dissolved solids resulting in an increase in turbidity) can have a profound effect on water quality and the ability of fish to spawn. Thus, even if a river is not impacted by pollution from point sources, improper timber management and clear-cutting can dramatically increase soil erosion in a watershed to the point of drastically reducing the quality of the river. Siltation of the Eel River system results from massive runoff during storms, and much siltation is due to improper logging practices in the past, impacting the fish population.

Dams and water diversions can also have profound adverse effects on water quality. Where cool, rushing rivers once existed, impoundments create flatwater reservoirs with higher temperatures, which often lead to increased algae blooms and low-quality water. Water quality problems during the 1976–1977 drought due to algae blooms in reservoirs is an example. Diversions lead to reduced water flow downstream and hence higher temperatures and decreased ability to dilute pollutants. The result is decreased water quality, a fact demonstrated in the Sacramento–San Joaquin Delta almost every year due to massive diversions of water to the south.

A Tour of California Waters

A "tour" of the major rivers and streams in California (see Figure 7.1) can be useful in describing water quality.[2]

North Coast Waters

The Smith, Klamath, and Eel rivers have some of the highest-quality water in California, in no case exceeding contaminant limits that the National Academy of Sciences (NAS) recommends for the protection of freshwater species. This is not unexpected, as these waters for the most part are not close to population centers, heavy industry, agricultural drainage systems, or mines. However, information on surface water in this area is also the most incomplete. Comprehensive studies of the effects of chemicals and herbicides used by the lumber industry have not been conducted. Elevated levels of arsenic, nickel, and chromium have been detected in the Smith River.[3] The arsenic and chromium could come from wood treatment chemicals. In the Klamath River, elevated levels of nickel were detected. Some levels of mercury and zinc in fish were found to be slightly elevated in the mid-1980s, along with levels of chromium, copper, and lead in water.[4] Copper levels could possibly have come from inactive mines. In the Mad River, the only pollutants were at the point of entry into Humboldt Bay, but the high levels of tetrachloro- and pentachlorophenol that were found were of great concern[5]; possible sources included the wood treatment industry. In the Eel River, water levels of chromium, copper, and lead were higher than average in the mid-1980s. The copper could have been coming from an inactive mine and the chromium from the wood treatment industry.[6] In the Russian River, slightly elevated levels of zinc in fish and chromium, lead, and mercury in water existed. There have also been problems with municipal

FIGURE 7.1
MAJOR RIVERS OF CALIFORNIA

wastewater discharges and industrial discharge of toxics into the Russian River.

Central Coast Waters

The Old Salinas River (the old river channel of the Salinas River) harbors some of the worst problems of any river in California. DDT, Chlordane, Endosulfan, and Toxaphene were all above NAS guidelines, with Chlorpyrifos and Dacthal also at high levels. Possible sources include agricultural return waters and/or storm drainage. In the Salinas River, DDT, PCBs, and Toxaphene were also above NAS guidelines. Dacthal was high, and cadmium, mercury, and chromium were slightly elevated.

Lake Tahoe

A masterpiece of mountain scenery and of water quality until recent years, Tahoe is the second-deepest lake in the United States, the tenth-deepest in the world, and holds more water than all other lakes and reservoirs in California combined. Worldwide, only Crater Lake in Oregon holds water as clear as Tahoe's. But between 1970 and 1978, nutrients from erosion increased by 20 percent and algae grew by 150 percent. In the thirteen years preceding 1983, lake clarity decreased from 100 to 75 feet, and a straight-line projection showed that the lake would lose most of its transparency in forty years. Efforts of the Tahoe Regional Planning Agency have sought, with only partial success, to halt the degradation of this unique feature of the California landscape. Clarity continued to decrease in the late 1980s and early 1990s.

Central Valley Waters

The rivers that drain the Sierra Nevada rival the North Coast rivers for exceptional water quality, but only for those sections in the mountains. Upon reaching the Central Valley, water quality deteriorates. In some sections of the Sacramento River, mercury and PCBs were above NAS guidelines. Silver, copper, nickel, zinc, cadmium, chromium, and Endosulfan were also elevated at times.[7] Sources of metal contaminants include an inactive mine on a tributary near Redding. The Department of Food and Agriculture's "Pesticide Use Report" for 1986 indicated that counties in the Sacramento River basin used 6.6 million pounds of pesticide active ingredients.[8] Rice growing also presents a unique situation for the movement of pesticides into rivers and the Delta. The herbicides Bolero, Ordram, and Basagran are applied at various times during the season and discharged into agricultural drains. Then, along with the irrigation water, they are discharged into the Sacramento River and eventually reach Sacramento and the Delta. Human exposure can also occur by ingestion of locally caught fish and ducks as well as by swimming in the river and Delta waters. Although changes in pesticide selection, application, and postapplication management reduced pesticide levels in the river, application to rice continues to be a major pesticide source in state waters.

In the Feather River, mercury exceeded NAS guidelines. Molinate, Thiobencarb, Ordram, and Bolero seasonally enter the river and represent the most serious risk. In the American River, trichloroethylene was high, and mercury, arsenic, cadmium, and lead were all higher than average in fish. A combination of industrial and municipal wastewater discharges are probably the sources. Fish from the Cosumnes River sometimes contain elevated levels of copper and zinc. Copper, probably from an inactive mine, was higher than average in fish from the Mokelumne River. Samples in the lower Stanislaus River contained toxaphene and PCBs above NAS guidelines, and fish contained above-average levels of cadmium and mercury. The Tuolumne River, of exceptional quality in the mountains, contains Toxaphene above NAS guidelines in the lower river, and mercury was above average in fish. The Merced River contains elevated levels of arsenic and cadmium, probably due to an inactive mine. Toxaphene is above NAS guidelines in the lower Merced.

Of the major rivers used for water supply, the San Joaquin at Vernalis is one of the most heavily polluted in California, primarily because of agricultural wastewater discharges. Voluminous data are available on the San Joaquin. To summarize, significant concentrations of toxic metals and pesticides were found in the water and/or fish and waterfowl, including mercury, Chlordane, Endosulfan, Toxaphene, PCBs, arsenic, cadmium, copper, chromium, lead, selenium, boron, and molybdenum.[9]

The issue of toxic agricultural drain water at Kesterson Reservoir and Wildlife Refuge has also been studied extensively. The San Luis Drain has deposited selenium at levels fatal to birds and fish. Less clear is the extent to which selenium has found its way into the Delta and San Francisco Bay, but there has been speculation linking the element to fish population declines.[10]

The Sacramento–San Joaquin Delta

The San Francisco Bay/Sacramento–San Joaquin Delta Estuary (Bay-Delta) is the largest and perhaps most important estuary on the western coast of North America. It is an extensive network of 700 miles of freshwater waterways and more than 350,000 acres of marsh, estuary, and open bay. The rivers and streams that feed this estuary drain 40 percent of California.

The Delta ecosystem is habitat for more than 100 fish species, 230 bird species, 43 mammal species, 15 species of reptiles, and 8 different amphibians.[11] Some of these animals are threatened or presently in danger of extinction. Some plant species are also listed by the state or federal government as rare, threatened, or endangered. Additionally, 450,000 to 600,000 migratory waterfowl winter at the Delta. Chinook salmon, striped bass, and American shad are the basis for important recreation and commercial fisheries, with an annual commercial value of about $20 million. Annual recreational use of the Delta is estimated at 12 million user-days.

From the Delta, two major water projects deliver about 6 million acre-feet to 20 million Californians and to several million acres of farmland in the San Joaquin Valley and Tulare Lake basin. In addition, water is delivered within the Delta boundaries to four cities, 515,000 acres of farmland, and many industries. Given the size of the land mass that drains into the Delta, it is not surprising that urban development, industrial and chemical facilities, agricultural runoff, and mines all impact on the quality of inflowing rivers.

Befitting the immense importance of the Delta, more studies, reports, and monitoring of water quality were conducted here than on any other body of water in the state. An SWRCB report determined that the Bay-Delta and the major tributaries that feed it (the Sacramento, American, and San Joaquin rivers) do not fully support all of the beneficial uses of these waters.[12] Water quality deteriorated to the point that some uses are no longer possible and others are threatened. Some fish populations declined almost to the point of disappearance, and concerns about contaminants found in fish and waterfowl tissue continue. The California Department of Health Services posted health warnings advising the public of mercury contamination of striped bass. Although mercury contamination is variable throughout the Delta, there are indications that mercury comes from the Coast Range drainages and from the Sacramento, American, and Feather rivers, which are contaminated by abandoned gold mines. At times, fish exceed the U.S. Food and Drug Administration (FDA) standards for protection of human health.

A San Joaquin River pulp mill discharges dioxins, which are persistent, toxic, and bioaccumulative contaminants. According to an EPA study, an effluent concentration of 2,3,7,8-TCDD exceeds the EPA ambient water quality criterion for protection of human health by a factor of 3,800. Dioxin-contaminated fish caught off the pulp mill discharge at Antioch pose a cancer risk slightly greater than 1 in 100,000. To meet the "no significant risk" level under Proposition 65, fewer than two meals of fish should be eaten per month. The Central Valley Regional Board issued a notification under the requirements of Proposition 65. Dioxin-contaminated fish were also found near the Port of Stockton (fish contained six times the equivalent concentration of dioxins as the bottom-dwelling fish caught off the pulp mill discharge at Antioch). The sources of dioxin at Stockton were not identified.

Pesticide contamination occurs in the Delta's upstream drainages and from within the Delta waterways. San Joaquin River fish consistently exceeded FDA standards for protection of human health, and pesticides such as Chlordane, DDT, and Toxaphene in fish tissue exceeded the NAS standard from 1978 to 1987. Similar yet less frequent pesticide contamination was documented in the Sacramento River. High pesticide levels may reflect illegal disposal as well as normal agricultural use.

The SWRCB developed a Pollutant Policy Document for the Bay-Delta estuary,[13] which identified fourteen pollutants of concern, including arsenic, cadmium, chromium, copper, chlorinated dibenzodioxins and dibenzofurans, hydrocarbons, lead, mercury, nickel, organochlorines, selenium, silver, tributyltin, and zinc, as well as the problem of cumulative pesticide loads. Additionally, an important water quality concept advanced in 1985[14] regarding the large amount of selenium entering the Delta ecosystem was embraced by the SWRCB by implementing a strategy to regulate mass emissions of arsenic, cadmium, copper, mercury, selenium, silver, and polynuclear aromatic hydrocarbons.

Southern California Waters

The New and Alamo rivers originate in Mexico and have been the subject of much negotiation. Industrial and municipal pollution from the Mexican side has been severe. DDT, PCBs, Toxaphene, Chlorpyrifos, Dacthal, and Endosulfan have been detected at high levels. California sources may be making a bad situation worse by inappropriate dumping into rivers that some people regard as irreversibly contaminated.

Surface Water Summary

Although presenting so much data about poor water quality can lead to a gloomy outlook, it must be emphasized that most of the state's rivers and lakes are of excellent to good quality. The focus on problems is perhaps the best way to dramatize that much work remains to be accomplished. Of the twenty-two surface waters listed here, thirteen contained at least one toxic substance at a level above NAS guidelines for the protection of predator species, a critical concern when bioaccumulation into the environment and the food chain is considered. Although only a few of these substances were at levels higher than FDA guidelines for the protection of human health, the importance of ecosystem protection by remaining significantly under the NAS guidelines cannot be overemphasized. The tragedy of selenium poisoning at Kesterson is a case in point; some of the selenium levels that caused deformities in wildlife were far below accepted standards.

Discharge of toxic agricultural wastewater is widespread throughout California from the Feather River to the New River. The failure of the Clean Water Act and state laws to control the discharge of agricultural wastes is well documented. Industrial, municipal, and logging/lumber industry sources are also known to discharge metals, organics, oil, and grease. What is surprising, however, is the extent and severity of contamination resulting from metals such as mercury, lead, copper, and chromium leaching from abandoned mines. From the Eel River to the Salinas River, abandoned mines continue to contaminate rivers and lakes.

Little is known about thousands of synthetic organic chemicals for which there is no monitoring. Trace metals such as selenium are essential for life but are toxic in slightly larger amounts. The preservation of California's water should be subject to the intense and lively scrutiny of a scientific process and increased protection efforts to match the increasing population of the state.

GROUNDWATER

About 40 percent of the drinking water (92 percent in rural areas) in California is taken from about 200 subterranean aquifers located 20 to 1,000 feet below ground surface. These provide all or part of the drinking water needs of 22 million Californians. In the past decade, chemical contamination of groundwater supplies has increased at a dramatic rate from four sources: leaking underground industrial storage tanks (in particular, from the electronics industry), nonpoint sources such as agricultural pesticides and herbicides, leakage from hazardous waste disposal sites, and discharge of leachates from municipal landfills.

Groundwater contamination has been detected in every major agricultural and urban area of the state, mostly resulting from the handling, storage, and disposal of industrial and agricultural chemicals, including fifty-seven pesticides. The number of wells contaminated with just one chemical—dibromochloropropane (DBCP)—increased from 40 in 1979 to 2,449 in 1984. Every hazardous waste disposal site was found to leak toxic wastes into the groundwater to some degree. The use of surface impoundments for the storage and disposal of hazardous wastes has been the leading cause of toxic contamination; eight of California's top ten dump sites were contaminated by unlined impoundments, incapable of containing hazardous liquids. In May 1991, it was discovered that groundwater in Yosemite Valley was contaminated from leaking underground fuel tanks; even the state's most prestigious park has not escaped groundwater problems.

A summary of many studies shows that surface waste impoundments have been responsible for extensive environmental contamination, that the continued use of thousands of unlined pits for the disposal of hazardous wastes poses an unprecedented risk to public health and groundwater quality, and that regulations affecting hazardous waste impoundments were inadequate to halt the widespread contamination of air, land, and water.

The scientific and regulatory response to this threat has been significant. Regional water quality control boards and local governments are imposing new requirements to clean up and prevent contamination. Some state and federal Superfund sites with groundwater contamination are being cleaned up.

PUBLIC HEALTH AND GROUNDWATER QUALITY

Groundwater is a crucial element in California's public health and water supply picture, with smaller water systems and private residences being especially dependent: 93 percent of these systems supplying 5 percent of the population rely on wells. Historically, groundwater has been considered safer than surface water because the soil acts as a natural filtering medium for surface pollution. However, the discovery of widespread contamination by synthetic organochlorine chemicals in the Santa Clara Valley, San Fernando Valley, San Gabriel Valley, and San Joaquin Valley has changed this perception. In 1980 and 1983, the California Department of Health Services was required to prepare and implement a program for detecting and monitoring organic chemical contaminants in drinking water supplies. With 2,947 large-system wells having been sampled initially, a total of 7,712 of California's public drinking water wells have been tested for organic chemical contamination.[15]

The results showed that among the larger wells, 538 (18.3 percent) showed some degree of contamination while 165 (5.6 percent) exceeded one or more of the state's "action levels" (ALs) or "maximum contaminant levels" (MCLs). ALs are informal health guidelines, whereas MCLs are enforceable water quality standards. Among the smaller wells, 383 (8 percent) showed some contamination. One hundred forty-nine of these wells (3.1 percent) exceeded one of the state's MCLs, and 100 (2.1 percent) exceeded one of the ALs. In most cases, water suppliers have closed troublesome wells or provided treatment.

While the sampling showed many areas for concern, widespread contamination of groundwater sources supplying large water systems is not a major problem. A small number of counties account for most of the contaminated wells; 41 percent of the contaminated wells found statewide were in Los Angeles County. Yet, in a disturbing finding, thirteen chemicals for which ALs or MCLs have not been developed were identified in 17 percent of the contaminated wells, and the impacts on public health are unknown.

A total of 248,000 tests for individual chemicals were conducted under the state's small public water system program. Among the 263 chemicals for which tests were conducted, 48 were contaminating small public wells, the most frequently detected contaminants being DBCP, perchloroethylene (PCE), and chloroform, all suspected human carcinogens. These were also among the most common contaminants found in large water system wells. Most of the counties showing large numbers of contaminated wells are heavily agricultural; the recurring problem is DBCP.

One water quality parameter bears special scrutiny because of its presence in Delta water supplies: salinity in the form of salt water.[16] In order to prevent intrusion of sea water into Delta supplies, adequate flows must pass through the Delta, undiverted, and into the sea. During drought, some sea water intrusion occurs, increasing the salinity of the Delta and impacting on public health.

THE FUTURE

The future of water quality in California lies in the hands of the State Water Resources Control Board, the regional water quality control boards, the U.S. Environmental Protection Agency, and ultimately the citizens. The outlook is unsure. Supported and sometimes pushed by a citizenry that demands superior water quality, the regulatory agencies have at times responded with ambitious plans for environmental and public health protection. Where one agency has faltered, another has sometimes picked up the standard. In September 1991, the EPA rejected the State Water Resources Control Board's Water Quality Control Plan for the Delta because the plan failed to protect the environment. The EPA stated that the plan lacked adequate standards for freshwater flow and salinity. The EPA further indicated that if the board did not develop an adequate salinity standard within ninety days, the EPA would develop the standard on its own.

One of the most ambitious water quality plans is the SWRCB agenda for the development of water quality control plans for inland surface waters,[17] including the development of numerical water quality objectives based on EPA criteria for human health or aquatic life and with schedules of compliance. Such plans will supersede regional water quality control plans where conflicts exist, thus assuring statewide consistency. In the past, water quality objectives have been developed and adopted by the nine regional water quality control boards in a time-consuming process. The statewide plans will now supplement the regional plans.

To address the problems of nonpoint sources of pollution, which includes agricultural runoff, Section 319 of the federal Clean Water Act requires each state to develop a nonpoint program. The SWRCB's 1988 report on nonpoint source pollution responds to this requirement and is being implemented.[18]

Finally, the Safe Drinking Water and Toxics Enforcement Act of 1986 (Proposition 65) is being implemented to protect drinking water sources from toxic contamination by prohibiting the "knowing discharge" of carcinogens or reproductive toxicants into drinking water sources.

The full implementation of these programs will increase the likelihood that surface and groundwater quality in California will be maintained and in some places enhanced. This is crucial to the viability of our state because we have learned from several years of drought that we cannot afford to contaminate our precious water resources. Quality and quantity are interdependent, and the lack of one affects the other.

CHAPTER 8

Troubled Shores: The Ocean, Bays, and Estuaries

BARRY NELSON

The gold that has attracted millions to the Golden State is not that of the mother lode, but rather that of the California coastline— golden sands, tans, and sunsets. Perhaps more than anything else, California is famous for its unique relationship with the water, from the beach communities of southern California and the rugged beauty of Big Sur to the Golden Gate and the fog-enshrouded North Coast.

At least in part, it is the ocean and the state's bays and estuaries that have attracted the 25.5 million people, 85 percent of the state's population, who live within an hour's drive of the California coast. The attraction is multifaceted: these bodies of water provide beauty, a wide variety of recreational opportunities, and a moderate cli-

Barry Nelson is the executive director of the Save San Francisco Bay Association and works on a variety of issues, including water quality, water diversion, wetlands protection, and increasing shoreline parks and trails. He joined the association in 1984 and in 1988 became its first executive director. Mr. Nelson holds a master's degree in rhetoric and a bachelor's degree in rhetoric and economics from the University of California at Berkeley.

mate, as well as tourism, commercial fishing, shipping, and other economic activities. In many ways, California's coastal waters are vital to the quality of life for which the state is famous.

However, many of the environmental ills associated with modern life—air and water pollution, habitat destruction, declining fish and wildlife populations, and more—have come to the coast. Perhaps nowhere else in the state have more environmental problems come together than along this 1,100-mile-long edge of the continent.

STATUS OF COASTAL WATERS

A quick tour will reveal that many precious marine, bay, and estuarine resources are at a critical point at which Californians must choose either to restore coastal waters or let them be ruined. A selection of problems facing the North Coast, San Francisco Bay, Gulf of the Farallon, Central Coast, and Southern California follows.

North Coast

Thousand-year-old redwoods, dozens of salmon and steelhead streams, Roosevelt elk on wind-swept beaches—the shores from the Oregon border to Sonoma County support a wealth of wildlife along one of the most stunning coastlines in the world. Some of these resources are publicly owned, such as Redwood National Park and the Sinkyone Wilderness State Park. Public ownership, however, is far from a guarantee of protection. National forest land has been logged at a staggering pace, leading to serious damage downstream.

Although it shelters so many species of wildlife, the North Coast is home to remarkably few people; less than 250,000 live in Del Norte, Humboldt, and Mendocino counties. Despite its isolation, the area has its share of environmental ills.

For the past decade, the hottest environmental controversy in this corner of the state has been the battle over the few remaining ancient forests. This debate is unavoidably linked with the fate of the region's marine resources, a relationship best illustrated by the marbled murrelet, which dives for fish in ocean waters. The state's few remaining murrelets are threatened by gill netting and oil spills as well as by logging, which is destroying old-growth forests—the murrelet's only nesting habitat.

This relationship is also illustrated by the fate of the freshwater lagoons and estuaries at the mouths of many of the North Coast's rivers, critical habitat for once-abundant salmon. A century and a half of logging has stripped bare riverbanks and entire hillsides. Estuaries such as those at the mouths of Redwood Creek in Redwood National Park and the Klamath River have been made far shallower due to sediment washed off logged hillsides by winter deluges, thus reducing habitat for migrating salmon.

The collapse of salmon and steelhead populations in many of these streams is caused by dams and water diversions, overfishing, the relatively new threat of deep ocean drift netting, degraded estuaries and lagoons, and the impacts of logging.[1]

The region also has urban environmental ills such as toxic pollution. In 1989, the Surfrider Foundation filed suit and later won a settlement against lumber and paper companies, charging that the mills violated waste discharge permits 15,000 times since 1984 and polluted a popular surfing area with 40 million gallons of wastewater a day.

San Francisco Bay

Famous for its scenic beauty, San Francisco Bay, along with the Sacramento and San Joaquin Delta, comprises the largest estuary on the western coast of the Americas. In 150 years, one-third of the bay has been diked or filled and the estuary has lost 95 percent of its tidal wetlands (see Figure 8.1). Many of the tidal wetlands were turned into garbage dumps, industrial parks, ports, airports, farms, and military bases. Some former tidal wetlands, however, were converted to salt ponds, duck clubs, and seasonal wetlands, all of which provide important habitat values.

The estuary is still one of the most important stopping points for water birds on the Pacific flyway. Each winter and spring, these bay wetlands support approximately 1 million migrating shorebirds in addition to hundreds of thousands of ducks, geese, swans, sandhill cranes, hawks, and pelicans. The estuary also supports important fisheries such as striped bass and produces approximately 70 percent of the state's salmon.[2]

These remaining values, however, give only a glimpse of the

FIGURE 8.1
SAN FRANCISCO ESTUARY WETLANDS

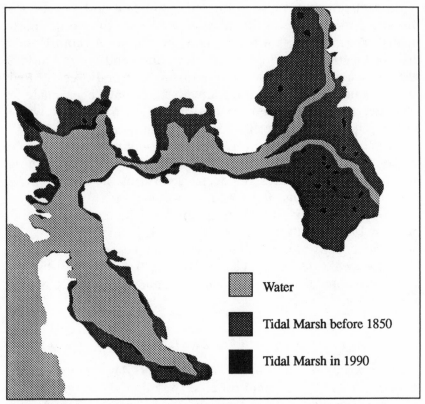

Water

Tidal Marsh before 1850

Tidal Marsh in 1990

SOURCE: Andrew Neal Cohen, *An Introduction to the Ecology of the San Francisco Estuary* (Oakland: San Francisco Estuary Project, 1990).

bay's historic riches. The abundance of wildlife attracted one of the densest populations of American Indians on the continent. Just over two centuries after the arrival of Europeans, the Bay Area now holds the fourth-largest metropolis in the nation, with more than 6 million people. And San Francisco Bay still plays an important part in the region's quality of life and economy. In 1990, for example, San Francisco's Fisherman's Wharf accounted for 14 million visitor-days, making it the second-largest tourist attraction in the state, surpassed only by Disneyland.

Today, San Francisco Bay is one of the most modified major estuaries in the world, and its fish and wildlife show increasing signs of collapse. At least fourteen animal species in the estuary are endangered or threatened—signs of an ecosystem in serious trouble.

The endangered salt marsh harvest mouse, which lives only in the bay's tidal and diked seasonal marshes, continues to lose habitat. Despite legal protections, many seasonal wetlands are illegally filled or degraded. Since 1956, 63 percent of the mouse's seasonal wetlands habitat in the south part of the bay has been filled or degraded.[3]

During the Gold Rush, the abundant California clapper rail, a striking resident of the bay's salt marshes, was a favorite target of market hunters. Due to habitat loss and excessive predation, the endangered rail's world population has now fallen to fewer than 500 birds.

The threatened winter-run salmon, one of four runs of salmon that pass through the estuary on their way to the Sacramento River, has fallen from 117,000 fish in 1969 to 200 in 1991. The population of adult striped bass has fallen 80 percent in the past two decades; virtually no young bass are surviving in the estuary.

Numbers of Delta smelt, a small fish that lives its entire life in the estuary, have plummeted by 90 percent. In 1991, this decline spawned an unsuccessful lawsuit against the U.S. Fish and Wildlife Service from water users who opposed the listing of the smelt as an endangered species.

During the past several decades, San Francisco Bay has seen steady progress in treating traditional household sewage. But dangerous levels of toxics, particularly heavy metals, are still a major problem in waterfowl, shellfish, fish, and in bay sediment and waters. The state has warned the public to restrict consumption of striped bass, surf scoter, and scaup. Bay clams off Palo Alto have been found with the highest levels of silver ever recorded in the world.[4]

Contamination has been linked with an increased incidence of tumors, reduced reproductive ability, and fin rot in fish, shell necrosis in shrimp, and missing limbs on crabs. Massive dredging projects exacerbate toxic problems by resuspending contaminants trapped in sediments.

One of the bay's greatest problems is the impact of massive water diversions. The watershed includes 40 percent of the state. The Sacramento, San Joaquin, and a dozen other rivers flow through the Central Valley and join in the Delta, once among the greatest

inland wetlands in the world. None of these rivers remain undammed; the Central Valley now contains one of the largest water
diversion systems on earth. Each year, approximately 50 percent of
the water that would otherwise flow into the bay is diverted. Up to
85 percent of spring water flows are diverted in dry years. During
the drought beginning in 1987, diversions increased.

Pumps in the Delta are so powerful that they actually reverse the
direction of flow in the lower San Joaquin River, wreaking havoc
on the homing instincts of migratory fish. The pumps suck millions
of fish, eggs, and larvae out of the system.

Diversion has also begun converting the unique, brackish Suisun
Marsh into a salt marsh. A tide gate pumps fresher water into diked
duck clubs, but tidal marshes have been left unprotected and conversion threatens unique plant and animal communities, including
one species that is being considered for endangered status—the
Suisun song sparrow.

The most productive part of any estuary is the mixing zone,
where fresh water meets salt water. This rich soup of nutrients is the
base of the food chain, supporting plankton blooms, which in turn
feed shellfish, fish, and birds. When spring diversions dramatically
reduce fresh water inflows, this mixing zone is moved upstream
from the rich shallows of Suisun Bay to the narrow and deep Delta
channels, resulting in a less productive estuary and dramatically
lower populations of many species.[5]

The introduction of nonnative species into the estuary can be just
as disruptive to the ecosystem as more obvious impacts. In 1879,
striped bass were introduced from the East Coast. Oysters were also
imported, and though they were unable to reproduce, many other
bottom dwellers came along with the oysters and thrived. With
increased global shipping came species from estuaries around the
world. Virtually all of the animals that now live in the mud on the
bay floor are not native.

The Chinese clam, for example, probably arrived in ballast water
after trade opened to China. By 1990 the clam had taken over parts
of the bay and has been found in concentrations of up to 10,000 per
square meter. These voracious creatures strain the equivalent of the
volume of Suisun Bay every day or two. The consequent loss of
plankton has further damaged the striped bass and other plankton-
dependent fish. The abundant clams, however, may be a boon to
bottom feeders such as sturgeon and diving ducks.[6]

Despite these impacts, San Francisco Bay remains a tremendously important natural resource. That so much life survives in such a hostile environment shows the tenacity of wildlife and provides at least some slim hope for the future.

Gulf of the Farallon

Just twenty-five miles off the Golden Gate, the Farallon Islands and the Gulf of the Farallon National Marine Sanctuary are home to the largest nesting site for seabirds south of British Columbia. At least twelve species nest here—more than 200,000 birds, including the world's largest colonies of Brandt's cormorant and western gull. These seabirds were nearly wiped out by egg hunting a century ago and still face threats today. As a result of El Niño currents and gill netting, the population of murres—138,000 in 1982—fell by 65 percent.

The islands are also home to seventeen species of whales, dolphins, and porpoises and five species of pinnipeds. Among these are grey whales, once on the brink of extinction because of whaling. They have rebounded to a current population of about 18,000, virtually all of which pass the California coast twice a year in their annual migrations.[7]

The waters around the islands contain radioactive and munitions waste dumped in the past. The sanctuary has also been threatened by oil spills. In 1984, the tanker *Puerto Rican* exploded and caused a 1.5-million-gallon slick that hit the sanctuary.

Central Coast

If any one animal symbolizes the California coast, it is the southern sea otter. Historically, the coast held 20,000 of these creatures. The fur bearer was hunted nearly to extinction for its plush pelt, but a few found sanctuary on Big Sur's isolated shoreline. Listed as threatened under the federal Endangered Species Act in 1972, the otter began a slow recovery. Now 1,600 otters live from Año Nuevo to Ventura County.

Although the otter is slowly expanding its range to the north, it has not been permitted to expand south into its historic range because of commercial fishermen. The otter eats up to one-third of its body weight in seafood each day. After its elimination from the southern coastline, the otter was replaced in the food web by shellfishermen, who have no desire for competition.

The greatest single threat to the otter is the possibility of a massive oil spill. A single large spill could coat much of the otter's habitat. In 1987, to reduce the risk of disaster, biologists began relocating the otter to its historic habitat on San Nicholas Island, the most remote of the Channel Islands. This controversial program has relocated 139 otters, but only 14 remained at the island as of March 1991.[8]

Monterey Bay, in the heart of the sea otter's range, holds the largest submarine canyon in North America. The nutrient-rich upwelling from this offshore chasm supports a remarkably rich marine life. One early missionary wrote that sea lions covered Monterey Bay "like a pavement," and another visitor wrote that "it is impossible to conceive of the number of whales with which we were surrounded, of their familiarity; they every half minute spouted within half a pistol shot of the ships and made a prodigious stench in the air."[9] Each year the waters off Monterey Bay still host thousands of porpoises and dolphins.

President Bush called for the creation of a Monterey Bay National Marine Sanctuary. The boundaries for the sanctuary have not been established, and environmentalists are urging the inclusion of sensitive areas to the north and south.

Gill nets, used to catch rockfish, halibut, and other fish, have long been known to kill marine mammals and diving birds. In northern and central California, a decade of legislation and negotiations among fishing interests and environmentalists led to gill net closures to protect marine resources such as the sea otter. In 1990, the passage of Proposition 132 banned gill nets within three miles of the southern California coast and attempted to ban the practice in federal waters. In 1991, however, the Pacific Fishery Management Council struck down the ban in federal waters as inconsistent with its management plans.

Abandoned nets, fishing line, and other plastics are another serious problem along the coast. During the 1990 Coastal Cleanup, 16,000 volunteers in just three hours scoured beaches and collected almost 150 tons of garbage, of which 61 percent was plastic.[10]

Morro Bay, an estuary south of Big Sur, suffers from a problem similar to the lagoons on the North Coast. The estuary holds important wetlands and shorebird habitat but is rapidly filling up because of agricultural erosion upstream. The Coastal Conservancy and local activists are developing a land use plan for the watershed to protect this beautiful estuary.

Southern California

In 1990, California received a graphic reminder that the state is vulnerable to a disastrous oil spill. Off Huntington Beach, the *American Trader* punctured one of its tanks with its own anchor, spilling 394,000 gallons of oil. Two days later a slick two miles wide and five miles long invaded the shore. Despite nearly ideal conditions, only a fraction of the oil was recovered by skimmers and shoreline workers. As a result of heroic effort by local activists, a sand dike was built to keep oil out of Talbot Marsh, an action that was not even considered in the official spill-response plan. Unfortunately, a storm destroyed the dike, contaminating the marsh. As in other wetland areas, cleanup workers were severely hampered because traditional cleanup techniques were destructive to marsh vegetation and wildlife.

Volunteers rescued and cleaned oiled birds. More than 1,000 birds were injured or killed, including 100 endangered brown pelicans. The long-term effects on the marsh, on ocean-floor biota, and on the grunions that were running during the spill will never be known.[11]

The spill was hardly the first threat to wetlands such as the twenty-five-acre Talbot Marsh. Southern California has lost 90 percent of its coastal marshes to diking, draining, and filling. In Marina Del Rey, the Ballona wetlands are remnants of the once extensive marshes that were transfigured into the world's largest marina complex. In 1986, the Coastal Commission approved a project that would have left only 178 of 260 acres of wetlands intact; the remaining habitat would have had a road through the middle of it. Friends of Ballona sued and won. By 1991 a new landowner had agreed to preserve the entire wetlands area.

Just as the loss of wetlands in San Francisco Bay led to a disastrous decline in the population of the California clapper rail, the loss of South Coast wetlands led to the disappearance of its cousin, the light-footed clapper rail, originally found from Santa Barbara to Baja California. By 1989 the total California population was estimated at 163 pairs.[12]

One of the most significant threats to the survival of the rail is the nonnative red fox. The rail evolved without this predator and has proven to be highly vulnerable. In just six years, the fox, probably a fur farm escapee, caused a decline—from thirty to six pairs—in the breeding population at the Seal Beach National Wildlife Refuge in Anaheim Bay. The fox has contributed to an equally disturbing decline in the population of California clapper rail in San Francisco Bay. To save these endangered rails from extinction, the U.S. Fish and Wildlife Service proposed predator management plans that include trapping and killing foxes. For a time, the Seal Beach plan was held up by litigation from animal rights activists. In 1991, the agency began trapping the fox at San Francisco Bay.

Other species are also endangered by the loss of South Coast wetlands. Belding's savannah sparrow lives in the fragments of wetlands south of Santa Barbara. In 1986, 2,274 pairs remained. The least tern, an acrobatic bird that plunges into bays and estuaries for small fish, nests from San Francisco south. Most of the marshes that produce its food supply have been lost, and it has been replaced in its nesting habitat—sandy beaches—by human, feline, and canine competitors. The resourceful tern has resorted to landfills and even airports. By 1989 only 1,200 pairs remained in California.[13]

One of the unfortunate side effects of Los Angeles's remarkable growth has been severe ocean pollution. For more than twenty years, large volumes of virtually unregulated industrial effluent flowed through Los Angeles County's outfall into the ocean off the Palos Verdes Peninsula. Tons of PCBs and DDT were dumped and concentrated in offshore sediments. An enormous "slug" of DDT still sits off Palos Verdes. Although the pesticide was banned in 1972, it remains in the marine environment and in marine biota. A commercial fishery for white croaker was lost due to contamination. In 1985, Dover sole averaged 6 parts per million (PPM) of DDT, exceeding the U.S. Food and Drug Administration's action level.[14] Coastal bottlenose dolphins, which feed on contaminated fish, have been found with blubber concentrations of DDT up to 929 PPM.[15]

Swimmers in Santa Monica Bay, at some of California's most famous beach communities, faced the prospect of diving into poorly treated sewage water and winter overflows of raw sewage. More than 1 billion gallons of wastewater were discharged into the ocean off Los Angeles each day, and only 25 percent was provided with biological (secondary) treatment in 1985. The Environmental Protection Agency (EPA) denied Los Angeles's petition for a waiver from Clean Water Act secondary treatment requirements. Since then, the city has improved its massive Hyperion treatment plant and begun construction of new facilities. Roughly half of the effluent now receives secondary treatment, and the city is nearing Clean Water Act standards. Santa Monica Bay, however, still faces serious problems from massive storm drains that funnel contaminated runoff from streets, roofs, and parking lots into creeks and the ocean.

The County of Los Angeles made significantly less progress than the city. The county also petitioned for a waiver of Clean Water Act requirements, arguing that it should be allowed to continue to discharge sewage sludge to the ocean because the sludge would cover and isolate the DDT contamination caused by past discharges. In 1991, the EPA denied this waiver. The county has asked for an administrative hearing and appears headed for an appeal.

Farther down the coast, a federal judge in 1990 fined the City of San Diego $3 million for 3,701 sewage spills and 15,000 wastewater treatment violations from 1983 to 1990. The court order will likely lead to a $2.4 billion upgrade of the city's sewers.[16] As a result of decades of abuse, scenic San Diego Bay is also suffering the avoidable fate of so many other urban estuaries: contamination by such toxics as PCBs, PAHs (polycyclic aromatic hydrocarbons), chlordane, organotin compounds, arsenic, lead, and mercury.[17]

Many southern California beaches are suffering from another problem—starvation. While, in some areas, changes to watersheds are smothering bays and lagoons with sediment, other areas are starving for natural flows of sand. Dams on rivers that once supplied sand for the beaches, jetties, and bulkheads that interfere with the longshore movement of sand have had unpredicted effects. As a result, most of southern California beaches, perhaps the state's most famous features, are artificially maintained at least in part.

Because of a jetty built to protect Camp Pendleton's harbor in 1942, the City of Oceanside found itself without a beach. The harbor and jetty became a sand trap, and Oceanside's beach became rocky shingle. Tourism in the city plunged. Because the buffering effect of beaches was lost, shoreline property was battered during storms. Between 1965 and 1981 the Army Corps of Engineers placed 5 million cubic yards of sand on the beach, only to watch it vanish. Many in the community have advocated a system of pumps to bring sand back. Similar problems in many beach communities are leading to cooperative planning and to a new area of legal controversy—sand rights.[18]

MYRIAD PROBLEMS

The plight of many ecosystems along the California coastline is the result of myriad problems, often having synergistic effects. The clapper rails would not be so vulnerable to the nonnative red fox if so much habitat had not been lost. San Francisco Bay's striped bass are made more vulnerable to toxic contamination because of the effects of water diversion.

Of all the threats to the state's marine, bay, and estuarine environments, none are as visible as the potential of a disastrous oil spill. The 11-million-gallon *Exxon Valdez* disaster provided a tragic worst-case scenario. A spill the size of the one created by the *Exxon Valdez* would stretch from Mendocino County to San Diego (see Figure 8.2), and California is uniquely vulnerable to such a catastrophe. Indeed, the *Exxon Valdez* and its captain were bound for California, as is much Alaskan oil.

The state's isolated coast, its unpredictable weather, and the sheer number of vessels combine for great risk. Together, the ports of San Francisco Bay, Long Beach, Los Angeles, and El Segundo saw more than 6,000 tanker trips and 16,000 barge trips in 1987.[19]

And tanker spills are not the only threat. Seventy percent of spills nationwide are from tank farms and on-shore facilities. In 1988, for example, San Francisco Bay was hit by a 420,000-gallon spill when valves at a refinery were left open in violation of federal regulations.[20]

The operation of existing offshore drilling rigs and pipelines presents another threat. However, the most volatile issue is the proposal for new drilling off the coast. In 1990, President Bush proposed delaying consideration of oil leases off the northern and central coast until the year 2000. Many, however, are concerned that this commitment may go the way of the president's campaign pledge for no net loss of wetlands. Indeed, there are already warning signs for the coast. The Bush administration energy policy downplays conservation and encourages drilling off other coasts. Concern continues for the potential impacts of new platforms,

FIGURE 8.2
AREA OF *VALDEZ* SPILL COMPARED TO THE CALIFORNIA COAST

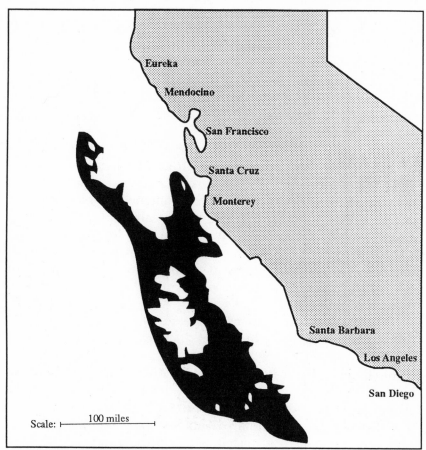

SOURCE: Natural Resources Defense Council.

wells, drilling mud, air emissions, on-shore development, and spills. In an attempt to provide permanent protection, California Congresswoman Barbara Boxer sponsored federal legislation to enact a permanent ban on new leasing and drilling on the outer continental shelf along the entire California coast.

Whether new wells are drilled or not, the threat of spills will remain. The lessons learned from California's recent spills are similar to those learned elsewhere. Response plans are inadequate. Even under ideal conditions, skimming and on-shore oil removal are ineffective. Containment booms do not keep oil from reaching the shore and sensitive habitats. Public involvement is critical in rescuing wildlife and in preparing and implementing cleanup plans.

In 1990, to address some of these problems, the state enacted legislation that will create the nation's most ambitious spill prevention and response program. The coming years will continue to see activists advocating energy plans that emphasize conservation rather than drilling, double hulls for tankers, improved navigation equipment and vessel traffic systems, and vessel-free zones in remote and sensitive areas.

But oil spills are not the only water quality problem faced by coastal areas. Contamination comes from a variety of sources: industrial and municipal discharges, contaminated agricultural and urban runoff, and resuspension of contaminated sediments through dredging. Even without considering upstream discharges, each day more than 16 billion gallons of wastewater flow into the ocean from 332 dischargers. The total amount of contaminants has never been calculated.[21] Despite progress in treating sewage, contamination still led to at least 338 beach closures in 1990, with just eight of thirteen counties surveyed.[22]

Oil refineries and pulp mills are the most visible industrial sources; however, many industries discharge directly into municipal sewers. Although regulated by the sewage treatment plants and required to pretreat waste, these hidden dischargers are often overlooked. The State Water Resources Control Board and the EPA claim to be unable to step in and directly regulate these industries. A recent report, which examined Santa Monica and San Francisco bays, found that up to 90 percent of the industries and 90 percent of the toxics dumped into sewers were unregulated. It also found that industry dramatically underestimates its discharges.[23]

Regarding water quality, perhaps the largest unregulated industry in California is transportation. Each year our cars, parking lots, and roadways dump tons of oil, antifreeze, and toxic metals into our coastal waters. People who use pesticides in their yards or dump paint down storm drains add to the problem. The EPA and the State Water Resources Control Board have only begun requiring permits for problematic urban runoff. At the current pace, programs to significantly reduce these discharges may be years away.

Water quality and aquatic biota in California's coastal environment also suffer from toxic hot spots caused by past pollution. These sites are only now being cataloged. Cleanup of many, where no responsible party can be found, will have to wait for scarce public funds. (See Figure 8.3.)

For decades, the state's wetlands were seen as mosquito-infested swamps good for nothing but cheap real estate. As the ecological importance of wetlands has become more accepted, the rate of wetlands destruction has been slowed but not halted. The campaigns to stop uncontrolled development, including wetlands filing in San Francisco Bay and along the coast, led to a national campaign and the federal Coastal Zone Management Act. The Coastal Commission and the San Francisco Bay Conservation and Development Commission (BCDC) now require the protection of wetlands. Serious problems remain, however, with both programs.

The BCDC does not have jurisdiction over diked seasonal wetlands, the most threatened habitat in the Bay Area. The Coastal Commission budget was slashed by the Deukmejian administration. The commission was also criticized for approving proposals such as that to fill fifty acres of marshlands in the Los Penasquitos Lagoon in San Diego County. Some coastal advocates have called for a revamping of the Coastal Commission, to strengthen policies and to prevent politically motivated votes.

Like California's state programs, federal regulatory programs have proven inadequate to protect coastal wetlands. Although the Army Corps of Engineers and the EPA have begun denying some wetland fill-permit applications under Section 404 of the Clean Water Act, many landowners intentionally destroy wetlands in hopes that the agencies will disclaim jurisdiction. Landowners and regulators engage in a complex legal dance in which filling and digging drainage ditches are used in attempts to skirt legal protections.

Finally, a major national fight has begun as development, oil, and agricultural interests fight to weaken Section 404. In the summer of 1991, these interests persuaded the Bush administration to propose a wholesale rewriting and weakening of federal wetlands protections. The changes could remove protections from 20 million to 40 million acres of wetlands nationally. Particularly threatened on the California coast are seasonal wetlands and high tidal marshes.

FIGURE 8.3
CALIFORNIA DUMPING
STATE-APPROVED WASTEWATER DISCHARGES AND FORMER FEDERAL
MUNITIONS DUMPS OFTEN COINCIDE WITH PRIME FISHING AREAS.

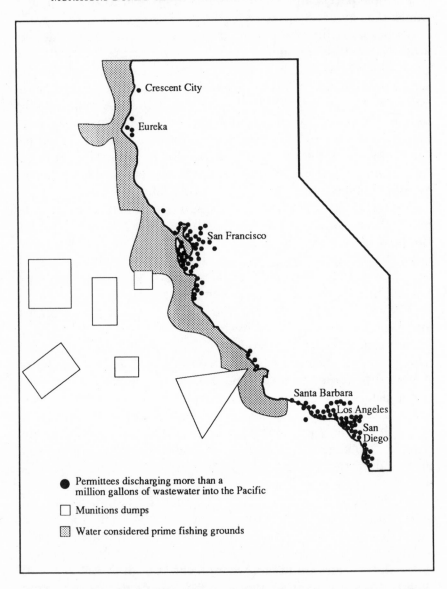

SOURCE: State Water Resources Control Board, Environmental Protection Agency's Toxic Chemical Release Inventory, and the National Oceanic and Atmospheric Administration. Published in *Coast and Ocean*, Winter/Spring 1991.

The interrelationships among the various threats to the coastal environment require planning at a level too often ignored. Upstream logging, agriculture, or urbanization can silt in coastal estuaries. Urban sprawl and pollution foul our waters and fill our wetlands.

Solving some of these problems will require broad planning efforts, including watershed and erosion management. It will require growth management, regional land use planning, and public transit. Ultimately, California's threatened coastal resources will be restored only if we appreciate the relationships among the many human activities that have caused the decline.

There is one wild card threatening California's coastal resources—the greenhouse effect and a rise in sea level. The burning of fossil fuels since the Industrial Revolution has dramatically added to the atmosphere's supply of carbon dioxide. In addition, deforestation is eliminating one of the world's greatest carbon traps, the plants of the tropical forests. The higher temperatures that will result from the build-up of atmospheric carbon will cause the melting of part of the polar ice caps and thermal expansion of ocean waters and, thus, a rise in sea level. The EPA estimates a rise of two to seven feet by 2100. The potential consequences are overwhelming—the destruction of coastal wetlands, flooding, and the loss of freshwater sources.[24] The potential costs are enormous. The solutions are necessarily global, but California has always been a global leader in environmental issues.

SIGNS OF HOPE

Despite a litany of problems, supporters of the coast have reason for hope. California and its coastline are in many ways the global epicenter of the environmental movement. The fights to stop the filling of San Francisco Bay and to halt the overdevelopment of the coast were among the significant early fights in the modern environmental movement.

If there is one example of the potential to bring natural resources back from the brink of disaster, it might be California's brown pelican. By 1968, Anacapa Island's historic population of perhaps 5,000 pairs of pelicans was reduced to 100 pairs. DDT contamination had caused the thinning of egg shells, and no young pelicans survived that year; breeding colonies were littered with broken eggs and dead chicks. DDT was banned in 1972, though production and export continued. But by 1989 the breeding population of brown pelicans was back to 5,000 pairs. DDT remains in the marine environment, though it no longer appears to be causing disastrous egg shell thinning. Although still listed as endangered, the brown pelican shows what a remarkable comeback natural resources can make if we give them a chance.[25]

THE FUTURE OF COASTAL PROTECTION

Up and down the coast, many Californians have concluded that the status quo is no longer acceptable, that we must begin the work of restoring the health of our coastal resources. In Humboldt Bay, San Francisco Bay, on the South Coast, and elsewhere, dozens of efforts are under way to restore not just individual species, but the productivity and health of entire ecosystems. Restoration efforts to date give only an indication of the full potential to restore our coastal marshes, bays, estuaries, and marine waters.

Ironically, the greatest hope for the California coast may come from the greatest threat to its future—the 25.5 million people who live near the shoreline. Many of them have chosen to live there because of the quality of life the coast offers. Many place a high value on a healthy natural environment. Despite the fact that they all have contributed to the coast's decline, they have the political and economic ability to reverse the trend of destruction. They have done it before.

CHAPTER 9

Land Use and Growth Management: The Transformation of Paradise

GARY A. PATTON

CALIFORNIA: A GARDEN OF EDEN

Woody Guthrie, folk song troubadour of the 1930s, wrote and sang movingly of the grandeur and greatness of the American land, and he made his songs into a profound and critical commentary on Depression-era America, pointing out the paradox of poverty and disenfranchisement amidst such plenty. California, he said, was a Garden of Eden. Still, despite the richness of the land, Guthrie advised those Dustbowl refugees who thought that moving to California would be their salvation that they'd better have some "do-re-mi."[1]

California has always been a golden land where promise and opportunity have waited. This has been the "California dream."

Gary A. Patton has been a Santa Cruz County supervisor since 1975. He is the author of that county's successful growth management and affordable housing program and has served on numerous local and state boards and commissions. Mr. Patton is president of the Planning and Conservation League.

Despite Guthrie's most appropriate warning, even those who didn't have the "do-re-mi" could strike it rich here. That's why they came. And if farm workers, factory laborers, and ethnic minorities have never shared proportionately, for many people California has made good on its promises. The beauty, fertility, and richness of the land have enriched a multitude of people. Today, this California paradise is in peril.

California's explosive growth is degrading and destroying the natural environment, undermining the foundations of the economy, and diminishing the quality of life for all Californians. People know this. They want changes, and they want real solutions. Richard Sybert, head of the State Office of Planning and Research, has called growth management "the foremost issue" in the state.[2] The time has come for a new approach to land use and growth management.

THE AMOUNT AND RATE OF CALIFORNIA'S GROWTH

The choices we make about how we use our land will determine the character and quality of life in our local communities and the fate of the natural world. Our land use choices are directly related to California's rapid population growth and to the economic growth that is both a cause and effect of the extraordinary, ongoing population increases. California's growth in 1990 was the equivalent of adding a city larger than San Francisco.

Growth, of course, can be measured not only in absolute numbers, but in rate; both factors are important. Los Angeles and San Diego counties are California's two largest in terms of population. In 1989, Los Angeles County grew by only 1.3 percent—slow compared to the state's overall rate of 2.6 percent. That "slow" growth rate in Los Angeles County, however, resulted in 117,100 new people—a medium-size city. San Diego County, which added 92,300 people in 1989, did so by virtue of a more rapid, 3.8 percent growth rate. The fastest-growing counties are growing far in excess of the state's average rate and are experiencing large increases in absolute numbers at the same time. In 1989, Riverside County grew by 8.3 percent, or 85,400 people; San Bernardino County grew by 6.6 percent, or 88,400 people.

The Problems Posed by Growth

Each increment of new growth places new demands on the natural environment—on air quality, open space, wildlife habitat, water supplies, and water quality. Growth also places new demands on the physical and social infrastructure of local communities. A community may have preexisting capacity in its infrastructure, which allows it to serve new growth without the need for new facilities. Often, however, new growth requires new roads, classrooms, libraries, parks, and housing—and if such facilities are not provided as population is added, the quality of life for existing residents declines. To provide the new infrastructure required by growth, communities need new sources of financing, but since the late 1970s, growth in California has not been generating the revenues necessary to provide the required infrastructure.[3] In many if not most regions, new growth now means a decline in the quality of life offered to existing residents and poses new threats to the natural environment.

Hundreds of local communities have tried directly to confront their growth management problems.[4] This has been true particularly where growth has been most rapid—the speed with which the community is changing tends to dramatize the problems. Sometimes local efforts have been successful,[5] but local successes can displace problems to other communities. In 1992, the state has no coordinated, statewide approach to land use and growth management that could eliminate such displacement effects.[6]

A Quick Tour of "The Californias"

The State Office of Tourism presents California as a composite— "The Californias"—a state comprised of many separate regions.[7] Each part of the state is experiencing growth in different ways.

The northernmost part of the state, encompassing the North Coast and the Shasta-Cascade regions, has an economy based on timber and tourism, with communities seeking to diversify as the timber industry fades. There is room for growth to spread out, and its effects are diluted. These counties make up 20 percent of the state's land area but contain only 1.5 percent of the population. Although the region is growing more rapidly on a percentage basis than California as a whole—2.9 percent per year compared to the statewide 2.6 percent—the absolute numbers of increase are small. While land use and growth management issues are of growing importance in many communities, these are not the issues of most critical concern for this region.

In the nine counties of the San Francisco Bay Area, land use and growth management are of paramount importance, reflected by the large number of local growth management measures enacted. At least twenty-six measures were adopted by 1989. Transportation and traffic problems feature prominently among citizen concerns. Air quality meets neither state nor federal standards, and open space and agricultural lands are being rapidly lost to development. Housing prices in the Bay Area are among the highest in the nation.[8]

Central cities are growing slowly if at all in the Bay Area. In 1989, San Francisco actually lost population, and Oakland added only 1,000 residents for a growth rate of 0.3 percent. The fastest-growing parts of the Bay Area are on the outskirts—in Solano, Sonoma, and Contra Costa counties. New residents are being attracted by Bay Area jobs but seek lower-priced housing on the fringe. Land prices are lower still in Tracy, Turlock, and Modesto in the Central Valley—another region entirely. Commuters from those areas are driving one or two hours to and from work in the Bay Area and are duplicating the destructive and traffic-intensive dynamic typical of southern California growth.

Los Angeles, Orange County, and the "Inland Empire" of Riverside and San Bernardino counties are essentially one region. The core areas of Los Angeles and Orange County continue to see rapid economic growth characterized by many new jobs. People attracted by jobs can't find affordable or desirable housing nearby, so they commute many miles, perhaps from a different county. Multihour commutes have generated sickening air pollution, crippling congestion, a loss of open space and agricultural lands on the ever-expanding urban fringe, and the disintegration of meaningful community. What were once separate regions have become a single, sprawling whole, and this megaregion lacks any adequate form of governance to meet the challenges that growth has posed.[9]

San Diego, Ventura, and San Luis Obispo counties all show the same pattern. The City of San Diego grew by 2.8 percent in 1989 while the county's rural, unincorporated areas grew by 6 percent. In Ventura County, the overall growth rate was a modest 2 percent, but the unincorporated area grew twice as fast. In San Luis Obispo County, overall growth was rapid—4.7 percent—but the unincorporated areas grew even faster, at 5.7 percent.

Growth pressures are at work in the Central Valley too. Sacramento County grew by 3.5 percent in 1989 as its population increased by 34,600. High-rise office towers are coming to dominate the Sacramento skyline, but the city's population growth is modest—only 1.5 percent, or 5,200 people, in 1989. During the same period, the unincorporated area grew 4 percent. Increasing traffic congestion and air pollution are caused by what has become the prototypical California growth pattern—jobs in the urban center, housing in the outlying areas.

Spurred by jobs in Sacramento and new employment centers in the suburbs, residential growth has spilled into adjacent mountain areas as well: Placer County grew by 5.6 percent in 1989, El Dorado County by 6.2 percent, and Amador County by 7 percent. Such fast-paced growth is typical of the Sierra region, although the absolute numbers are small.

In San Joaquin County, the 1989 growth rate was a modest 2.3 percent, but Tracy—a bedroom community for the Bay Area—grew 11.2 percent. Stanislaus County grew by 5.5 percent in 1989. Merced County grew by 3.8 percent and Fresno County by 3.5 percent. A big problem in the Central Valley is the impact that growth is having on agricultural land. The American Farmland Trust reported that, in 1989, 335,274 acres of Central Valley farmland were included within urban limit lines and thus slated for development.[10]

The counties of the Central Coast region are having a somewhat different experience. San Mateo County, one of the nine Bay Area counties, is growing slowly—1.2 percent in 1989—and has managed to preserve its rural and agricultural coast. Santa Cruz and Monterey counties, which also have significant rural and agricultural areas along the coast, are growing slightly slower than the state average, even though both are subject to growth pressures from the San Francisco Bay Area and from the Silicon Valley communities of Santa Clara County.

Several factors seem to set the Central Coast apart. While the

Monterey, Santa Cruz, and San Mateo county coastlines are all close to the Bay Area and Silicon Valley, the mountains of the Coast Range pose a transportation barrier that makes commuting difficult. Additionally, the most developable lands in all three counties are in the coastal zone and are therefore subject to the land use restrictions in the 1976 Coastal Act. Voters in San Mateo and Santa Cruz counties have also enacted local ballot measures imposing growth management restrictions not found elsewhere. The Santa Cruz system, adopted in 1978, has been particularly effective in stopping sprawl and in preventing the development of agricultural lands. In Monterey County, water supply moratoria have played a part in slowing growth. These restrictions could become less severe as water efficiency improves or new water sources are found.

WHY OUR LAND USE DECISION-MAKING SYSTEM DOESN'T WORK

There is a great deal of agreement that the state's current system of land use decision making isn't working well. A group of thirty-one business, government, education, and community leaders constituting the Bay Vision 2020 Commission stated that the "beauty, livability, and economic strength" of the Bay Area is in jeopardy because "we have no effective means for addressing the problems that cross city and county boundaries. Only by some changes in the structure of government in the region can we tackle increasing traffic congestion, long commutes between home and job, shortages of affordable housing, loss of valued open space to urban sprawl, predictable air pollution, and deterioration of our economic base."

The Los Angeles 2000 Committee—made up of eighty-five civic leaders appointed by Mayor Tom Bradley—came to virtually the same conclusion in its 1988 report: "Waves of newcomers have literally overflowed the borders of the city into surrounding spaces. . . . The problems have increasingly become regional in scope and magnitude. As Los Angeles becomes more job-rich, it will also become housing-poor as the number of affordable housing units declines. Approximately two-thirds of the added population will settle in outlying neighborhoods. This imbalance could increase the number of vehicle hours travelled by more than 300 percent." The committee called for "a new perspective" and "reform or improvement of current institutions."

The Assembly Office of Research reported that the California dream may be "turning into a nightmare" because the state is not adequately addressing the impacts of growth; it, too, suggested that a new system of land use governance is needed.[11] The California Council for Environmental and Economic Balance (CEEB), representing major California corporations, reached the same conclusion. Hopeful about the future, the CEEB forecast a California "urban renaissance" but added that we "must reform our planning policies at the state, regional and local levels."[12] The Sierra Club likewise saw the need for change: "The negative effects of undirected growth ignore legal boundaries, agency jurisdictions, economic status, or cultural differences. Air pollution, traffic, skyrocketing housing prices, deteriorating roads, overcrowded schools, failing waste water treatment systems, and closed landfills are just some of the problems created by an increasingly complex, distant and byzantine hodgepodge of paralyzed governmental authorities. The system is not working."[13]

What is wrong with California's land use decision-making process? In order to prescribe the right remedy for what afflicts us, we need to do more than just describe the symptoms of our affliction; we need to analyze the cause.

The root cause of most of our land use and growth-related problems is our long-standing and profound bias toward individualism with respect to land use. In 1776, the year that the Declaration of Independence was signed, the English economist Adam Smith published *The Wealth of Nations*, in which he contended that an "invisible hand" is constantly at work turning private selfishness into public benefit. Smith theorized that the public good is simply the sum of all of our individual and special interests. The best way to achieve the public good is to encourage each individual to pursue his or her own private good.[14]

In many ways, Smith's theory seems plausible; it is taught in our schools and has deeply influenced both American history and our legal system. The problem is that the premise is wrong. It is simply not true that each individual, set free to pursue his or her individual agenda, will necessarily aid the public interest. Nothing demonstrates this more clearly than the urban sprawl, air pollution, and traffic congestion that have resulted from the application of Smith's theory in the arena of land use. In Sacramento, for example, large lowland areas are being developed in spite of flood hazards. If a development is profitable to even one person, it is likely to get approval, regardless of public costs, overtaxing public facilities, and the presence of alternate, more suitable locations.

The California courts and land use statutes do uphold the right of government to regulate land uses in order to achieve the public good,[15] but despite the government's clear, constitutional, and legal power to regulate individual land use activity, strong land use regulations are the exception. The state government has simply not seen fit to establish hard and fast rules for land use, such as state-level zoning guidelines, protection for critical habitat, and open space requirements for flood plains, ridgetops, and steep slopes. A profound bias against regulation itself, and against community control as opposed to individual control over land use, is the root cause of the state's current land use and growth problems.

Consider the loss of agricultural and open space land. State law contains no specific mandate that open space and agricultural land be preserved. Except in the coastal zone, the land use directions provided by state law are almost totally procedural. Local governments, for example, must have an open space element in their general plans, and land use decisions must be consistent with that element. Nowhere, however, does the state tell a local government what the content or substance of an open space element has to be. Local governments can do what they think best, and most let individual property owners have just as much flexibility as the state provides to local government.

This nonmandatory approach applies to virtually every land use issue. Because the state has not established performance standards for major new developments or most other land use matters, local governments usually don't establish rigorous standards for individual landowners or developers. There are, of course, exceptions to this. As growth-related problems grow, local governments sometimes make more use of their powers to manage growth, such as building restrictions in Marin County, steep slope restrictions in Palo Alto, and efforts to preserve the seaside character of Carmel. Reflecting the state's own bias against hard and fast rules, however, most local governments tend to allow individuals to pursue their individual self-interest.

Would establishing new regional governments solve the land use problems of the state? Not unless the state were to give the new regional agencies much better and more certain direction on policies and performance standards with respect to regional-scale commercial or industrial development, transportation systems, critical habitat, and hazardous zones involving floods, earthquakes, and landslides. Without new policy direction from the state, shifting decision-making authority from the local level to the regional level would simply remove land use decisions further from the people most directly affected, making it easier for special interests to gain approval for their individual projects. Such a "reform" could place us in a situation even worse than the one in which we now find ourselves because it would eliminate the ability of local governments to enact strong growth management programs.

THE COASTAL ACT: A GROWTH MANAGEMENT SUCCESS STORY

In 1972, Californians adopted Proposition 20, which established special rules and procedures to govern development in the coastal zone. The legislature subsequently enacted the California Coastal Act of 1976, which established a permanent system of coastal zone protection with a state-level Coastal Commission to ensure local compliance.

The Coastal Act establishes development policies that specifically constrain development choices regarding the siting and amount of development permitted. State laws, not local decisions, determine project requirements. Comprehensive planning requirements are imposed on local governments, and local plans become effective only when approved by the Coastal Commission. Certain projects that might have a significant impact on coastal resources must receive approval from the state. Local decisions may be appealed on the grounds that local government has failed to follow the state-approved plan.

According to the League for Coastal Protection, a citizen-based environmental group, the net result of the Coastal Act has been "impressive and overwhelmingly positive."[16] Coastal Act policies mandate that "the maximum amount of prime agricultural land shall be maintained in agricultural production." Subdivisions of agricultural land in the coastal zone have been significantly reduced, and in several coastal counties no such subdivisions have occurred since 1976.

The success story of the Coastal Act can be summed up easily: strong and clear state policies, enacted in state law, constrain local choice where new developments in the coastal zone are proposed. State-required planning is effective because local plans must receive state approval before they can be implemented, and local plans must comply with state-mandated performance standards. Coastal Commission review of key decisions at both a planning and project level ensures compliance with Coastal Act policies.

Similar successes have been achieved by both the San Francisco Bay Conservation and Development Commission and the Tahoe Regional Planning Agency. In both cases, the state delineated a specific objective to be achieved, and this specificity of direction from the state has been the key ingredient.

Strategies for Growth Management

Our tour of the state demonstrates what's wrong. Throughout California, new economic growth and development associated with the creation of jobs are attracting newcomers to rapidly growing urban and suburban areas. Because of the need for affordable housing, landowners and developers are able to gain local government approvals for housing developments located far from job centers. The resulting long-distance commutes cause air pollution, congestion, and contribute to the disintegration of both family and community life, as hours that might have gone to family or community activities are spent on the highway. Sprawling growth destroys both open space and agricultural land. The rapidity with which growth proceeds outruns both the physical and social infrastructure of the region, overtaxes natural resources, and convinces local residents that growth is an autonomous and uncontrollable force.

Nothing about this pattern of growth is inevitable. The realities of growth in California are realities that we have created by allowing individualistic decision making, instead of requiring a greater level of community management and control. We can model a new statewide growth management program on the success stories we know about. Changing the faces of the people who make the decisions is not enough. True land use reform will require:

- State-mandated performance standards so that new developments meet minimum criteria for public services and environmental protection.
- Limit line boundaries that separate the cities from the countryside. Oregon uses an "urban growth boundary" to establish an edge to cities and to help redirect growth and new investment into urban areas. In California, the establishment of a large "greenbelt zone" around each of our major metropolitan areas is a particularly promising approach to protect open space and agricultural lands and to eliminate sprawl. The inner edge of the greenbelt is the urban growth boundary, or publicly acquired lands, and the open space beyond is regulated for conservation or managed resource production, plus some rural enclaves and service centers. Such an approach, advocated most forcefully by the Greenbelt Alliance/People for Open Space,[17] has been widely and successfully used in England for forty years and in other countries as well.
- Strong and certain protection for natural resource and constraint areas, such as wetlands, flood plains, steep slopes, ridgetops, and wildlife habitat.
- A requirement that roads, water supplies, sewers, sewage treatment systems, and social infrastructure be provided concurrently with new development.
- Transportation pricing mechanisms, such as those that have been outlined by the Environmental Defense Fund and the Regional Institute of Southern California, that will discourage the long-distance, single-occupancy vehicle commutes that are now causing both traffic congestion and air pollution.[18]
- A requirement that all jurisdictions in the state must permit and promote housing for people with average and below-average incomes, with a requirement that such housing be provided in connection with the approval of new, job-generating developments, and that it be included in housing developments constructed for people with average and above-average incomes.

A TIME TO ACT

It is both legally and constitutionally appropriate that the state require individual decisions to be consistent with an overall plan, that certain areas be declared off-limits to growth, and that new growth provide for needed infrastructure as that growth occurs. The state needs to mandate local and regional planning, subject to state review and approval, and to ensure that local plans are implemented. The people of the state need to "lay down the law" for California's future growth, and they need to act soon.

A professor at the University of California at Santa Cruz tells a memorable story as a way of convincing his students that it's later than we think with respect to growth. "Think of yourselves," he says, "as bacteria in a bottle." Suppose that the bacteria in the bottle are growing at a rate that doubles their population every minute, and that given its size, the bottle will be completely filled with bacteria in one hour. If that's true, and if it's eleven o'clock in the morning, and the bottle will be completely filled at noon, then when is the bottle going to be half-full?

Did you guess 11:30? Well, that's not quite right. The bottle will be half-full at 11:59, one minute before noon. One minute later, it will be completely full. That's the nature of exponential growth—the same kind of growth we're experiencing in California.

The political and governmental lesson is clear. If you were one of the bacteria in the bottle, you might not recognize how quickly things could change. At around 11:58—just two minutes before the bottle would be completely full—you would see that there was 75 percent open space in your bottle. Would you vote to control growth? Maybe not. In California, our doubling time is measured in years, not in minutes, but the lesson is the same. It's definitely not too early to take growth issues seriously. But is it too late?

CHAPTER 10

Conserving the Land That Feeds Us

BRIGGS NISBET

WHY PRESERVE CALIFORNIA AGRICULTURE?

California is losing more than 50,000 acres of farmland each year to urban development. Soil erosion, salinization, and air pollution are reducing agricultural productivity on millions of additional acres, and an exponentially expanding population is vying for a limited water supply. Still, the sheer magnitude of California's agriculture industry—$18 billion in annual revenues from 250 different commodities—would seem to make concern over its demise presumptuous, or at least premature.[1] But California has also been the fastest-growing economy in the nation and has experienced an unprecedented population boom. Much of that growth will be spilling onto farmland in some of California's most productive farming regions. Concern over the fate of agriculture in California is certainly warranted. Particularly worrisome is the fate of agriculture's most important resource—land.

Briggs Nisbet has been writing about California resource and land conservation issues for the last decade. As staff analyst for the American Farmland Trust, a national nonprofit conservation group, she researched and wrote a 1989 report on Central Valley agriculture. Ms. Nisbet has a master's degree in geography from the University of California at Berkeley.

WHAT IS CALIFORNIA AGRICULTURE?

The strength of the state's agricultural industry lies in its diversity. California leads the country in the production of fifty-eight crops and livestock commodities, and many are crops grown nowhere else. Compared to the American Midwest, where agriculture is characterized by vast stretches of a single crop—wheat, soybeans, or corn—California agriculture encompasses everything from a few acres of kiwi fruits, strawberries, or avocado trees to hundreds of acres of tomatoes, rice, and cotton. Several distinct growing regions are renowned for their specialty crops—Napa Valley for wine grapes, Salinas Valley for lettuce, and Madera County for olives, to name just a few. California is the only U.S. producer of such commodities as walnuts, prunes, and pistachios. Perhaps more important even than diversity and specialization, California-grown fruits, nuts, and vegetables provide Americans with more than half of their fresh market and processing vegetables, including lettuce, tomatoes, broccoli, cauliflower, carrots, and celery.

The most economically productive sector of California's agricultural economy is fruit and nut production, ranging from oranges and almonds to strawberries, raisins, and wine grapes (see Figure 10.1). This sector, along with vegetable production, accounts for about half of the state's annual farm revenues. Field crops contribute nearly one-quarter of total annual agricultural receipts, with alfalfa seed and hay, cotton, and rice providing most of the value. Both cotton and rice are important export crops. The market for alfalfa is the state's dairy industry, which produces the top-grossing farm commodity, milk and cream, worth $2.4 billion in 1989, or 13 percent of total annual farm sales. Completing the list of billion-dollar farm sectors is livestock, providing about 10 percent of annual farm revenues.[2]

The core of California's farm economy is the Central Valley, a 450-mile-long basin in the center of the state that contains both the Sacramento and San Joaquin valleys. Fertile soils, an extended growing season, and the existence of a vast water delivery system for irrigation have all contributed to making the Central Valley one of the world's great gardens. Two-thirds of the state's irrigated cropland is located here. Most of the cotton, almonds, grapes,

FIGURE 10.1
SHARE OF CALIFORNIA FARM REVENUE,
1989 TOTAL VALUE = $18 BILLION

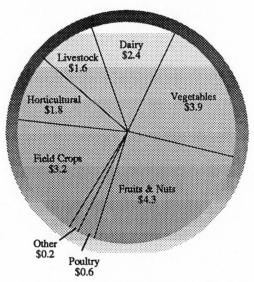

SOURCE: California Department of Food and Agriculture, *California Agriculture: Statistical Review 1989* (Sacramento: California Agricultural Statistics Service, 1990).

walnuts, alfalfa, prunes, rice, tomatoes, and other farm commodities shipped or flown outside California are grown on Central Valley farms. Three Central Valley counties—Fresno, Kern, and Tulare—together contribute 34 percent of the state's annual farm sales, as well as the bulk of California's farm exports.[3]

FARMLAND: HOW MUCH IS ENOUGH?

There are about 31 million acres of agricultural land in California— about a third of all the land in the state. Of that, 9 million acres are irrigated and planted in field crops, fruit and nut trees, and vegetables. Another 1.5 million acres are dry-farmed, mostly for grains, and at least 21 million acres are pasture and grazing land.[4] Another way of looking at farmland is in terms of soil quality. The best, or "prime," farmland has the potential for significantly higher crop yields with fewer restrictions than nonprime farmland. Out of 7.8

million acres of cropland that have been mapped and analyzed for soil quality in California, 3.1 million acres are prime.[5] More than half of this is in the Central Valley.

Much farmland remains; so why do we need to worry about preserving it? As the state's population increases, agricultural land is converted to other uses, such as housing, shopping malls, golf courses, and landfills. Between 1986 and 1988, more than half the land converted to urban use was former farmland.[6] New agricultural land has been brought into production also, but nearly half has been located on lesser-quality soils. Only crops that bring the highest market prices—such as avocados or citrus—can balance out the increased costs of producing crops on poor-quality soil.

Beyond growth pressure, additional threats make farmland preservation important. Environmental problems such as soil erosion, salt deposits from irrigation water, and air pollution affect millions of acres of California crop and grazing land. Reduced yields and the possibility of productive land being idled as a result of these effects will ultimately diminish the total agricultural land resource.

Another reason for concern is the uncertainty of California's water supply. As the largest user of the state's developed water resource, agriculture is vulnerable to decreases in irrigation allocations. The combination of cyclic droughts and increased demand from urban water users will put pressure on the state's farmers to produce more efficiently with less water. As water allotments are cut, farmers may have to strive for the utmost irrigation efficiency. Higher prices for water may force some farmers to change cropping patterns or to cease marginal production altogether.

THE WATER EQUATION

Today's agriculture industry could not exist without irrigation. Farming has been a feature of the California landscape since before the Gold Rush, producing crops for export even without irrigation; dry-farmed wheat and other farm commodities exceeded the value of gold production in the late 1800s. Still, it was not until farmers began to irrigate—first with pumped groundwater and later using surface water from extensive canal systems—that year-round production and crop diversity were possible.

Irrigating farmland requires, of course, a supply of water, determined in part by the amount of yearly precipitation that fills reservoirs and rivers that feed the irrigation delivery system. An important component of the state's water supply is groundwater, crucial to Central Valley production. The amount of water needed depends on the crop, the local climate, and the characteristics of the soil. Irrigated crops in California have varying water requirements, ranging from rice and fruit trees—which need, on average, three acre-feet of water per acre—to wheat and barley, which require less than half that amount.

AGRICULTURE'S SHARE OF WATER USE

In an average, nondrought year, 34 million acre-feet (an acre-foot equals 326,000 gallons) of water are used by the people of California. Of that, about 27 million acre-feet, or about 80 percent, goes to irrigate 9 million acres of California farmland, 6 million acres in the Central Valley.[7] From a third to half the water going to agriculture is used to irrigate four crops: alfalfa, pasture, cotton, and rice (see Figure 10.2). The rest irrigates about 3 million acres of fruit and nut orchards, vineyards, vegetables, and melons.[8] This distribution is better understood in terms of the roles these commodities play in different agricultural sectors. Alfalfa hay is crucial to the dairy industry, providing high-quality feed; even though a great quantity of it is produced in California, a considerable amount of hay is imported from other states. Irrigated pasture provides cattle feed, particularly important in drought years, when forage production on rangelands is minimal. However, the trend is toward decreasing acreage of this very water-intensive field crop. Cotton is produced entirely in the arid San Joaquin Valley and is the state's leading agricultural export. Ninety percent of California's rice crop is grown in the Sacramento Valley, where irrigation water is locally available (as opposed to imported via water projects) and clay soils permit little else to be grown. Cotton and rice are two California crops that benefit from federal farm subsidies that pay farmers the difference between the government's "target price" for crops and the actual market value. Wheat is another crop for which farmers receive federal subsidies.

During the last fifty years, California has benefited from above-average precipitation, although historically drought has been a

FIGURE 10.2
SHARE OF CALIFORNIA IRRIGATED FARMLAND, TOTAL IRRIGATED
FARMLAND = 9 MILLION ACRES

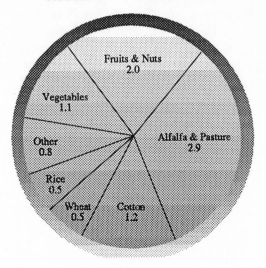

SOURCE: Harold O. Carter and Carol F. Nuckton, eds., *Agriculture in California: On the Brink of a New Millennium 1990–2010* (Davis, Calif.: Agricultural Issues Center, University of California, 1990).

regular occurrence. Not only is the total water supply level likely to fluctuate, with periodically severe dips in quantity, but in the future an increasingly thirsty urban population will be competing with agriculture for a water supply that has effectively reached its limit of development. In addition to potential shortages of surface water, the amount of groundwater currently being withdrawn statewide each year exceeds the amount being replaced. This groundwater overdraft amounts to more than 2 million acre-feet in an average year but increases during droughts.[9] That is enough water to irrigate all the almond orchards in the state for a year, or provide a year's water supply to the city of Long Beach.[10]

SOIL SALINITY AND DRAINAGE PROBLEMS

Irrigation of the arid San Joaquin Valley has helped to create a prodigious agricultural region. It has also been the source of soil and drainage problems that are now reaching the critical point in some areas. Salt, found naturally in California soils, is carried to fields in irrigation water, gradually accumulating in the soil if it is not flushed away by seasonal rainfall. Excessive salt reduces crop yields and limits what can be grown. As much as 7 million tons of salt is deposited on San Joaquin Valley soil each year from irrigation water. A total of 3 million acres of California farmland (2.2 million of it in the San Joaquin Valley) is affected by high concentrations of salt, and by the turn of the century this could increase to 5 million acres.[11]

Other farmland is affected by the presence of saline groundwater just below the soil surface, much of it owing to irrigation flows. About half a million acres of such land in the San Joaquin Valley are already suffering declines in yield. Eventually these soils will be unfarmable unless the fields are drained. But even if drainage systems are installed to remove used irrigation water, the drain water itself must be disposed of. Some farmlands have natural outlets, such as rivers, but thousands of acres have no such natural drain, and farmers must build storage ponds for the irrigation runoff. An artificial channel, the San Luis Drain, was built in the 1970s to alleviate the San Joaquin Valley's saline drainage problem, but it was closed in 1986 when it was discovered that high levels of selenium—a naturally occurring mineral that accumulated in irrigation drainage water—was causing deaths and deformities in large numbers of waterfowl. The only solution to some of these dilemmas is to retire the lands where irrigation is causing the most problems.

Soil erosion is another effect of irrigating farmland. In California, millions of acres of farmland are affected by sheet, rill, or gully erosion as a consequence of irrigation. In the San Joaquin Valley alone, this erosion affects 1.5 million acres of cropland.[12] Soil erosion resulting from irrigation is also a problem in other areas of California where new vineyards and orchards have been planted on hillsides as the availability of flat farmland dwindles.

Ozone Pollution

California has some of the highest ozone levels in the United States. In addition to adversely affecting human health, ozone pollution from automobiles and other sources causes reduced yields in many of the state's leading crops. Ozone is causing a 20 percent to 30 percent loss of cotton, grape, and orange crops grown in the San Joaquin Valley; the economic effect of this is a loss of hundreds of millions of dollars annually.[13] Increasing population poses the threat of increased levels of ozone, particularly in the Central Valley, where more cropland is at risk.

THE LAST CROP: URBANIZATION AND FARMLAND CONVERSION

It is a sight familiar to anyone driving the interstate highways between California's coastal urban centers and the rural inland valleys—hundreds of skeletal house frames clustered on the horizon or sprawling alongside the road. For farming regions, these suburbs are the last crop, completing the cycle of conversion from wildlands to farmlands to urban land. A new wave of farmland conversion is occurring as California's rural hinterland becomes the target of urban growth and expansion. Migration from urban centers to outlying areas is now greater than net migration into California from other states. In 1990, more than 100,000 people moved from urban core areas to inland counties, twice the number that did in 1987. More than 70,000 left the Los Angeles/Orange County urban area to take up residence in outlying Riverside and San Bernardino counties.[14] The California Department of Conservation reported that 200,000 acres of farmland were lost to urban growth between 1984 and 1988 and warned that the equivalent of another San Francisco peninsula is being created from converted farmland each year.

At the southern end of San Francisco Bay, in the Santa Clara Valley, fertile alluvial soils, plentiful groundwater, and a fog- and frost-free climate provided ideal conditions for growing walnuts, peaches, plums, and apricots. In 1950, as the first postwar housing began to rise from the orchards, there were 135,000 acres of agricultural land in the county. By 1978, the region now known as Silicon Valley had lost 90,000 acres of farmland to urban development. A similar scenario was taking place in southern California surrounding Los Angeles. Irrigated acreage—largely orange groves—in Orange County fell from a peak of 130,000 acres in 1948 to less than 25,000 acres by 1981. The remaining groves will likely disappear within the next decade.[15] Figure 10.3 illustrates California's increasing farmland conversion from 1970 through 2000.

FIGURE 10.3
FARMLAND CONVERSION 1970–2000

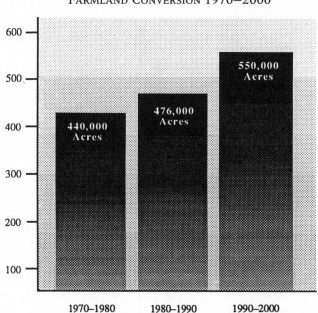

The 1990 census revealed that the fastest-growing counties in California—those with population increases of 30 percent to 76 percent in the last ten years—are all in predominantly rural regions, including eight Central Valley farm counties. For more than half the cities in the Central Valley there is more farmland than urban land within their "sphere of influence" or urban growth boundaries (a legal designation for all the state's incorporated cities defining land that is projected to be developed). If all this land is converted to urban uses, more than 335,000 acres of farmland will disappear from the heart of California's most productive farming regions.[16] Urbanization is also taking place on farmlands throughout the state. Conversion of productive soils to low-density "ranchette" development and idling of agricultural land takes almost as much productive farmland as direct conversion—more than 36,000 acres yearly.[17]

The realities of farm production aren't always apparent to the traveler on the road to somewhere else. But when former city-dwellers move to agricultural areas, the country scene can be unexpectedly disturbing at close range. Noisy irrigation pumps that chug through the night, aromatic livestock, flies, and dust may all be part of normal agricultural production. But to the nonfarming neighbor they can be a nuisance, prompting complaints and even lawsuits. As a result of these conflicts, farmers may have to limit activities, change cropping patterns, or incur the costs of a court action. Even without the threat of nuisance suits, farmers at the urban fringe are subject to theft and vandalism of farm property, crops, and livestock. The ultimate cost of these urban/rural conflicts is a decrease in the profitability of farming in the area and an increase in the willingness of farmers to sell their land for development. When development encroaches on agricultural land, some farmers take the attitude, "Why fight it?" Others hope to save their farmland, becoming advocates of local land use controls such as exclusive agriculture zones or protective ordinances that shield farmers from nuisance lawsuits. Those farmers choosing to switch rather than fight may oppose any attempts to limit their ability to cash in on ballooning land values. Some go so far as to declare that farming is no longer a viable option on land that can produce only $5,000 worth of crops but is worth ten times that for development. Agricultural land conservationists, however, think it is possible to save farmland and allow development on land not suitable for agriculture.

How does it all add up? Not all farmland in California is equal in quality, in the value of crops produced, or in its importance to the state's agricultural economy. Up to half of California's irrigated farmland is susceptible to productivity losses from environmental problems, and an unknown quantity of land with the most severe problems will eventually be removed from production altogether. Much of the remaining farmland is at risk of conversion as a result of urbanization. The state's monitoring program has documented annual losses of farmland at more than 50,000 acres.[18] But there are crucial gaps in this data, including several unmapped counties containing some of the state's richest farmland. In the Central Valley alone, projections of farmland loss based on population growth are estimated at 360,000 acres by 2010.[19]

VALUING AGRICULTURAL LAND

According to the economic "law of highest use," land will tend to be converted to the use that brings the highest economic return to the landowner. As a private asset, agricultural land is subject to the same economic market as housing and high-rises. A farmer can choose to grow tomatoes on the land or sell the land to a developer. As a public resource, however, farmland is worth something more than just the cost of the space the dirt occupies. There are values external to the marketplace inherent in good farmland. The value of farmland in a given location will determine what crop is best grown and even whether farming makes economic sense, but the larger question for the public is how to value the beneficial "externalities" of farmland, such as farming's contribution to the local economy, or as a reliable source of high-quality produce. As urbanization takes place in farming regions, the demand for housing or commercial development can create a speculative market for farmland that, in effect, devalues its agricultural use. As the price for farmland rises in response to development pressure, even those who want to remain in farming must find ways to get more value out of the land.

How people see farmland has a lot to do with how it is valued in the public mind. A pretty farmscape is as much a part of the mythical geography of the American dream as highways are part of the real American landscape. As such, farmland is perhaps prized foremost in the public's mind as open space, particularly as increasing numbers of Americans live "enclosed" by urban environments. However, the principle that necessarily must guide planning and protection efforts in farming areas defines agriculture as primarily an economic activity that is dependent on a network of local businesses and services whose land uses must also be incorporated into the planning picture.

FARMLAND CONSERVATION IN CALIFORNIA

The idea of protecting farmland is not new. Twenty-five years ago the state passed the California Land Conservation Act; other land use policies enacted in the 1960s and 1970s established a review process for city boundary changes and an environmental review of proposed development projects and required consistency between local general plan policies and zoning. More recently, private, non-profit land trusts have been successful in protecting farmland in a few locales, such as Marin County. These programs and policies have proved more or less effective in preventing or slowing the urbanization of farmland, depending on location and the degree of growth pressure. Statewide, however, farmland conservation is fragmented by the number of policies administered at various levels of government, most of which are vulnerable to political and economic pressure.

THE WILLIAMSON ACT AFTER TWENTY-FIVE YEARS

In 1965, the state legislature passed the California Land Conservation Act, known as the Williamson Act, a preferential assessment program that reduces property taxes on farmland in return for an agreement to restrict development for ten years. In contrast to similar programs in other states, the Williamson Act combines a tax break with restrictions on the future use of participating farmland, and it is administered by county governments, which have some discretion over its implementation; participation is voluntary for both the county and the landowner. In 1976, a subvention formula was incorporated into the Williamson Act that allocated state funds to counties participating in the program to replace a portion of the property tax revenues lost on contracted lands, offset some local administration costs, and provide an incentive to local governments to take on contracts.

The Williamson Act has helped to protect the economic viability of California agriculture—as judged by the current enrollment in the program of 15 million acres of farmland, half the state's agricultural land base. This does not appear to translate into the preservation of agricultural land, based on the loss of more than 50,000 acres of farmland each year. A clear failure of the program has been its inability to protect prime farmland at the margins of growing cities or in the path of development, and research conducted in the 1970s showed that landowners who perceived development as imminent were not likely to participate in the program.[20] More recently, it appears that the amount of land in Williamson Act contracts is declining. In one Central Valley farm county, agricultural landowners failed to renew their contracts on 5,295 acres from the time of the program's inception to the end of 1988; however, in 1989 and 1990, nonrenewal of contracts affected more than 25,000 acres.[21]

ACQUIRING DEVELOPMENT RIGHTS ON FARMLAND

Unlike legislated policies and programs or local land use planning decisions that are by nature subject to change, acquisition of development rights on farmland is a method of permanently protecting the agricultural use of land. This involves a legal transaction between a landowner and a qualified agent, such as a nonprofit land conservation organization, to restrict use of the land to farming. The transaction is a deed of easement placed on the property that in effect removes the right to subdivide the land or develop it. Once the easement is placed on the land, it cannot be removed except by a court action.

A number of private, nonprofit land trusts have acquired development rights to farmland, notably in Marin County, where more than 15,000 acres of farmland adjacent to the densely populated San Francisco Bay urban area have been protected by the Marin Agricultural Land Trust. In addition to local land trusts, several counties have implemented farmland conservation programs based on the purchase of development rights. In 1988, Californians passed a statewide bond measure to fund the purchase of parkland and wildlife habitat that also included funding for the purchase of development rights on farmland in five counties.

NEW PRESCRIPTIONS FOR FARMLAND PROTECTION

Recent policy initiatives to protect farmland have focused on several areas of vulnerability in the land use planning process at the local level. One in particular would strengthen the role of the California Environmental Quality Act in local land use decisions. County governments would be required to establish a threshold for the conversion of agricultural land to nonagricultural uses; any proposed land use action to convert farmland beyond the established threshold would trigger preparation of an environmental impact review, or require mitigation if the conversion was approved. Other proposed legislation would require local governments to include a separate element for agriculture in their general plans, and a right-to-process law would protect agricultural processing operations from nuisance complaints. What is lacking, however, is a truly comprehensive approach to the problem of urban encroachment in highly productive farm regions.

The solution to this problem is of global importance. The farmlands of California are among the few prime agricultural regions upon which a geometrically expanding world population must depend.

AN INSIDER'S VIEW: A TALK WITH RICHARD ROMINGER

As a fourth-generation farmer, Richard Rominger has a perspective on farming that is keener than most. As a former director of the California Department of Food and Agriculture and board member of the American Farmland Trust and the Yolo Land Conservation Trust, he is in a special position to speak on the issues. This conversation took place on the Rominger farm in Winters, where two generations of Romingers are growing wheat, tomatoes, popcorn, and rice.

Q: In your opinion, what are the most pressing problems facing farmers in California today?
A: The most pressing problems are generated by the increase in population—competition for water, air pollution, and the conversion of farmland to nonfarm uses. I think my sons feel that the problems caused by population pressure are of more concern than whether there is going to be credit available, or whether they're going to be able to farm with fewer pesticides.

Q: What can farmers do to reduce the negative effects on the environment resulting from agricultural practices?
A: More and more farmers have been working on decreasing pesticide use. Farmers have a number of incentives for trying to limit the amount that they use, and one is economics. Pesticides are expensive. If they can keep their yields up without using as much pesticide, they are interested in that. Farmers have been pressing the

universities and private research firms to do more work on the whole system of agriculture, getting back to some of the ideas that we haven't paid any attention to for the last forty or fifty years—trying to nurture beneficial insects, for example. I think the focus of agricultural research needs to be on long-term sustainability. We can't just continue with what we've done in the last fifty years. In many parts of the country the soil erosion rate has been much too high to sustain agriculture over the long term. In other cases, the problem is salinization and overgrazing.

For the individual farmer, there has to be economic viability as well. If you're not making a living at it, you're not able to carry out the conservation practices that need to be done. In many cases, it takes a large, long-term investment to stop soil erosion, and it's not something that the farmer can afford to do alone.

Q: How can the goals of farmland preservation be achieved in California?
A: I think we have to take a longer-term view. Depending on which annual farmland conversion figure you use, maybe it's a hundred, maybe it's two hundred years before we pave over all the good farmland in California if we don't make some public policy decisions on where this growth is going to take place. I don't think you can depend on market forces to do that for you. So you have to make those decisions, and then you have to have a mechanism to accomplish them. And I think the easement programs, purchase of development rights, and transfer of development rights are all mechanisms that need to be used in order to achieve the goal of preservation. You can't do it with general plans and zoning; the county board of supervisors can change the general plan and the zoning any time they can get a majority to agree on it.

We have a local land trust here, the Yolo Land Conservation Trust. Our interest is in getting programs in place in Yolo County—easement programs, purchase of development rights programs—so that we can preserve farmland permanently. These are programs that will work. They can be financed in a number of ways. You can put most of the burden on the newcomers through development fees or developer extractions or mitigation fees, or you can spread the costs of the program to the general public as Sonoma County has done by increasing its sales tax. We need to decide that we want to save some of our farmland and then do it.

CHAPTER 11

The Forest: Fragmented Remnants of an Ecosystem

TIM PALMER

When the Spanish and later American settlers arrived in California, they discovered a great Central Valley grassland and savannah of oaks ringed by millions of acres of wooded hills and mountains. Vast ancient forests, with many trees more than a thousand years old, appeared to offer an inexhaustible supply of lumber for gold mines, railroads, towns, and cities. Waves of immigration, beginning with the 1849 Gold Rush, have greatly changed that landscape.

Despite California's increasing population, there remain areas of forest where people are few. How these lands are managed and how old-growth trees will be preserved are issues that have been debated at least since the establishment of the first California redwood park at Big Basin in 1901. The debate continues today, even though the amount of old growth remaining has dwindled to isolated tracts and to a scarcity that endangers many species of wildlife.

Forests are more than trees. Forests and rangelands provide more than 90 percent of the annual runoff of water in the state, support

The author would like to acknowledge the research assistance of Taylor Miller and Kathrine Currie concerning background information in this chapter. The opinions expressed are those of the author.

650 species of wildlife, provide recreation for millions, and maintain climate and chemical balances of global significance to the atmosphere.

Production of material goods has been an important use of California's natural forest endowment, but forests are also prized for the wildlife, water, scenic wonder, and recreational opportunities they provide. Though owners of forest lands sometimes speak of "tree farms," persistent controversies concerning management and protection reveal the broader social values that people place upon forests. Perhaps because of their age and size, trees arouse human passions in ways that corn fields cannot. Forests are not just "tree farms" to most people.

With the changing population and values in California, conflicts regarding forest land uses and management have grown dramatically since the early 1970s. The once apparently inexhaustible supply of timber has dwindled, particularly on forest industry lands, so that increasingly smaller and younger trees are being logged to meet demand and keep mills running, and many of the remaining old trees are being cut.

How these and other issues are resolved will affect the nature and condition of the forest that will be available to future generations. What kind of forest do we want? What resources should be used now and at what rate? How much should be preserved? Who makes the decisions, and how?

A Changing View of the Forest

Until recent years, a dominant view of forests was as a marketable commodity—a farm for logs and pulp. The 1980s and 1990s have brought an increased and widespread awareness of the forests as far more than that, indeed—as reservoirs of biodiversity, as islands of ecological complexity housing myriad species that live nowhere else, as governors of climates, and as essential fabrics in the stability and health of streams, fisheries, watersheds, and water supplies.

Controversy over the northern spotted owl is just an indicator, regarded as the proverbial "canary in the coal mine." The most important point is not that the owl is endangered, but that its ecosystem is endangered, along with all its attendant values.

The rate of deforestation of northwestern forests exceeds that of the celebrated tropical rain forests, and the ancient forests cannot be recreated simply by replanting trees. The complex of young and old trees, related plant life, microorganisms, and dead snags are all vital, along with the fallen timber that may take 200 years to decompose, yielding vital nutrients around living trees as old as 1,000 years.

Along with the principles of production that have dominated professional forestry for many years, new principles are ascending: do not reduce the capability of the land, and do not extirpate wildlife species. Though only remnants of ancient forests remain outside Alaska, those in northern California and the Northwest are our last chance to sustain a temperate, old-growth forest; except for tiny acreages, all the others have been cut. Ecologist and author Elliott Norse calls for a "new forestry" that recognizes the dependence of commodity products on the integrity of forest ecosystems.

CALIFORNIA FORESTS AND TIMBER HARVESTING

California forests include the oldest living tree on earth (the bristlecone pine), the largest living organism on earth (the giant sequoia), and the tallest tree on earth (the coast redwood). Species that are uniquely Californian include the Catalina ironwood, Washington palm, California nutmeg, Santa Lucia fir, and Monterey cypress.

Of California's 101 million acres, some 33 million are forests, including conifers such as Douglas fir, redwood, and ponderosa pine, and hardwoods such as oaks. Hardwoods are broadleafed and irregular in shape. The oaks, cottonwood, willows, and other hardwood species play a vital role in the ecology, economy, and desirability of California. The cottonwood, for example, is the major tree of the riparian zone—one of the two most important habitats for wildlife but reduced to 10 percent of its original extent. Oaks are likewise important but threatened (see Chapter 17).

This chapter focuses on conifers, which cover 23 million acres and account for 70 percent of California's forests. These trees grow straight and tall, and their lumber can readily be used for buildings; most commercial timber is conifer. Douglas fir, redwood, and mixed species predominate in northern and coastal areas; ponderosa pine, white fir, red fir, sugar pine, and jeffrey pine are numerous in the Sierra Nevada. About 18.5 million of the 23 million acres of conifer lands are classified by the state as "productive forest," meaning commercial harvest is feasible, about 2 million acres of which are in parks and reserves, leaving 16.5 million acres potentially available for logging. The timber industry owns about 3.7 million acres of these lands, and another 3.9 million acres are held by nonindustrial private forest land owners. The balance of commercially harvestable trees, nearly 9 million acres, is owned by the American public and is part of the 20.4 million acres of land managed in the eighteen separate national forests within California.[1]

Most of the remaining old-growth or ancient forests are in the national forests, where about 2 million acres support such old-growth trees. Of the 1.6 million acres of forest land on which redwood dominates, only 12 to 15 percent contained old growth in 1988. Cutting since 1988 has significantly reduced this old-growth acreage. About 105,000 acres lie in state or federal reserves (less than 6 percent of the original redwood forest).[2]

The industrial lands are owned by some 120 corporations. There have been fourteen sales of these lands since 1978, accounting for a shift of 2.4 million acres of the 3.7-million-acre total. One of these marked a new era of timber land sales supported by leveraged buyout financing: the Pacific Lumber Company of Scotia, California, was acquired by Maxxam Corporation of Houston, Texas, which doubled the cutting of old-growth trees to service corporate debt. Such sales have sparked intense public concern for the consequent pressure to increase cutting for short-term profits.

Timber cutting in California peaked in the 1950s at 6 billion board feet (BBF) per year. The annual average between 1978 and 1985 was 3.4 BBF, and recent harvest levels have been 3.9 BBF. About 1.65 BBF currently comes from national forests and other public lands, 1.9 BBF from industry lands, and 0.3 BBF from nonindustrial private lands. The North Coast and interior regions account for most of the timber harvested. Much of the timber in the north comes from private lands, while in the northern interior and Sierra, logs come more from national forests. During the harvest peaks of the 1950s, 90 percent of the timber came from private lands, much of it in the North Coast area. During the 1975–1985 period, 59 percent of the state harvest came from private lands, primarily in industrial ownership.

On the average, according to the State Department of Forestry, statewide forest growth has exceeded harvest during the 1978–

1985 period by 21 percent; however, the picture is dramatically different when the three ownership categories are separately considered. Cutting during the period was 69 percent of growth on public lands and only 29 percent of growth on nonindustrial private land. In contrast, harvest is 122 percent of growth on forest industry land.

In 1988, the Department of Forestry projected that total annual harvest can be maintained at 3.9 BBF through the year 2000 and then will drop to a stable 3.2 BBF per year by 2030. The industrial component was projected to drop from about 1.7 BBF per year to only 950 million board feet per year during the 2020–2030 decade. The forest industry share of total cutting was projected to decline from 46 percent to just over 30 percent, and the national forest share was estimated to rise to 60 percent. The Forest Service predicted that its annual timber sale volume is likely to decrease slightly from 1.9 to 1.6 BBF.

The decline of the industrial forest seems to have already arrived; trees as small as fourteen inches and as young as thirty-five years are proposed for logging. Ballot initiatives and legislative proposals have been introduced to impose a sustained yield standard on private land cutting.[3]

JOBS AND PRODUCTION

California consumed a total of 10 BBF of lumber in 1985. The state projects that this rate will rise at about 2 percent per year. About 25 to 30 percent of demand is met by California forests. Only about 1 percent of the private land logs is exported (exports are prohibited from public lands). Oregon sent 1.8 BBF to California (one-third of the trees cut in that state) in 1984. Canada provided 6 percent of the imported lumber.

There were eighty-nine sawmills in California in 1990 and thirty mills and processing plants of other types, compared to 1,000 mills in 1947. There were twenty-six plywood plants in 1968; in 1991, there were none. The large-diameter trees used for plywood are gone. The number of sawmills has continued to drop as the supply of old growth has been exhausted and mills have been consolidated into fewer, larger facilities. Those mills that remain are concentrated into ownership by a smaller number of companies; five of the ten mills in Mendocino County were owned by one company in 1990.

Many mill workers have lost their jobs to automation. While seven jobs were needed to produce a million board feet in 1975, only three jobs for the same amount of production were required by Mendocino County mills in 1985. Employment declined from 85,000 California timber-industry workers to 58,000 between 1975 and 1985. The average wage is below the state average ($8.15 per hour in 1983 compared to the state manufacturing average of $9.19). Although the timber industry accounts for only 5 percent of manufacturing employment and 1 percent of total employment in the state, it accounts for 10 percent of the manufacturing jobs in eleven counties and more than half the jobs in some sparsely populated counties.[4]

In addition to issues raised by the current rate of harvest, there are other concerns about the condition of California's forests. Ozone is affecting conifers, particularly ponderosa pine in the Sierra and southern California.[5] Years of extracting higher-value trees and conversion of lands to grazing have left vast areas of damaged forest. Soil loss from some cutover areas is extreme, raising questions about long-term sustainability of the forests if cutting and erosion persist at current levels.

Because of soil loss, nutrient depletion, and complex interactions between trees and soil microbes that are damaged or eliminated by modern logging practices, widespread concern exists that this renewable resource may not be renewable at all; that, in fact, we are mining the forests of California and will fail to see their replacement by forests of comparable diversity, productivity, and ecological value.

THE ROLE OF THE STATE

The California Department of Forestry and Fire Protection (CDF) is the lead agency for private and state owned forest lands, requiring permits for commercial harvests. About 1,500 timber harvest plans per year are approved under the State Forest Practices Act, which calls for maximum sustained production of high-quality timber products while giving consideration to recreation, watersheds, wildlife, range and forage, fisheries, regional economic vitality, employment, and aesthetic enjoyment.[6] Persistent controversies provoked by approved plans show that a consensus is yet to be reached on the proper balance of these values; some fifty lawsuits have been filed challenging timber harvest plans since 1986.[7]

The CDF director issued a "new directions" policy in 1990 announcing that greater attention will be given to maintaining the productivity of the forests and to ensuring that a thorough and complete analysis is made of the environmental effects of timber harvesting.[8]

Although individual environmental impact reports are not required for timber harvest plans, the environmental policy provisions of the California Environmental Quality Act do apply. A number of court decisions have held that CDF must consider a range of significant environmental effects, including cumulative effects of past, current, and foreseeable timber harvest on watershed and wildlife values.

THE ROLE OF THE FEDERAL GOVERNMENT

Day-to-day management of national forests is under the direction of a forest supervisor in each national forest, regulated under three acts of Congress. The Multiple Use and Sustained Yield Act of 1960 established a policy of multiple use management. The Resources Planning Act of 1974 requires that plans for the forests be completed, and the National Forest Management Act of 1976 established guidelines for plans and standards as more definitive controls on the discretion of the Forest Service, particularly with regard to such matters as clear-cutting.

The forest land management plans include voluminous amounts of information on each national forest. Developed in the 1980s under commodity- and production-oriented mandates of the Reagan administration, the plans attracted widespread public comment and appeals. Responding to criticism of these policies, the chief of the Forest Service in 1991 announced a "new perspectives" policy designed to remedy at least some of the conflicts with environmental values. Jeff DeBonis, a Forest Service timber sale planner who founded an organization of employees dedicated to reforming the agency, said in July of 1991 that he saw very little evidence of the new policies "on the ground," adding, "The rhetoric is wonderful, but is very different from what is happening in the forests." The celebrated case of John Mumma, a regional forester in Montana who was transferred because he didn't sell timber in critical habitat areas, is only one example that the agency is still governed by western congressmen pushing for heavy, subsidized cutting of the nation's forests, no matter what. Just one example of these subsidies: new roads built by the government for logging and having a twenty-five-year life are amortized by the Forest Service over a period of a hundred years, and sometimes much longer, making their cost appear to be lower. Only time will tell how substantive the reform-oriented policy changes will be.[9]

Of the eighteen plans required for California forests, ten were completed by mid-1991, though aspects of each were appealed.

FOREST POLITICS IN CALIFORNIA

In 1990, many long-simmering issues were brought to the forefront of California politics. Following expensive and agonizing initiative battles in which both conservationist and industry-sponsored efforts failed, 1991 brought an historic meeting of the minds—indeed, a model of consensus among differing groups. Environmental organizations, logging companies that own 66 percent of the private timber lands in the state, the California Labor Federation, and water agencies all agreed on a timber cutting reform package. Supported even by North Coast legislators, the bill passed the state Assembly and Senate as a model of compromise. To the complete amazement of political observers in California and the nation, Governor Pete Wilson, under intense lobbying pressure from three timber companies owned by out-of-state corporations, vetoed the bill. The governor then reconvened negotiations between environmental and industry representatives, which resulted in a new proposal that became stalled in the legislature. In the meantime, destructive methods of logging proceeded faster than before.

The Northern Spotted Owl

Logging can destroy habitat to the degree that areas must be set aside to avoid certain species' extinction. This is the case for the northern spotted owl, each pair requiring three square miles to survive. In 1991, the U.S. Fish and Wildlife Service identified 11.6 million acres of habitat necessary to the owl, 3.2 million of them in California and 1.5 million in national forests of the northern state. Clear-cutting was found responsible for the fragmentation of spotted owl habitat.[10]

The State Board of Forestry passed rules in 1990 providing for protection of potential owl habitat, and CDF is preparing a habitat conservation plan to avoid a taking of owls in violation of the act. The Bureau of Land Management has pressed for an exemption to Endangered Species Act requirements that limit its ability to cut timber. The Fish and Wildlife Service's proposed rulemaking asserts that logging and other projects may still be carried out in owl habitat, but each project must be assessed to determine if it is likely to harm critical areas.

In spite of the National Forest Management Act, which requires the agency "to maintain viable populations of existing native and desired non-native vertebrate species," and in spite of Congress ordering the development of a protection plan for the spotted owl in 1990, Bush administration officials ordered that work on the plan be stopped. A lawsuit was required to halt Forest Service timber sales in old-growth habitat, critical for the owls. U.S. District Court Judge William Dwyer ordered the Agency to stop the sales and found "a deliberate and systematic refusal by the U.S. Forest Service and Fish and Wildlife Service to comply with laws protecting wildlife." Bills have been introduced to gut protections for the owls.

Even with some revision by the Fish and Wildlife Service and possible intervention by Congress, it seems likely that spotted owl habitat preservation will protect at least some old growth and reduce cutting somewhat on national forest and private land. Whether or not it will be enough to assure the owl's survival is not known. Concerns have also been raised regarding other potentially threatened species, such as the marbled murrelet, red tree vole, fisher, and pine martin, all of which depend on old growth.[11] In the past species have gone extinct through people's ignorance; that is not the case with the old-growth forests of today. The vulnerability of species is well known; the political response, however, has thus far failed to take adequate steps for protection.

CLEAR-CUTTING

Perhaps the most hotly contested forest management issue is the practice of clear-cutting, a factor in the creation of national forests and in the reform of their management. Clear-cuts—where all trees in a particular area are cut at once—appear devastating and often are. The land is scraped raw by heavy machinery, no trees are left, soil temperatures can be extreme with no shade, and erosion can be severe.

Clear-cutting is often done to achieve "even aged management." Under this approach, the forest is made up of a mosaic of areas, each with trees of the same age. Theoretically, the larger forest will have all age classes represented in blocks of various ages.

There is disagreement about the revegetation aspects of clear-cutting. Some believe that it is the best method for reforestation of shade-intolerant trees. Others argue that even these species require some shade to survive the damaging effects of sun-heated soils.

Controversy is aggravated by the fact that reforestation after clear-cutting often involves the use of herbicides temporarily banned on national forests in California by the regional forester in the 1980s, after a federal court upheld a challenge to herbicide use in Washington and Oregon. After upgrading the environmental impact statement, California's regional forester again allowed the spraying of herbicides, a decision that has been appealed.

Clear-cutting is often the most economic method to the logging company. Under state regulations, clear-cuts are limited to 120 acres. Forest Service regulations limit clear-cuts to 40 acres, but in practice they are usually limited to about 20 acres. State legislative proposals in 1991 would have limited clear-cutting to 20 acres on private land and prohibited it in ancient forests. Federal legislation has also been introduced that would restrict or eliminate clear-cutting on federal lands. In an environmental agenda released in 1990, the Forest Service regional forester announced an intention to use methods other than clear-cutting on about 70 percent of the areas to be harvested.

ANCIENT FOREST PROTECTION

Ancient forests, which have never been harvested, are one of the highlights of the California landscape. Redwoods are a symbol of the state and one of the major tourist attractions. More important than this scenic splendor, ancient forests are one of the vital habitats in the West, housing an abundance of life that may be incapable of surviving anywhere else. Species such as the fisher, pine martin, spotted owl—160 wildlife species in all—are associated with the undisturbed forest, as are the qualities of important watersheds and fisheries. Plants found there have medicinal value, and much remains to be discovered. Nearly all of the old growth on private forest lands, and much of it in national forests, has been cut. Only 10 percent of the original old-growth redwood and Douglas fir remain, though some estimates of old growth in the Northwest, including northern California, are as low as 2 percent.

On Forest Service lands, about 1 million of the 2 million remaining acres of old-growth forests are preserved in wilderness areas or under provisions of national forest plans.[12] In 1990, the chief of the Forest Service announced a policy of treating old growth as a resource in itself and requiring that it be managed to preserve intrinsic characteristics. Yet critical areas of old growth remain unprotected.

Raising the ire of forest conservationists, local communities, and the public at large, the Forest Service allowed the cutting of all trees but sequoias in some showcase groves of the giant redwoods in Sequoia National Forest. Besides ravaging the landscape in these groves of the world's largest species of organism, the logging deprives remaining redwoods of protective windbreaks that had been provided by the ancient sugar pines and cedars.

Two bills have been proposed in the U.S. House of Representatives addressing ancient forest protection. The legislation would direct the secretaries of the Interior and Agriculture departments to designate an ancient forest reserve system, including lands managed by the Bureau of Land Management and the Forest Service. The legislation also directs the secretaries to enhance the economic stability of the Pacific Northwest.

The California Forest Practices Act does not impose special restrictions on the harvesting of ancient forests. Though outright prohibition on cutting old-growth trees would be challenged as a taking of private property requiring just compensation, recent efforts have been made in initiatives and statutory proposals to slow the attrition of old-growth forests and expand the protection of more mature forest stands. In the proposed state legislation, clearcutting would be banned in all ancient forests. Removal of various sizes of trees would be limited to a given percentage, such as 50 percent, during a certain period of time, such as twenty-five years; however, in all cases at least six of the old, large trees per acre must remain. Timber harvests within all ancient forests would be required to be conducted in a manner that preserves the "mature character" of the forest.

A central theme of ancient-forest supporters is that the timber industry could be allowed to go ahead and cut the remaining 1 million acres of unprotected ancient forests on public lands within the next decade or two and *then* adjust to the inevitable economy lacking old-growth trees, or the industry can make the adjustment now and leave this irreplaceable remnant of the original California for the survival of a vital, endangered ecosystem and for growing public use and appreciation.

Sustained Yield

Sustained yield is cutting that does not exceed forest growth. The practical goal is to limit cutting today in order to have regularly available timber in the future. Unfortunately, some mills have been managed with an economic dependence on harvests that exceed the sustained yield capacity of the forests, an apparently suicidal strategy in the long term. While assuring stability for the future, sustained yield could disrupt local employment and local economies in the short term.

National forest lands have theoretically been subject to sustained yield policies since at least the enactment of the Multiple Use and Sustained Yield Act. General requirements were made more specific through a "non-declining even flow policy." This requires the Forest Service to set caps, known as the allowable sale quantity, on the amount of timber that can be sold. In 1990, this amount was 1.6 BBF in California.

The California Forest Practices Act does not contain provisions specifically addressing sustained yield on private forest lands. The act does state that the legislature intends that the goal of maximum sustained production of high-quality timber products should be achieved. Nevertheless, in practice, decisions about timing and intensity of harvest have been left to the private landowner.

In recent years, timber harvest plans for some private lands have been submitted for relatively young, small trees of thirty-five to fifty years of age. Though it approves most plans, the Department of Forestry denied at least one plan and withheld decisions on others because of concerns that harvest of the fastest-growing young trees would deplete site productivity and reduce future timber supplies available for harvest. The department subsequently proposed to prohibit the harvest of trees less than fifty to eighty-five years old and limit cutting to once every ten years. Legislative proposals in 1991 called for limiting the annual cut to 2.2 percent of inventory, calculated to be a sustained yield rate.

Sustained yield requires consideration of trade-offs between current harvest and conservation for future use. Imposing a decision upon private land management is difficult since it limits the rights of ownership. Yet, as timber supplies dwindle on private lands, particularly on forest industry lands on the North Coast, pressures to prematurely dip into future timber supplies have thus far been insurmountable. In a November 19, 1991, *Time* interview, state Department of Forestry head Richard Wilson said, "The loggers put money into buying more old growth rather than regrowing our forests, and the trees are not there to feed the mills. The M.B.A.s have turned forestry into a mining exercise."

Social and Economic Change in Forest-Dependent Communities

The economic and social climate in forest-dependent communities has changed dramatically in recent decades. Most of the large, high-quality trees have been harvested, jobs have dwindled, and new residents oppose cutting of the little that remains of the old growth. Long-time residents of logging communities often feel that their way of life is under attack; others perceive that the old way is simply a thing of the past.

Social problems such as drug abuse, spousal and child abuse, and alcoholism have increased while available state and local taxes and social services have declined. In some areas newer residents, attracted to the "nonmarket" values of the forests, have arrived with little or no connection to the timber industry.

Responses to these problems are easier to catalog than to implement. They include efforts to diversify the markets for timber products, such as developing more uses for hardwoods. Diversification of local economies is another obvious approach. Tourism—California's top industry—may be the economic future of many forest-dependent communities. The need for healthy and stable rural communities must be integrated into state and federal policies for healthy and stable forest ecosystems.

CONCLUSIONS AND TRENDS

Numerous forest policy and management issues require attention by the California public, lawmakers, agency regulators, forest managers, and users. Recent events indicate that the following trends are likely to continue.

California policy is increasingly being set by the politically dominant urban voters. Forest management concerns have moved into the main arena of statewide environmental policy and politics, as evidenced by the initiative and legislative campaigns of 1990, 1991, and 1992.

Regulation of timber harvesting on private and public lands will increase, particularly in the areas of wildlife protection, stream protection, cumulative effects, and sustained yield. For many people forests will be seen as more valuable for water, fish and wildlife, recreation, and aesthetic enjoyment than for timber production. Intense political battles, however, will be fought every step of the way.

Forest harvests are likely to decline significantly on private industrial and national forest lands during the next several decades because of declining mature timber inventories. Additional mill closures will occur, and industry consolidation is a continuing trend.

The decline of harvest and structural change of the industry will create social and economic problems in local communities that deserve the attention of forest policy makers.

Old-growth and mature forests, and the fish and wildlife that depend upon them, have become recognized as a resource in their own right deserving of long-term protection. The policy and management challenge will be to determine how old-growth forests can be protected, consistent with the rights of private land ownership. Some private forest lands will be good candidates for public acquisition, but this will be a challenge in an era of budget deficits.

Nonindustrial private lands, which are forecast to contain 29 percent of the timber inventory but contribute only 7 percent of the harvest volume, will receive more pressure for cutting.[13] The long-recognized challenge of devising management approaches that will allow logging consistent with "nonmarket" owner objectives will be even more important.

Controversies concerning the role of clear-cutting and herbicide use will continue. Opponents will seek more limitations while many foresters will continue to argue that clear-cutting and herbicides should be allowed.

Long-term regional plans for private lands will be a necessary complement to greater regulation of timber harvest. Plans are needed for sustained yield, wildlife management, and watershed protection.

Rapid and continuous change will characterize California's private and national forest land management during the 1990s. This will be a time of stress, but also an opportunity to place forestry more firmly on a path of sustainable management for the many values Californians place upon their forests.

FURTHER INFORMATION

Michael D. Lemonick, "Whose Woods Are These?" *Time*, December 9, 1991, 70–75.

Donald G. McNeil, Jr., "How Much of the Public Forests Are Sold to Loggers at a Loss," *New York Times*, November 3, 1991.

Elliott A. Norse, *Ancient Forests of the Pacific Northwest* (Washington, D.C.: Island Press, 1990).

Gordon Robinson, *The Forest and the Trees* (Washington, D.C.: Island Press, 1988).

"Why Let Chainsaws Pare the Old Forests at All?" *New York Times*, November 3, 1991.

CHAPTER 12

Solid Waste: To Recycle or to Bury California

WILLIAM K. SHIREMAN

In the time it takes you to read this sentence, Californians will buy, consume, and throw away *ten tons* of raw materials. Before we manufacture these materials into products, we call them trees, rocks, hillsides, canyons. Afterward, we call them garbage.

Californians generate solid waste at the rate of a ton and a half *every second*. That works out to 50 million tons per year, or nearly two tons for every man, woman, and child.[1]

Eleven percent of our waste is recycled, and 2 percent is incinerated in so-called "waste-to-energy" facilities. The rest—87 percent—is dumped into the more than 650 landfills scattered throughout the state.[2]

Lately, it has become more and more difficult to take out the trash in California. As the true environmental costs of landfills have been unearthed, costs have surged, and local opposition to new landfills has become intense.

William K. Shireman is president of California Futures, a Sacramento-based environmental and economic think tank. He serves as editor of *Profit the Earth*, a monthly newsletter that shows how companies can increase profits by protecting the environment. He was previously executive director of Californians Against Waste and developed many of California's recycling laws and policies.

When local citizens organize to oppose a landfill, the waste management industry refers to them as NIMBYs—adherents to the "not in my back yard" syndrome. But, in actuality, these activists have sound cause for concern. Landfills can lead to groundwater and surface water pollution, traffic congestion, noise, emissions of methane gas, and even toxic waste pollution. More than one in five Superfund hazardous waste sites in the United States is a landfill.[3] All of this can translate into a lower quality of life and the potential of much lower property values for residents of an area.

So acute has the landfill crisis become that, at current rates, all the remaining capacity in the state's landfills will have been used up by 1999. In southern California, the situation appears more dire: its capacity will be gone by 1996 (see Figure 12.1). Capacity in Los Angeles will be spent by 1994.[4]

What then? Few experts predict that garbage will pile up in the streets in California, as it has for brief periods in other states. In all likelihood, some existing landfills will be expanded, a few new

FIGURE 12.1
LANDFILL CAPACITY IN SOUTHERN CALIFORNIA

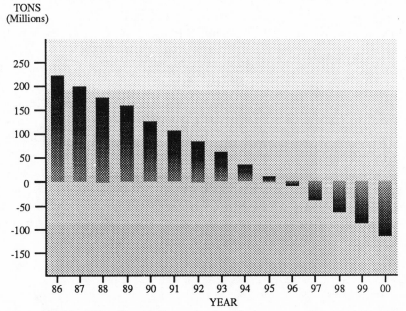

SOURCE: Assembly Office of Research, *Integrated Solid Waste Management: Putting a Lid on Garbage Overload.* April 1988, p. 17.

ones may be opened, and hundreds of recycling programs will divert materials for more useful purposes. We will probably squeeze by.

Or will we? For as serious as the landfill crisis is, its environmental impacts pale by comparison to the waste and pollution caused by the process of creating things to be thrown away. Most of the environmental damage caused by the throwaway system is caused not when a product is discarded at a landfill, but much earlier, when the product is first manufactured, and before.

Central to this damage are the hidden wastes from mining. Extracting and processing raw materials from the earth mean tearing apart mountains, canyons, and forests, extracting a small percentage of valuable materials, and discarding what remains as tailings. For every ton of garbage discarded at the municipal level in the United States, six to seven tons of mining wastes are generated. That equals 1.0 billion to 1.3 billion tons nationally; based on our population, California's share would exceed 250 million tons per year. Acidic or toxic drainage from mines has damaged nearly 10,000 miles of streams in the western United States.[5]

Other damages result from waste of energy and water. Any given product "contains" much more than its physical composition might imply. An enormous quantity of energy and water is needed to transform raw ore into a finished metal, to produce a product, to transport it through an elaborate distribution network to a consumer, and finally to collect and move it to a dump for disposal. It takes almost half a can of petroleum energy—five ounces—to make a single 12-ounce aluminum can (if you don't recycle it). It takes 381 ounces of water to make a glass bottle holding 12 ounces of soda, but only 97 ounces to make and wash it if it is refillable.[6] (See Table 12.1.)

The garbage we throw away also spews garbage into the air and water—and not just at a landfill. Making aluminum from bauxite ore creates twenty times as much air pollution and thirty times as much water pollution as recycling it.[7] Table 12.2 presents some of the environmental benefits of recycling.

TABLE 12.1
AMOUNTS OF ENERGY AND WATER IN A 12-OUNCE SOFT DRINK

Type	Energy (*Petroleum Equivalent*)	Water
Aluminum Can	5 ounces	181 ounces
Glass Bottle	4 ounces	381 ounces
Plastic Bottle	3 ounces	382 ounces
Recycled Aluminum	2 ounces	Not available
Refilled Bottle	1 ounce	120 ounces

SOURCE: William K. Shireman, *Can and Bottle Bills* (Stanford, Ca.: Stanford Environmental Law Society, 1982), pp. 28, 36.

NOTE: "Aluminum" assumes 25 percent recycled content. "Refilled bottle" assumes ten or more fillings.

TABLE 12.2
ENVIRONMENTAL BENEFITS OF RECYCLING

Environmental Benefit	Aluminum Percent	Steel Percent	Paper Percent	Glass Percent
Reduction of:				
Energy Use	90–97	47–74	23–74	4–32
Air Pollution	95	85	74	20
Water Pollution	97	76	35	—
Mining Wastes	—	97	—	80
Water Use	—	40	58	50

SOURCE: Robert Cowles Letcher and Mary T. Sheil, "Source Separation and Citizens Recycling," in *The Solid Waste Handbook,* ed. William D. Robinson (New York: John Wiley and Sons, 1986).

WHAT CALIFORNIA THROWS AWAY

Of the 50 million tons of garbage we generate, almost one-third is paper. Perhaps 40 percent is organic yard and food waste, much of which is compostable. More than 20 percent is glass, metals, and plastics, nearly all recyclable. Less than 1 percent is household toxic products, of which three predominate: paints, motor oils, and car batteries.[8] (See Table 12.3.)

TABLE 12.3
CALIFORNIA'S WASTE STREAM, 1990 ESTIMATES

Type	Percent	
Paper		30
Newsprint	10	
Organic Waste		40
Yard Waste	30	
Food Waste	10	
Plastics		8
Glass		7
Metals		7
Household Toxic		0.5 to 1
Other		7

SOURCE: California Futures, 1991. Waste composition estimates will vary based on sampling and categorization methods. ·

Waste generators can be divided into categories, such as residential, single-family, multifamily, commercial, industrial, agricultural, and others. Fifty-five percent of California's waste stream is residential; 45 percent is commercial.[9]

WHY WE GENERATE SO MUCH TRASH

Why do we create so much garbage? Much has been written about the wastefulness of Californians and of Americans. But wastefulness is not a character flaw that especially afflicts people between the 25th and 49th parallels. It is a systemic problem, the result of policies of a bygone era—outdated policies explicitly intended to encourage the consumption of raw materials and generation of waste.

Very simply, we pay people to generate waste and we penalize them for reducing it.

We encourage companies to extract raw materials by offering depletion allowances that enable them to erase much of the cost of extracting finite raw materials from the earth. Originally intended to accelerate industrial development, these allowances typically range from 7 to 22 percent of gross annual income. They are not available to those who produce the same products from recycled materials. The federal government also subsidizes timber harvesting. In 1989, the United States lost money on timber sales in 102 of 120 national forests.[10]

We price energy and raw materials not according to their cost of creation but merely their cost of extraction. For example, the cost of petroleum is based not on the cost of actually making it, but merely on the cost of withdrawing it from the earth. This would be like valuing your life savings according to the cost of driving to the bank to withdraw them.

We make waste a "free good" for product manufacturers—and as economists tell us, all free goods get overused. When manufacturers first design products or packages, they figure the costs of buying the raw materials that comprise them, but seldom the cost of throwing away or recycling them. That means manufacturers overuse materials *and* overuse production systems that render the materials nonrecyclable. Why should manufacturers care about the costs of disposal when someone else will pay them no matter how high they go?

Finally, we create the illusion of free disposal for consumers by charging residents a single all-you-can-excrete price for most garbage collection. Whether a family discards one can or five every week, most city refuse services will charge them the same fee. In Los Angeles, the system is even more convoluted: residents pay nothing at all for garbage collection, directly. The service is "free," subsidized by general revenue taxes. Politicians are reluctant to explode the myth of free garbage collection; hence, garbage keeps piling higher, and the costs of handling it rise even faster.

WHAT ARE WE DOING ABOUT IT?

After years of burying our garbage in the ground and our heads in the sand, Californians have finally awakened to our solid waste problems. Two pieces of legislation show how we are tackling garbage: the beverage container refund law, or "bottle bill," and the state's comprehensive local recycling mandates, referred to as AB 939, or the Integrated Waste Management Act.

The Bottle Bill

After two decades of battles over beverage container deposit proposals, the California legislature passed AB 2020 in 1986, a product of a unique compromise forged between environmentalists and their traditional adversaries: beverage and container manufacturers, distributors, retailers, and some recyclers.

The bill, authored by Assemblyman Burt Margolin (D–Los Angeles) was modeled on bottle bills in nine other states but differed in key respects. In a capitulation to industry, refund values began very low—at a penny—but were quickly increased to at least two for a nickel. And in order to bring aboard retailers and recyclers, an alternative system of redemption was established. Retailers had always opposed the law because they lost money sorting returned containers. Many recyclers opposed it because they feared it would divert containers away from them and toward retailers. Both groups opposed the law on economic grounds: by starting deposits with beverage wholesalers, the traditional bottle bill required that containers be sorted by brand for return to those same distributors, adding as much as a nickel in processing costs for every container.

Environmentalists devised a new redemption strategy: rather than forcing containers back through retail stores that didn't want them, they would enable consumers to return them to a variety of programs that *did* want them: curbside recycling programs, buy-back recycling centers, and charity drop-off sites. But to ensure that every consumer would have at least one convenient place to obtain a refund, they required that new "convenience zone" recycling centers be set up by recyclers or retailers around most supermarkets in the state. Furthermore, to cut the operating costs of the system, all deposits are paid into a central state fund. That way, containers could be collected and crushed at recycling centers, eliminating the need and cost of sorting by brand.

The original one-cent refund turned out to be too low. But today, at two and a half cents, the system is recycling more containers than any other state, at a cost per container 90 percent lower than traditional deposit laws.[11]

The original measure called for gradual increases in the refund. But starting in 1990, the legislature jump-started the process, increasing refunds to two for a nickel for small containers and a nickel for large ones, such as two-liter plastic soft-drink bottles. Under that system, refunds would double to five cents for small containers and ten cents for large ones in 1993 if a minimum 65 percent redemption rate is not achieved.

When two-for-a-nickel refund values took effect, the result was an explosive increase in recycling—more than 40 percent overall, comparing 1990 to 1989. More than eight out of ten beverage containers were recycled through the AB 2020 program in 1991— more than under New York State's traditional bottle bill, which costs more than ten times as much to operate.[12]

The most significant attribute of the California system may be the low cost at which containers are recycled. By eliminating costly sorting requirements for retailers and recyclers, the system saves from $245 million to $390 million per year in the state compared to a traditional bottle bill, or $32 to $52 per family of four (see Figure 12.2).[13]

That savings is not merely a generalized financial benefit to the state. Most significantly, by making recycling profitable, it has helped to drive an explosive growth in the number and size of recycling programs of all kinds. The program has dramatically reduced the costs of handling containers, compared to alternative programs. Hundreds of cities, counties, and private businesses have initiated or expanded recycling programs, using beverage containers as their financial foundation. In 1987, only 500 recycling

FIGURE 12.2
SAVINGS UNDER CALIFORNIA'S 1990 RECYCLING PROGRAM

$32 to $52 a Year for a Family of Four

13¢ to 19¢ on every six-pack of cans

SOURCE: California Department of Conservation.

centers operated in the state, and 30 communities offered curbside recycling services to their residents. By 1990, more than 2,500 recycling centers had opened for business and 200 communities offered curbside collection.

Nevertheless, recycling is still not profitable in many instances. "Convenience zone" recycling centers often require additional funds from the state to cover their costs. These centers process just 10 percent of all redeemed containers.[14]

In addition, many recycling programs contend that they still lose a significant amount of money on glass recycling. Glass manufacturers reply that paying higher scrap prices might put many glass producers out of business. In 1991, the state Department of Conservation implemented a glass market development program that paid rebates to companies that purchased glass for recycling. The department also imposed new, higher processing fees on glass to make up the difference between average scrap values and the costs of glass recycling. The issue is likely to continue to be debated in the legislature and at the department.

The Integrated Waste Management Act

If the Bottle Bill provides financial incentives and funding for recycling, then AB 939 provides the political impetus. Authored by Assemblyman Bryon Sher (D–Palo Alto) and passed in 1989, the law mandates that all cities and counties implement plans to recycle 25 percent of their solid waste by 1995 and 50 percent by the year 2000. To enforce these goals, the act requires that cities and counties prepare waste reduction plans, called source reduction and recycling elements.

The act is already forcing cities and counties to rethink age-old practices with regard to solid waste management and to reveal the fallacies of certain commonly held recycling myths, one being the "magic box" theory—the idea that disposal and recycling challenges can be met the old-fashioned way, with one single system doing the whole job (a landfill or incinerator, for example). There simply will not be sufficient landfill capacity in the years ahead to meet the projected increase in waste, and incineration is not the option it was once thought to be. In the early 1980s, at least thirty waste-to-energy incinerators were projected to be on line by the year 2000. By 1989, only three were operating.[15] Many of the state and federal subsidies that used to make incinerators viable have since been eliminated. While markets exist for fuel pellets of waste paper and plastics, large-scale waste-to-energy facilities have little support. Given environmental objections regarding air pollution and toxic wastes, imposing capital requirements, and high operating costs, it is doubtful that incineration will make significant inroads in the foreseeable future.

Not even the best-run recycling program will single-handedly solve our solid waste dilemmas. A typical curbside recycling program targets newspapers, glass, and aluminum containers, together less than 20 percent of the waste stream. Curbside programs have participation rates of two-thirds or less; those who participate set out two-thirds of the materials that qualify. In addition, residential waste is perhaps half a program's total waste. Thus, curbside programs recycle 5 percent of the total waste on average. A 1990 California Futures review showed that a typical program diverted 8.1 percent of residential waste and 3.2 percent of total municipal waste.

The only way 25 percent and 50 percent recycling rates can be achieved and sustained will be through an integrated package of programs that collects an array of materials and identifies quality markets where the materials can be reused.

RECYCLING CHALLENGES OF THE 1990S

The only problem with all this recycling activity is that it may ultimately seem futile. Even if we are able to reduce and recycle 50 percent of our waste by the end of the decade, soon thereafter we will be producing twice the volume of garbage we do today, given today's garbage growth patterns. Ultimately, the only way we can meet the crisis will be to deal with it at its root, by reducing waste at its source. We might be able to do this by imposing tough standards on products and packages. But the variety of materials that would need to be regulated, the costs of administration, and the restrictions on the marketplace make this an expensive and ineffective option. The larger need is to create a system of financial and other incentives that cultivate the emergence of smaller, more durable, less wasteful, and more recyclable products and packages. Accomplishing that objective will require that we undo the financial subsidies that presently encourage the generation of waste. Some of the proposals now being considered for accomplishing this include the following.

Variable Can Rates

Most communities charge a flat fee for garbage service no matter how much waste a family generates. By contrast, Seattle residents are charged according to the amount of garbage they set out for disposal. The result has been a major reduction in waste. After two years of operation, the average number of thirty-gallon cans (or equivalent) set out per family per week declined 60 percent, from 2.6 to 1. About one-third of a can was diverted to curbside recycling. One-fourth of a can was diverted to yard waste composting. The remaining reduction—about a can per week—was apparently diverted into a combination of recycling, source reduction, and increased compaction of waste.[16]

Advanced Disposal Fees

Legislation has been introduced to establish "advanced disposal fees" on various products and packages. Part or all of the solid waste costs of a targeted product would be imposed on the manufacturer or wholesaler. In theory, this would provide a strong financial incentive for businesses to reduce the disposal costs of these products by making them smaller, more durable, or more recyclable.

Landfill Surcharges

Every dollar added to the cost of landfill disposal adds a dollar to the value of recycling. Some recycling companies have suggested that a new fee should be assessed at the landfill to raise money for recycling. But its most important impact might be to improve the cost-effectiveness of recycling and source reduction. A fifty-dollar-per-ton landfill surcharge would make glass and many other types of recycling profitable for nearly all recycling operations and would raise an estimated $2.5 billion per year.[17]

Recycled Content Standards

Perhaps the most obvious market for recyclable materials is the products that we throw away. Requiring that beverage containers have a 50 percent recycled content could automatically generate a market for 50 percent of the containers we use. The state has recently established recycled content standards for newspapers, glass bottles, and fiberglass. New content standards are expected to be proposed for a variety of other materials, including plastics, metals, and office papers.

Procurement Policies

Like other products, recycled products may need to achieve a high level of sales before economies of scale provide cost savings that make them affordable. To encourage the development of such a market, many recycling advocates support the establishment of tough procurement policies for government. California already has a procurement policy for paper: whenever the cost of recycled paper is within 5 percent of the cost of primary paper, the state is to purchase the recycled paper. Additional procurement policies have been proposed for other materials, ranging from construction materials to motor oil.

CONCLUSION

California has made great strides in its efforts to implement comprehensive, effective recycling programs. But much work remains to be done. The future of recycling and source reduction depends on our ability to move beyond the mere imposition of new and costly programs; the key to our success is to institute the market development and recycling incentives that will automatically bring about reductions in wastefulness and increases in recycling. The end of the throwaway ethic is within our reach, but it will depend on our ability and willingness to charge waste generators the full cost of throwing away the earth.

CHAPTER 13

Toxic Wastes:
Proliferating Poisons

JODY SPARKS

In the mid-1980s, residents of Westminster Tract, a neighborhood in Orange County, complained of a tarlike sludge seeping to the surface in their backyards, into their pools, and breaching the foundations of their homes. People complained of respiratory problems and eye irritation from fumes coming from the sludge. Investigation by state health officials revealed that oil field and refinery wastes had been deposited earlier on the land presently occupied by the homes. The dumped waste was seeping to the surface. Groundwater has been contaminated. The site is currently proposed for listing on the National Priorities List of the most contaminated sites in the country, which would make it eligible for federal cleanup funds. In the meantime, residents must notify state officials of seepage in order to have it removed.[1]

The residents of Westminster Tract are not alone in their encounter with historically mishandled hazardous substances. Stories like this one are far too common. Homeowners, workers, and their families have suffered the consequences of the "out of sight, out of

Jody Sparks is president of the Toxics Assessment Group, a Davis-based research and consulting firm specializing in policy analysis, public records access, and regulatory aspects of hazardous waste management.

mind'' approach to hazardous waste management prevalent in the past. It has not been easy to gain control over pollution from the vast quantities of toxic chemicals produced every day.

HAZARDOUS WASTE GENERATION

In 1989, approximately 1.6 million tons (or 3.2 *billion* pounds) of hazardous waste were generated in California.[2] This amount is well over 100 pounds of hazardous waste for each resident of the state. In the same year, manufacturers reported that 21.7 million pounds of toxic chemicals were transported to hazardous waste management (treatment and/or disposal) facilities. In addition, 10.6 million pounds were released to surface waters, 81.3 million pounds to air, 47.3 million pounds were discharged directly into sewers, and 6.1 million pounds were applied to land at the site where the waste was generated.[3] (The U.S. Environmental Protection Agency [EPA] defines a hazardous substance as one that poses a threat to human health and/or the environment and a toxic substance as one that may present an unreasonable risk of injury to health or the environment. The terms are often used interchangeably.)

Every household is stocked with products that contain or were manufactured with toxic chemicals. Some examples are obvious—cleaners and detergents, plastics, electronics, and appliances. But many people would be surprised to learn the quantities of toxic chemicals used by other industries. The use of these chemicals results in tremendous amounts of hazardous waste—chemical residues that are potentially dangerous to humans or the environment. These wastes are generally defined by their toxicity, or the extent to which they are poisonous. A study of New Jersey manufacturers revealed that sausage and prepared meat manufacturers used almost 2.4 million pounds of toxic chemicals in one year; for canned fruits and vegetables, almost 2.6 million pounds; for bottled and canned soft drinks, 44.6 million pounds; and for women's outer wear, 11.7 million pounds.[4] These figures reveal the magnitude of our reliance on toxic substances and translate into vast quantities of hazardous wastes that threaten our air, water, land, and our health and safety every day.

Toxic chemicals are persistent poisons. The use of polychlorinated biphenyls (PCBs)—lethal chemicals used in electrical equipment—was banned in 1979. Of the 1.4 billion pounds of PCBs manufactured before the ban, only 4 percent has been disposed of safely. More than 50 percent is still found in electrical equipment and other products. But more than 32 percent is lost to landfills (which are leaking), to the air, and to bodies of water. PCBs have even been discovered in ice at the North and South poles.[5]

HAZARDOUS WASTE REGULATION

Hazardous waste in California is handled by about 200 hazardous waste management facilities.[6] All of them are regulated by the California Environmental Protection Agency's Department of Toxic Substances Control (DTSC). Some of these facilities are also regulated by the federal government under the Resource Conservation and Recovery Act (RCRA), enforced by the U.S. EPA. Only California regulates "small quantity" generators (generators of less than 100 kilograms per month of hazardous waste) as well as companies that treat wastes prior to discharge to surface waters or sewers, recycling facilities (including incinerators that use the heat generated from waste incineration as an energy source), and facilities that manage wastes considered by the state but not by the federal government to be hazardous, such as petroleum wastes, asbestos, PCBs below federal limits, and auto shredder wastes. These are known as "California-only" hazardous wastes.

Although the DTSC is the state authority for regulating the generation, transport, and off-site management of hazardous wastes, the program relies on cooperation among state agencies and local and regional governments. The State Water Resources Control Board and the Air Resources Board have the authority to enforce requirements designed to protect water quality and control air emissions respectively. Primary decisions regarding the siting of hazardous waste facilities are made by local government. Conditional use permits are issued by local agencies and are intended to ensure that any development will comply with local and regional zoning and policies. The California Environmental Quality Act requires all local, regional, and state agencies to consider environmental impacts in making decisions regarding proposed developments. Any waste facility must undergo an environmental evaluation.

These agencies and programs have formed the framework for California's regulation of hazardous waste management for years; yet pollution caused by toxic materials is widespread, and the true magnitude of the problem has not yet been defined. Why have these programs been unsuccessful?

HAZARDOUS WASTE DISPOSAL

Traditionally, regulation of toxics focused on controlling the spread of pollution from waste disposal facilities. Land disposal in landfills, surface impoundments, or wells was the predominant method for managing hazardous waste. This approach proved inadequate; one by one, even the so-called "state-of-the-art" landfills were found to be leaking pollutants. In 1985, one report found that all eight hazardous waste disposal sites in California were out of compliance with federal and state requirements and were leaking wastes into or toward groundwater or surface water.[7] Since that time, five of the original eight sites have closed, due in part to the extensive costs of cleaning up the existing contamination.

The EPA estimates that 30,000 to 50,000 hazardous waste sites exist in the United States. In 1989, 1,200 sites had been included or were proposed for inclusion on the National Priorities List eligible for cleanup under the Superfund program. This means that half of the U.S. population now resides in a county where a Superfund site is located, and the list is expected to grow to 10,000 sites in fifty years. California has forty-eight Superfund sites, the fifth-largest number of any state. A government report estimated that the average cost for cleaning up one Superfund site is $21 million to $30 million.[8]

California has its own hazardous waste site cleanup program. The California Expenditure Plan for Hazardous Waste Cleanup listed approximately 273 sites in 1989. Cleanup of known sites is estimated to take ten to fifteen years. State officials have reported that up to 5,600 additional sites may require some sort of evaluation or cleanup.[9] Cleanups involve exhaustive studies to determine the extent of the problem and can involve removal of large amounts of soil or equipment, long-term treatment, fixing contaminants in place, "sealing" the site to prevent further exposure, or other measures. Contaminated sites can rarely be restored to a pristine condition, and cleanup often generates litigation because of the huge amounts of time and money involved.

As of 1987, 60 percent of the hazardous waste generated in California was still destined for land disposal where pollution led to "land ban" legislation. The Hazardous and Solid Waste Amendments of 1984 required the EPA to determine which wastes should be restricted from land disposal and to require a minimum level of treatment prior to land disposal. The California Hazardous Waste Reduction and Management Act prohibits all untreated waste from land disposal as of 1992 and requires California to determine treatment standards for California-only hazardous wastes.

The DTSC has established a Research, Development, and Demonstration program to help generators meet treatment standards and land disposal restrictions. The program has prepared guidance documents for use by industry, as well as conducted demonstration projects in the areas of mercury recovery from fluorescent tubes, thermal drying to separate organics (including PCBs) from inert materials, incineration of spent rocket propellant, and solidification of heavy metals.[10] These processes must be thoroughly evaluated, however, to ensure that one source of pollution is not substituted for another.

Waste Minimization

No matter how effective treatment methods and land bans are, they do not address the immense quantity of toxic materials manufactured and used daily, and the generation of hazardous waste is only one of many impacts. Exposure in the workplace, accidents, and spills during transport continue to occur despite the best efforts to prevent pollution. Nowhere have risks from transporting these materials been more evident than in California.

On July 14, 1991, a Southern Pacific train derailed on a bridge near Dunsmuir, spilling a toxic weed killer into the Sacramento River. Forty-five miles of river to Shasta Reservoir were polluted, killing fish and vegetation. At least two miscarriages and a hundred cases of persisting symptoms, such as coughing, rashes, and headaches, were reported after the spill. Residents still fear the possibility of birth defects and prolonged health effects. Later the same month, another Southern Pacific train derailed near Seacliff, California, dumping a potentially lethal chemical and closing U.S. 101 for five days. Hundreds of people were evacuated from their homes as a toxic cloud spread through the neighborhood.

Although the Federal Railroad Administration has a hazardous materials safety program, records show that risks from rail accidents increased 40 percent from 1985 to 1988. The Association of American Railroads found that 94 percent of the rail-related releases were due to defects in tank cars and equipment, and not due to accidents.[11] The Federal Railroad Administration has come under fire for its failure to ensure safe transport of these materials, but improvements have not come quickly.

The widespread use of toxics has its greatest impacts on our state's minority residents. Throughout California, the highest concentrations of toxic chemical use or disposal are found in poor and minority neighborhoods. Although siting toxic waste dumps or incinerators in minority neighborhoods is an old practice, only recently has the problem been recognized as a form of discrimination known as "toxic racism."

For example, a one-square-mile section of Los Angeles County is home to 18 companies that in 1989 released 33 million pounds of waste chemicals into the surrounding environment. The population of the area is 59 percent black and 38 percent Hispanic. The Barrio Logan area of San Diego County generates 63 million pounds of hazardous waste from 127 companies. This is one-third of all chemical waste generated in the county, from one community that is 99 percent Hispanic. And in Richmond, the most heavily industrialized community in the San Francisco Bay Area, 100 manufacturers released 1.7 million pounds of chemicals in 1989. In the neighborhoods closest to industrial areas, the population is 72 percent to 94 percent black.[12]

These communities are organizing and fighting to end the overwhelmingly disproportionate share of the burden of toxic chemical use and pollution they have carried thus far. In the Los Angeles area, the Concerned Citizens of South Central and the Mothers of East L.A. successfully blocked the siting of a toxic waste incinerator in their neighborhoods. The West County Toxics Coalition in Richmond is attempting to make "good neighbor agreements" with local companies to set deadlines for improving operations and reducing air emissions and other pollution sources. These groups are forming throughout the state and are confronting the toxic chemical industry's long-held belief that poor and minority communities are least able, or least likely, to take an interest in toxic substance problems.

Shifting the Focus

During the 1980s, legislative and regulatory efforts began to shift toward a more comprehensive program to reduce generation and control the treatment or disposal of hazardous wastes. Waste reduction efforts include three methods: avoiding the generation of a waste (source reduction), recycling or reusing a waste, and treatment to reduce hazardous characteristics. The California Hazardous Waste Management Act of 1986 requires the development of programs to promote source reduction, recycling, and treatment, and to limit the amount of waste destined for land disposal. The state legislature set the following priority for waste management activities: (1) reduction of the amount of waste generated, (2) recycling wastes, (3) treatment of wastes, and (4) land disposal of residuals.

The California Hazardous Waste Reduction and Management Review Act of 1989 was designed to reduce the generation of hazardous waste by promoting the exchange of information about reduction and recycling between the government, industry, and the public. The law requires industries that produce more than 12,000 kilograms of hazardous waste annually to submit hazardous waste reduction reports, available for public review. The goal is to achieve a 150,000-ton decrease in hazardous waste generation by 1994 through source reduction and recycling.

In order to promote waste reduction efforts, the DTSC's Waste Reduction Program provides technical information and grant assistance for reduction, treatment, and recycling. In addition, the state has formed the California Waste Exchange to disseminate information regarding recycling, to provide technical and regulatory assistance to recyclers, and to draft legislation and regulations regarding recycling. An annual directory of hazardous waste recyclers listed 129 facilities in 1989.

In conjunction with the U.S. EPA, the state DTSC has been working with industry to develop innovative technologies for reducing hazardous waste generation. The state has worked with Hewlett-Packard to recover and recycle nickel and copper plating solutions and with the Orange County Transit District to reuse bus oil filters. Other studies are aimed at reducing or eliminating the use of solvents in fourteen industries.[13]

THE RIGHT TO KNOW

The 1980s brought about a greater public awareness of the environmental dangers posed by toxics. As a result, right-to-know and citizen enforcement laws have been enacted, recognizing that the public must have the opportunity to participate in decisions affecting health and environment. Many new laws include provisions to enable state and federal agencies to compile and disseminate data regarding the quantities and types of toxic chemicals and hazardous wastes produced. The Superfund Amendments and Reauthorization Act of 1986 calls for state and local committees to compile information regarding hazardous materials handling and releases from industry (including information previously considered trade secrets) and to prepare response plans to deal with emergencies. The act empowers citizens to sue facility owners who fail to release information regarding hazardous substances.

California's Air Toxics "Hot Spots" Information and Assessment Act of 1987 requires reporting and risk assessment of specified toxics routinely released into the air in an attempt to determine who is at risk. Communities must be notified of significant risks from air pollution. Proposition 65, the Safe Drinking Water and Toxic Enforcement Act of 1986, was mandated by California voters and requires the governor to compile a list of chemicals known to cause cancer or reproductive toxicity. The discharge of these chemicals into any source of drinking water is prohibited, and no one is to be exposed to listed chemicals without first being warned. Citizens may file suit against any facility in violation of the act if the public prosecutor fails to do so.

EXPORTATION

One of the most glaring loopholes still present in California's regulatory structure is the ability of generators to export wastes out of the state, thus circumventing the source reduction and land ban regulations in California. It is difficult to determine how much waste is leaving California, but it is estimated that hazardous wastes leaving the state increased from 39,036 tons to 253,718 tons between 1986 and 1989.[14]

Many of the exports are California-only hazardous wastes, which might not be regulated in the receiving state and therefore may be disposed of in a municipal landfill in another state. Utah, Nevada, and Arizona receive most of this waste.[15]

Between 1987 and 1989, 3 million tons of hazardous waste were shipped from the United States to foreign countries. Mexico is the largest importer of California wastes, although it nominally accepts hazardous waste destined for recycling or use as a product, and not for disposal. California's hazardous wastes are also exported to Canada (overall, the largest importer of wastes from the United States), Germany, Belgium, the Philippines, Australia, Japan, and England.[16]

The United States and Mexico have had an "Agreement to Cooperate to Address Environmental Problems Along the Border" since 1983, which requires that U.S. companies operating in Mexico and importing raw materials from the United States export resulting waste back to the United States for recycling, treatment, and/or disposal.

Over several years, the EPA has received fewer than ten notifications that hazardous waste from U.S. industries in Mexico was being shipped back to California. The state has suggested that this low number of notifications may owe to illegal transport and disposal of wastes, that the wastes may be handled at Mexican facilities and recycled, or that industries may be paying duties on their raw materials, which would "nationalize" them and allow disposal in Mexico.[17]

The DTSC has found evidence of illegal practices in exporting wastes from California, including waste laundering (mixing hazardous waste with nonhazardous materials for illegal disposal), midnight runs (particularly a problem along the U.S. border with Mexico), and sham recycling (disposal of wastes under the guise of recycling).[18] The federal government recently obtained its first conviction for illegal export when a California resident pleaded guilty to charges that he illegally transported hazardous waste to Mexico.[19]

EXEMPTIONS TO REGULATIONS

An exemption from many of the strict regulatory requirements imposed on traditional hazardous waste management facilities is enjoyed by recyclers. This exemption has led to the practice known as sham recycling, which poses environmental threats of its own. At the heart of regulations and legislation regarding recycling is the assumption that hazardous wastes may actually be *useful* and can be reclaimed and reused or otherwise recycled into a valuable product. Recently, however, a trend has developed known as "use constitutes disposal," in which useless hazardous wastes are simply added to a product, such as an asphalt or cement mix for road construction, without actually contributing to the production process or the product itself. Road construction using such a mixture is not really a "use" but disguised land disposal. The products manufactured with hazardous waste in them offer an inexpensive method for disposing of waste. In addition to the potential environmental impacts of this process, it creates a disincentive to source reduction and recycling efforts.

MILITARY EXEMPTIONS

The military may be the largest generator of hazardous waste in the United States. Toxic contamination has been found at many military bases here and abroad, including Hunters Point Naval Shipyard in San Francisco, McClellan Air Force Base in Sacramento, and the Barstow Marine Corps Logistics Base. In addition, private contractors producing goods for military use create huge volumes of toxic waste. Although the Pentagon announced plans to cut waste generation by the military in half by 1992, military facilities remain one of the largest generators of hazardous wastes as well as one of the deadliest polluters from their misuse.[20]

The military has long been considered outside the jurisdiction of environmental regulations in effect for the private sector. In 1978, President Carter ordered that all federal facilities comply with environmental regulations, but the Reagan era was a decade of "self-regulation" during which the EPA's power was severely curtailed.

The Pentagon was assigned sole responsibility for cleaning up military bases, and the EPA was prohibited from suing, issuing cleanup orders, and fining other federal agencies.[21]

The military has also been exempt from public participation requirements, such as community right-to-know laws, because of claims that our national security is at stake. Our security may be more threatened by the enormous potential for personal injury and environmental degradation posed by contamination at military sites. Public involvement is vital to compelling the military to accept responsibility for conditions at bases and other installations. Community right-to-know legislation should be expanded to require military installations and military contractors to report use and release data on toxic materials.[22]

WHITHER NOW?

The DTSC has estimated that between 1987 and 1995, the generation of federally regulated hazardous waste will be reduced by 84,000 tons. This prediction, however, is due largely to the assumption that the quantity of wastes generated during cleanup of abandoned or inactive sites will diminish from 272,200 tons in 1987 to 9,300 tons in 1995.[23] This is not consistent with estimates by the U.S. EPA and others; in fact, the EPA estimates that the number of hazardous waste sites requiring cleanup will increase. The state has also noted that by 1995 generation of wastes at active industrial facilities will increase.[24]

Although the state's policy is that waste reduction and recycling will be the primary methods for managing future wastes, with only secondary reliance on new disposal sites, implementation of this policy will be difficult. The exemptions and loopholes provided in current law and regulations must be eliminated. Military facilities, as well as other publicly owned generators or hazardous waste management facilities, must be brought under the full purview of existing regulations. Taxes and fees can be structured in such a way as to remove the economic benefit that generators may now achieve by exporting their wastes elsewhere. The true environmental costs of various methods of treatment or disposal must also be incorporated into fee and tax structures. In this way, economic incentives to reduce or recycle can provide a powerful catalyst to industry.

Companies may also find internal savings resulting from reduction and recycling efforts. Good housekeeping practices, such as segregating various waste streams in house for reuse, can save companies the cost of buying raw materials, in addition to the cost of disposing of the waste. Substituting less toxic materials may also reduce waste streams and result in substantial cost savings. Although equipment and process changes to achieve waste reduction may be costly, these are one-time costs and are usually recovered in the reduction of costs incurred for worker safety, accidents, spills, and waste management.

As part of the state's efforts to promote source reduction, the first annual Hazardous Waste Reduction Award for Innovative Technology was given to General Dynamics' Pomona Division, together with the U.S. Navy, for achieving a 96 percent reduction in the amount of hazardous waste shipped off-site for disposal. This reduction was achieved through a number of process substitutions as well as resource recovery and recycling of remaining wastes.[25] Other companies have had positive experiences with waste reduction efforts. At a Hewlett-Packard plant in Santa Rosa, the company found it could save approximately $90,000 per year by recycling solvents used at the facility. The cost of installing and operating the necessary equipment was paid back in eleven months. Small businesses also have been able to achieve cost savings through waste minimization efforts. An automotive repair shop was able to reduce the amount of caustic waste requiring disposal from 200 gallons per month to 22 gallons per month by changing the process used to clean parts coming into the facility for repair. The company was able to save $1,895 per month in disposal and energy costs and to recover the cost of the new equipment in five months.[26]

Source reduction and alternative technology may have become buzz words for government and industry, but only careful scrutiny by the public will lead to widespread implementation of laws and policies to achieve reduction goals. Waste reduction policies are still not afforded the same degree of time and resources invested in pollution control and remediation. Just as individuals living near toxic waste dumps raised concerns in the past and provided the impetus for legislation controlling the disposal of hazardous wastes, the public must take the lead in influencing policy toward limiting the use of toxic substances and generation of hazardous waste.

Hazardous waste is a collective responsibility. We all enjoy the fruits of a consumer society, but we must face up to its costs, including those of dealing with hazardous materials.

CHAPTER 14

Pesticides: In Our Food, Air, Water, Home, and Workplace

RALPH LIGHTSTONE

CALIFORNIA, A LEADER IN PESTICIDE USE

California leads the nation and the world in the extensive use of pesticides—poisonous chemicals used to control unwanted organisms. California is also a leader in problems associated with pesticide use, including the poisoning of farmworkers and others, and contamination of air, food, drinking water, rivers, and wildlife.

This state is home to the nation's most diverse and profitable agricultural system, the farmworker labor movement, and many environmental groups. California is the nation's leader in the organic food production industry and has the most complex system of

Ralph Lightstone is an attorney with California Rural Legal Assistance (CRLA) and the CRLA Foundation. He coordinates the organization's pesticide task force, which works to prevent the poisoning of farmworkers and their families. He has worked on state and federal legislative reforms and represented workers in personal injury and regulatory reform cases. He is co-author of "How to Handle a Pesticide Case," in *A Guide to Toxic Torts*, and "Pesticides" in the *Products Liability Practice Guide*.

pesticide regulations. Yet the state has failed to prevent thousands of worker poisonings and widespread environmental contamination. California's failure or success in controlling pesticides and pests will undoubtedly point the way for the nation and the world.

California uses 500 million pounds of pesticide (active ingredients) annually. This represents 20 percent of all pesticides used in the United States and 10 percent of world use (see Figure 14.1).[1] About 650 of these active pesticide ingredients are registered in California. They are formulated into thousands of products sold to growers, structural pest control companies, lawn-care companies, and the general public.

This chapter will review the fundamentals of pesticide use, unwanted toxic effects of pesticides, gaps in data, and problems in the workplace, in food, in water, in air, and in the home. Finally, it looks to the future and a better way to handle pest control problems.

THE PESTICIDE STRATEGY

Under California law, pesticides are called "economic poisons," a term coined in the 1930s to convey that pesticides are poisonous

FIGURE 14.1
1980 WORLD PESTICIDE USE, POUNDS (BILLIONS) ACTIVE INGREDIENT

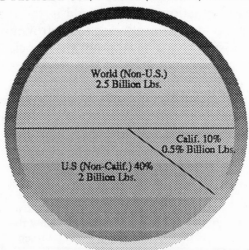

World (Non-U.S.)
2.5 Billion Lbs.

Calif. 10%
0.5% Billion Lbs.

U.S (Non-Calif.) 40%
2 Billion Lbs.

SOURCE: California Department of Food and Agriculture, *Pesticide Usage in California and the United States—Report HS-1071* (Sacramento: K. T. Maddy, 1983).

but useful. The term *pesticide* usually conjures up the image of a substance used to fight off a voracious insect, such as a locust, that is devouring a crop. But pesticides are also designed to kill weeds, rodents, predators, fungi, nematodes, snails, spiders, mites, fish, and birds.

The basic idea of pesticide use is simple: the chemical must be toxic, and it must be delivered to the target pest. This simple strategy results in complex problems that have never been solved.

Chemicals toxic to pests are usually toxic to nontarget organisms, including humans; the pest and human often share the same biological vulnerability. This effect can be seen in the history of organophosphates, which were produced as World War II nerve gas agents in Germany. Adapted to agricultural use production after World War II, they remain in military and pest control arsenals today. Humans and insects share similar nerve enzyme systems, which are attacked by the poisons. In addition to their intended acutely toxic effects on target pests, many pesticides have now been linked to unforeseen effects on nontarget organisms, such as birth defects, sterility, cancer, neurotoxicity, and chronic diseases in humans.

The poisonous chemical must be delivered to the target pest without contaminating the surrounding environment—air, water, other crops, wildlife, domestic animals, and people. Hitting the target is quite difficult. Not contaminating the surrounding environment is virtually impossible.

Pesticides are sprayed from planes and helicopters, blown out of high-pressure power-blast units and foggers, misted and dusted from tractor-pulled equipment, hosed onto crops, injected into soil, dripped into irrigation water, and applied by hand from backpack spray tanks. Aerial spraying is notoriously inefficient; only a small fraction of the pesticide ever contacts a pest.[2] Even accurately delivered pesticides don't stay put—they leach into water and volatilize into the air.

Another pesticide delivery strategy is to bring the pest to the poison through the use of systemic pesticides. These are put into the soil and absorbed by the plant, which becomes poisonous to any sucking insect ingesting plant nutrients. The goal is to render the plant itself fatal to insects that eat it but harmless to human consumers. Systemic animal pesticides are used as well. In the 1980s, larvadex, a "feed through" pesticide, was developed for chicken feed. The chicken manure becomes poisonous to flies. Residues in the chicken and egg have been deemed by the manufacturer and government as "safe" for humans.

The efficient delivery of a pesticide to a target pest does not assure success because pests are notoriously unaccommodating to being controlled by poisons. Due to frequent reproduction and short life spans, insects, mites, weeds, and other pests have an ability to adapt rapidly to pesticides. The resulting resistance and secondary pest outbreaks lead to a striking anomaly. Although food crop insecticide use increased by 1,000 percent from the 1940s through the 1970s, insect damage doubled during that period in the United States.[3]

During the past forty years, the pesticide strategy has dramatically increased pesticide use and related pest control costs and caused enormous collateral damage, including worker poisonings, environmental contamination, and increased pesticide resistance.

ACUTE TOXIC EFFECTS OF PESTICIDES

Pesticides are generally designed to kill the target pest. The more acutely toxic the pesticide, the less of it is required. The most toxic pesticides, then, are effective on pests and dangerous to humans in minute amounts.

Acute toxicity is expressed scientifically as the LD50, or lethal dose that kills 50 percent of the exposed laboratory animals. The LD50 is measured in milligrams of pesticide per kilogram of body weight of the exposed organism. In human terms, it takes fewer milligrams of a pesticide to poison a small person than a large one.

Aldicarb is so toxic that the infamous watermelon poisonings in 1985 were caused by levels below that of detection of the chemistry then used to routinely screen food for pesticide residues: the laboratory equipment didn't detect the pesticide, but an inspector biting the melon would have been acutely poisoned. More than 300,000 pounds were used in California in 1988, principally on cotton.

A quarter of a million pounds of the highly toxic insecticide mevinphos are used annually in California on crops such as lettuce and broccoli. Mevinphos degrades within a few days after it is applied to the crops, but during those days it is extremely toxic. More than a hundred mevinphos-related worker poisonings were reported between 1982 and 1988 in California.

Mevinphos and aldicarb are among the class of most acutely toxic pesticides that are deemed Category 1 by the U.S. Environmental Protection Agency (EPA). California allows the use of twenty-seven pesticides listed as Category 1 that are lethal at doses of one tablespoon or less on the skin or one teaspoon or less orally. In 1988, 45 million pounds of these pesticides were used in California. Metam sodium, which sterilized forty-five miles of the Sacramento River in 1991, is a Category 2 ("moderate") toxicity pesticide. The state has no plans to require replacement of the most toxic pesticides with less toxic alternatives.

CHRONIC TOXIC EFFECTS OF PESTICIDES

Chronic toxic effects, including cancer, sterility, neurological damage, and pulmonary disease, may manifest themselves years after long-term, low-level exposure to pesticides. Other effects, such as birth defects, may be caused by a single exposure.

One tragic chronic effect was uncovered in California in 1977. A group of men employed as pesticide formulation plant workers in Lathrop discovered that they were unable to conceive children. They initiated their own investigation and discovered that they were producing few or no sperm. DBCP, a pesticide used to kill nematodes, was the cause. Similar DBCP-induced effects were then discovered in other plant workers worldwide and in banana plantation workers in Central America.

DBCP had been tested on laboratory animals at the University of California in 1958. Sponsored by DBCP manufacturers, the tests showed severe testicular damage at the lowest dose. DBCP was widely marketed anyway until the sterility discovered by Lathrop workers nineteen years later. Further testing showed that DBCP caused additional chronic health effects, such as cancer.

California temporarily suspended DBCP use in 1977, but the federal government initially declined to ban DBCP, except on crops where food contamination was expected. This action reflects a common theme: consumer concerns are placed ahead of concern for workers. DBCP would likely be in use today if it had not been subsequently found leaching into groundwater. This find compelled both California and the federal government to eventually ban all uses of DBCP. The ban on its use in growing Hawaiian pineapple was delayed several years due to the assumption that unique hydrological conditions would prevent contamination of Hawaiian groundwater; the assumption was wrong.

Molinate, an herbicide widely used on rice, has also been shown to cause sperm damage in animal tests. In 1991, California's Department of Food and Agriculture officials approved continued molinate use, despite concerns of the Department of Health Services. The Department of Food and Agriculture asserted that full-body protective gear and respirators for the workers using molinate would provide for safety.[4] Molinate has also been found leaching into river water and offgasing into the ambient air of nearby towns.

At least nineteen pesticides in use are classified as probable human carcinogens.[5] Federal and state agencies have allowed the continued use of these carcinogens based on the theory that the risks of cancer to the general population are acceptable. The estimated risk varies enormously depending on the risk assessment theory that is applied. The countervailing view is that carcinogens should be banned because scientists cannot predict the number of people who will get cancer. In 1954, Congress adopted the no-carcinogen view when it enacted the Delaney Clause, which outlaws any food additive that causes cancer in humans or animals. Cancer-causing pesticides, however, are allowed in food because they are treated separately, under the law, from other food additives.[6] A campaign has been waged for decades by the chemical industry to repeal the Delaney Clause and substitute the risk assessment approach.

Epidemiology, the study of disease in humans, is unable to settle many disputes regarding pesticide hazards. Clusters of childhood cancer have been identified in the Central Valley agricultural communities of McFarland and Earlimart. The McFarland researchers suspected but could not prove that pesticide exposure was a cause of the cancer.[7] They documented high rates of anemia, other health problems, and lack of access to medical care among McFarland's children.[8] A series of studies indicated a link between elevated cancer deaths among farmers and pesticide use in the Midwest.[9]

As with potential risks for cancer and sterility, most pesticides were approved without premarket testing for potential to cause birth defects. Several pesticides, including nitrofen and dinoseb, were removed from the market after years of sale when they caused birth defects in animal testing.[10] Others remain on the market despite positive tests because the government believes that an adequate margin of safety exists. The theory assumes that a pregnant woman will not be acutely poisoned. Unfortunately, this is not the case. Farmworker crews, including pregnant women, are acutely poisoned. In one such episode, a child was born with severe congenital defects and died.[11]

The herbicide paraquat has been linked to pulmonary disease from dermal exposure. After a federal employee who applied paraquat died of pulmonary disease, his family successfully sued the manufacturer for failing to warn of this chronic effect on the label.[12] The family won the case in 1984, but the paraquat labels still omit the warning. Pesticide labels rarely contain warnings of chronic hazards known to the manufacturer. This is common even in cases where the manufacturer has disclosed such effects to its employees on a material safety data sheet. Pesticide companies are presently challenging the right of victims to sue for inadequate label warnings.

Because the science of toxicology remains in its infancy, new chronic risks may be uncovered as the science improves. Industry and government assurances that certain pesticides are safe have repeatedly proven to be incorrect as more was learned. This pattern is likely to continue as further research is conducted. In the meantime, widespread exposure of workers and the public continues as pesticides are assumed to be safe until proven otherwise.

DATA GAPS: MISSING AND INADEQUATE STUDIES

Consumers who purchase pesticides will see a U.S. EPA registration number on the label. No pesticide may be sold in the United States without EPA approval, and no pesticide may be sold in California without a separate approval by the state.

Neither the U.S. EPA nor California conducts basic pesticide safety studies. Instead, they decide what types of tests should be conducted and require the pesticide companies to undertake or contract for the tests. Unfortunately, this plan of scientific study and government review has proven to be a colossal failure. Although every pesticide product carries the stamp of government approval, very few have been fully tested. Nearly all pesticides have data gaps—key safety tests are missing or inadequate.

Tests for cancer, birth defects, sterility, and other diseases were not required until the mid-1960s or later, after most pesticides now in use had already been approved. As new test requirements were added, they were not applied retroactively. In 1977, the EPA discovered that hundreds of previously submitted tests had been altered, faked, or botched.[13] Officials at the nation's largest pesticide-testing laboratory were convicted of fraud in relation to pesticide and drug safety tests. Many companies have continued to resist meeting new test requirements.

Congress ordered the pesticide data gaps to be filled by the pesticide companies beginning in 1972, but it hasn't happened. In 1984, California enacted a landmark statute, the Birth Defect Prevention Act, requiring full testing of 200 pesticides for chronic health hazards, including birth defects, sterility, cancer, and other diseases. Tests were to begin by March 1987 and be completed by March 1991. Of the 200 priority pesticides, 104 did not meet the 1991 deadline. Many of the studies had not begun on the date they were due. Five of the ten required studies of metam sodium had not been done when that pesticide catastrophically spilled into the Sacramento River in 1991.

In 1988, Congress followed California's lead by adopting a nine-year plan to fill the data gaps for all pesticides. By July 1991, the U.S. EPA reported that only 6 of 612 pesticides had completed the data-gap filling process.[14]

As long as these data gaps remain, scientists cannot determine the hazards. The pesticide industry often labels its critics as antiscience, but in fact the industry has failed to produce the required scientific data on its products.

PESTICIDES IN THE WORKPLACE

Workers who mix, load, and apply pesticides, and those who work in fields, are at highest risk for pesticide poisoning. These workers also share the public's normal pesticide exposure in food, air, and water. Neither worker protection standards nor food and water standards acknowledge these multiple routes of exposure. In the world of pesticide regulation, workers don't eat and eaters don't work.

The pesticide industry and regulators advance two strategies to protect workers. Applicators and handlers are to cover themselves with equipment such as rubber suits and respirators to keep the pesticide off themselves. The strategy for people entering treated fields is to quarantine the sprayed area until the residues have degraded to a safe level. These strategies have a long history of failure.

The quarantine strategy has repeatedly failed because the established quarantines are too short to allow degradation. In the spring of 1986, chemical burns began to appear on 114 orange harvest workers in Tulare County. Redness, pain, and burning progressed to weeping and oozing, followed by crusting, scaling, and skin loss.[15] A miticide, propargite, had been applied to the trees. Ten years earlier, California officials had determined that the propargite worker safety quarantine of one day was too short and proposed a regulation to increase the quarantine from one day to fourteen days. Growers and the manufacturer protested, and the state dropped its proposal. Propargite became a leading cause of worker poisonings.

In 1986, state investigators determined that the one day propargite quarantine needed to be changed to forty-two days for the special propargite formulation that poisoned the crew of 114. The manufacturer had advertised the new version, formulated with a secret ingredient, for its ability to persist longer and kill mites for four to twelve weeks, but had failed to change the one-day worker protection quarantine.[16] Moreover, the quarantine for other propargite formulations on citrus was increased from one day to fourteen days in 1986 and then to forty-two days in 1989.

The quarantine period for one of the most acutely toxic insecticides, ethyl parathion, was initially established at forty-eight hours. Before it was banned for use on most crops, the quarantine reached up to ninety days on citrus, following the same pattern of trial and error. The parathion quarantine was repeatedly ratcheted upward over the years while hundreds of workers were poisoned. In 1991, the U.S. EPA announced a plan to ban most uses of parathion.

These cases illustrate a systematic chain of failure by those who should have prevented worker poisonings. The manufacturer failed to prescribe the correct quarantine. The federal government approved the product. California approved it as well. Instead of preventing poisonings, California has witnessed an ongoing experiment on workers.

Quarantines do not work unless workers know which field is under quarantine. Posting of warning signs in the fields is a basic method to warn workers. Under California law, warning signs must be posted for some crops, such as grapes and peaches, but dozens of others, including apples and oranges, are not posted unless the quarantine is eight days or longer. The U.S. EPA has proposed posting regulations, but dropped the skull and crossbones symbol from the proposed signs when growers objected that the public would be alarmed by the widespread appearance of signs with the international symbol for poison.

The people who mix, load, and apply pesticides are most at risk for death or severe acute poisoning because they handle the concentrated pesticides. The strategy to protect them relies on the use of personal protective gear that is difficult to fit, requires meticulous daily care, and often leaks or fails. California's summer heat often renders this equipment unusable. Nevertheless, state policy is directed toward improving the gear rather than seeking safer pesticide substitutes. This violates the fundamental principles of industrial hygiene, which recommend the use of personal protective equipment only as a last resort.

In 1990, a Kern County man died of acute poisoning while applying parathion to almonds from a spray rig. The U.S. EPA determined that parathion, which was originally developed in 1944 in Germany, resulted in ninety-nine fatalities between 1966 and 1980, when the agency discontinued its program to monitor cases involving fatalities and hospitalizations.[17] In California, growers used more than half a million pounds annually until the partial federal ban in 1991.

Thousands of workers, agricultural and nonagricultural, personally attest to the failure of the system to prevent pesticide poisonings. The state's data do likewise. In 1973 and 1974, doctors reported 1,474 and 1,272 poisonings. In 1987 and 1988, doctors reported 2,650 and 2,996 poisoning cases.[18] State officials cite improved reporting to account for this increase. Worker advocates believe that poisonings remain greatly underreported.

The leading crops in California for physician-reported pesticide illness between 1982 and 1988 were, in descending order: grapes, citrus, nursery/ornamental, almonds, cotton, lettuce, peaches, tomatoes, broccoli, and cauliflower. The leading agricultural counties for reported poisonings were Kern, Fresno, Tulare, Monterey, and Madera. The leading urban counties were Los Angeles and Alameda.

Enforcement of pesticide laws has also been historically weak. For example, county agricultural commissioners, who are charged with policing pesticide use, annually report finding many violations of law but levy few sanctions. In 1988–1989, they issued 5,766 warnings and notices but only 517 agricultural fines (8 percent) and 215 nonagricultural fines (3 percent).[19]

PESTICIDES IN FOOD

During the Fourth of July weekend, 1985, three adults who ate a watermelon purchased in Oakland rapidly became nauseous, vomited, then experienced diarrhea, profuse sweating, tearing, muscle twitches, and rapid heartbeats. They had eaten a watermelon that was contaminated with aldicarb, a systemic pesticide not registered for legal use on melons. They were among more than 1,000 victims, the largest North American outbreak of food-borne pesticide illness ever recorded.[20] The state legislature used public funds to reimburse other melon growers, shippers, and supermarket chains who claimed economic losses from the depressed melon market that followed.

The melon poisonings kicked off a round of concern about pesticides and food safety. Most controversies focus on chronic risks of cancer from low-level exposure rather than acute poisoning episodes.

Pesticide contamination of food is licensed through a system of tolerances. A tolerance permits contamination up to a limit and prohibits sale of food contaminated above that limit. A single commodity, the tomato, has more than 100 tolerances—multiple pesticides that may be legally present in and on the tomato within the prescribed limits.[21] (Only a few such pesticides would be used in a given tomato field.) Criticism of this tolerance system has focused on the allowance of carcinogens, failure to consider realistic dietary patterns, failure to consider the special vulnerabilities of children, lack of toxicity data, failure to consider exposure to more than one pesticide at a time, failure to consider the interaction of multiple pesticides, and failure to consider nonfood exposures.

Congress has been unable to reform the tolerance system. As the nation's leading food-producing state, California has been a focal point of the food safety debate. States have the authority to establish food tolerances but have not exercised that authority to a significant degree. A coalition of pesticide, agriculture, and food marketing interests has been seeking to have Congress preempt state control if California moves forward with tolerances.

In the meantime, nonregulatory food-safety strategies have evolved in California. The United Farm Workers Union has sponsored a boycott of table grapes, linking food safety and worker safety issues. A California company developed a private laboratory certification of residue-free food used by supermarkets as a selling point for their produce. Organic food sales have increased.

California not only leads the nation in pesticide use, but in organic farming as well, with 1,200 organic farmers (out of 85,000 farmers total) in 1991 who did not use synthetic pesticides at all. The California Certified Organic Farmers certifies that 670 farmers are growing organic food on 70,000 acres. The state estimates that farm gate revenues of the organic farming industry exceeded $170 million in 1991.

PESTICIDES IN WATER

Prior to 1979 it was widely believed in academic and government circles that pesticides could not leach into groundwater. It was assumed that a pesticide applied to the soil would degrade within the root zone of the soil before it could migrate down to a groundwater aquifer. In 1979, this assumption was proven wrong when the pesticide DBCP was first discovered leaching into groundwater in the Central Valley. The discovery marked the beginning of an entirely new view of this problem and triggered a series of state actions relating to pesticides in groundwater. In 1985, the Assembly Office of Research produced a seminal report on pesticides in groundwater, *The Leaching Fields: A Nonpoint Threat to Groundwater*. Fifty-seven pesticides had been found in the groundwater of twenty-eight counties in California; twenty-two of the pesticides were probably from agricultural use. Most water in the state had not been monitored for pesticide contamination. The state legislature then ordered every water system in California to test for toxic contamination, but the most likely pesticide contaminants, atrazine and simazine, were often not looked for in the water samples.

Once a pesticide has leached into groundwater, the contamination is permanent for all practical purposes. This leaves water users with two choices, both quite expensive. They can develop new sources of uncontaminated water or they can install filtration systems. In the case of DBCP, thousands of wells providing drinking water to millions of people have been contaminated. Huge sums have already been expended to dig deeper wells or filter existing water sources. In Fresno County alone, more than $10 million was spent by 1985 to dig wells to DBCP-free water sources. Prevention of contamination is clearly preferable to the postcontamination options.

The drinking water law regulates the delivery of contaminated water to consumers but does not prevent contamination. The Health Services Department sets limits on the amount of each pollutant allowed in drinking water at the tap, but the agencies that deliver this water are often unable to prevent contamination of the water sources. The law is effectively a pollution-licensing law, allowing pollution up to an established "safe" level. As pesticide contamination is found, levels will be established. Eventually, dozens of pesticides will be permitted in drinking water, all at government-approved "safe" levels. The science of determining these safe levels is ever-changing, but the contamination, once permitted, is irreversible. Unlike setting "safe" levels for food, a discovery of additional hazards in pesticide water pollutants cannot be reversed in groundwater.

In 1985, the state legislature enacted the Pesticide Contamination Prevention Act, requiring a pesticide to be banned if it is found leaching into groundwater from agricultural use. The ban can be avoided if the manufacturer proves that mitigation measures will prevent future contamination. Although the law shifts the burden of proof to the manufacturer, the State Food and Agriculture Department construed the law to allow continued use of leaching pesticides except in locations where the state finds that groundwater has already been contaminated. If sustained, the state's policy would reverse the goal of prevention; it would not protect any water in California from pesticide contamination until after it is contaminated. Environmental and public interest groups are challenging this approach in court. The outcome is critical, because 40 percent of California's drinking water is from groundwater sources, including large areas of Los Angeles County, which has many pesticide contamination sites.

Surface water contamination by pesticides has historically been viewed as a problem of agricultural runoff. For example, rice water discharges have contaminated the lower Sacramento River for years. The residues chronically accumulate in fish and wildlife and contaminate downstream drinking water sources. The 1991 spill of 20,000 gallons of metam sodium from a rail car sterilized a forty-five-mile section of the Sacramento River. A state that permits the use of half a billion pounds of pesticides is vulnerable to that type of catastrophe at any time when vast quantities of poisons are being transported.

PESTICIDES IN THE AIR

In 1986, California's routine pesticide-residue food monitoring program detected illegal residues of four insecticides, including the extremely toxic parathion, on vegetables that had been grown and shipped from the Central Valley. The growers had not applied the illegal pesticides at all. The solution to this mystery has profound implications for the residents of California and other agricultural regions of the United States.

The crops had been grown in the Central Valley in the winter, when orchards are sprayed with insecticides and thick layers of fog cover the valley floor. Researchers discovered that the fog absorbs pesticides from the air and concentrates their levels in fog droplets at a much higher rate than expected.

In 1989, the State Food and Agriculture Department launched a study that acquitted the growers and convicted the fog. The crops were contaminated with detectable residues of parathion, diazinon, chlorpyrifos, and methidathion, which were not applied in the vicinity of the crops.[22] The fog had absorbed the pesticides from the air, transported them many miles, and deposited them on the untreated crops. At a lower rate, the transport even occurred on nonfoggy days.

Contaminated fog contacts everyone and everything in the valley. The implications for public health are not known. In 1989, a study of hawks living near Butte County almond orchards showed insecticide-induced chronic depression of a nerve enzyme. Dermal exposure via preening of fog-contaminated feathers is a suspected route of exposure.

In April 1990, the California Air Resources Board conducted ambient air monitoring at five sites in Merced County and found alarming levels of telone, a cancer-causing pesticide used widely in agriculture. The initial estimates of cancer risk for the general population were so alarming that the state immediately suspended use of the pesticide pending further investigation. Telone is injected into the soil nearly a foot deep to kill worms and soil organisms before planting. It escapes from the soil and finds its way into the ambient air of nearby towns. And, it is not unique.

Many pesticides have been found in the air of cities throughout California. In 1987, researchers monitored Bakersfield and five other Kern County sites for six pesticides at schools or other public buildings.[23] In McFarland, all six pesticides were detected. Guthion appeared in central Bakersfield. The effects of continuous exposure to these pesticides on the entire population at very low levels are currently presumed to be insignificant, a hopeful assumption.

An immediate health impact has been found in cotton-growing areas of California. The crop is defoliated with def, folex, or paraquat to prepare the plants for machine harvesting. Def and folex don't remain in the cotton field but permeate the ambient air after application. They also metabolize to a highly odorous compound, butyl mercaptan, enabling people to be acutely aware of the air contamination. The industry has added other scents to the mix, but its efforts have not allayed public opposition. A Health Services Department study found higher levels of allergy, rhinitis, throat irritation, asthma symptoms, nausea, and diarrhea among people exposed to the cotton defoliants.[24]

Although California enacted a toxic air contamination law in 1983, the pesticide industry succeeded in placing pesticide jurisdiction under the agriculture department while all other toxic air contaminants are under the jurisdiction of the air board. With the exception of the emergency suspension of telone, the department has not designated any pesticide as a toxic air contaminant to be regulated.

The fate of pesticides has generally been viewed as a chemical process of degradation into innocuous compounds that remain in the orchards or fields where they were sprayed. Research is now pointing to a different environmental fate. Pesticide residues are leaving the orchards and fields by volatilizing into the air we breathe and seeping into the water we drink.

PESTICIDES IN THE HOME

Acute pesticide poisonings occur in the home. California's regional poison control centers receive 12,000 pesticide-related calls annually.[25] Up to 30 percent of these involve children from one to four years of age. Emergency rooms report pesticide poisonings from home exposure. As in agriculture, alternative methods of pest control exist but have not been widely adopted.

TRANSITIONS AWAY FROM PESTICIDE USE

As the nation's leader in pesticide use, farm labor, pesticide poisoning, and agricultural production, California must become a leader in finding a path toward reduced pesticide use. The dominant strategy has been to preserve the widespread use of these toxic chemicals while trying to improve regulatory controls. This strategy has clearly fallen short. It can always be argued that conditions would be even worse if those efforts had not been made, but the strategy has clearly failed in efforts to make California a safe place for people to live and work, not to mention widespread and tragic impacts on fish and wildlife that are scarcely mentioned in this chapter.

California must move to alternative methods of pest control. Part of the solution will come from new research priorities into alternative farming and urban pest control methods. Part will come from strengthening the voice of farmworkers and others on the front lines of pesticide exposure. If they are protected through collective bargaining and a vigorous regulatory system, the public and the environment will likewise be protected. Part of the solution will come from an orderly but rapid program to phase out the use of many of the most toxic pesticides in the existing arsenal.

In 1991, California transferred the pesticide program from the State Food and Agriculture Department to the new state Environmental Protection Agency. This does not assure a change of direction; a similar federal transfer in 1972 was a dismal failure. The new agency may seek to improve enforcement of pesticide laws. This is helpful but ultimately cannot protect workers, the public, or the environment from the effects of pesticides that are dangerous at every step of the way, from manufacturing, distribution, and storage to application, residue contamination, and disposal of containers. The most toxic pesticides must be eliminated, and use of the others must be reduced to a minimum while nontoxic methods can be developed.

On occasion, a pesticide is banned or dropped by the manufacturer, typically following media attention and public outcry. Alar (apples), EDB (breads), and 2,4,5t (Agent Orange) are examples. In most cases, the hazards of the pesticide were known for many years before the action was taken. Many pesticides now in use will inevitably be banned or dropped. Manufacturers and commercial users are seeking to delay such action, workers and environmentalists to accelerate it. Since the government has no plan for orderly transition and development of alternatives, the current pattern will probably continue. Unfortunately, the law—drafted under the influence of the pesticide industry—fosters delay, and there will be many human and environmental casualties of these pesticides before they disappear.

An overhaul of the federal and state pesticide laws is needed, but in the near term, legislation will probably not be enacted in Washington, D.C., or Sacramento unless grower organizations abandon their traditional alliance with the pesticide industry and support a program of orderly transition to nontoxic agriculture. The two elements of such a program are an orderly phase-out and reduction of pesticide use and well-funded research into nontoxic alternatives. In the meantime, progress will be driven inevitably but unpredictably by catastrophes both large and small.

CHAPTER 15

Parks and Recreation: Vital to a Way of Life

PETE DANGERMOND

The Quality and Character of California

In the 1840s, one of the first public parks in the nation was created in Boston to improve the social condition of the citizens and to serve the youth of the city. In 1864, Yosemite Valley was designated as a state park through an act of Congress, the first park in the world created to preserve a natural, scenic resource and make it available for the enjoyment of all the people. In California today, we find that on these two conceptual foundations stand dozens of classifications of parks and thousands of individual parks encompassing millions of acres and hosting approximately 2.5 billion visitor days of use per year.

The tremendous richness and diversity of California's natural resources span from the Big Sur coast to Santa Monica beaches,

Pete Dangermond is president of Dangermond & Associates, Inc., a Sacramento-based firm that specializes in park planning, land resource protection, and project financing. His life-long professional career has been devoted to parks and recreation and allied fields of wildlife conservation and open space preservation with a focus on the state's environmental problems. He has served as director of the California Department of Parks and Recreation and as director of the Monterey County and Riverside County parks departments.

giant redwoods to a pygmy forest, vast deserts to open spaces within urban areas. Portions of these natural landscapes are protected within public lands and managed by many different agencies.

The people of California are another measure of the state's diversity, having emigrated from every nation on earth. Many remnants of their cultures are represented and preserved within our museums, historic parks, and culturally oriented spaces found in and near our cities. Innovation and a sense of place have combined to provide both a Mission Bay and a Capitol Park; a Santa Monica Bay Trail and a Palm Springs swim complex; a sports complex in Bakersfield and a Japanese Tea Garden in San Francisco's Golden Gate Park.

If one focuses on what has been accomplished, it might be easy to become complacent. Our park and recreation systems are, however, threatened. Four major influences are combining to put immense strains on park spaces and the agencies that provide them.

The first issue is the dramatic, continuing influx of population to California that began in the early 1980s. During the last decade, 25 percent of all the population increase in the United States occurred here, and 1990 was an all-time record year, with a nearly 3 percent increase. The characteristics and location of this growth have also had significant implications on parks and open space systems.

Second, the effects of Proposition 13 and federal tax cuts have caused budget crises at every level of government, forcing cutbacks in services year after year.

Third, our communities are plagued by a deterioration in social stability; increasing crime and gang problems are just two indicators of how our social fabric appears to be rending apart.

Fourth, a climate of rising expectations has led to a desire to create better communities for the future. This is particularly felt in the drives for open space preservation but is widespread, including efforts for sports fields, trails, museums, senior centers, and even landscaped medians.

There are many other issues of great importance, but the response to these four will largely shape the rest and will determine much about the quality and character of California during the next century.

A Measure of the Quality of Life

Californians participate in a wide variety of recreation activities. In 1987, the California Department of Parks and Recreation undertook a statewide survey of outdoor recreation use patterns, including estimates of the percentage of the population that participated in various activities and the average days of use per person (see Table 15.1).

A number of interesting facts were documented by the survey:

- More than two-thirds of the total use and all of the top ten use categories are inexpensive and require no special equipment other than a car.
- Approximately one-fourth of all out-of-car use is jogging, walking, biking, and horseback riding, much of it the result of increased concerns over physical fitness. Although the majority of this use does not take place in public parks, new trails in and near urban areas are tremendously popular.
- When all the beach and swimming activities are lumped together, they are the second-most popular activity—more than 20 percent of all recreation in California. ("Swimming," of course, is probably as much a social experience as it is actual water contact.) Recreation areas with water features are the most desirable, and their protection for public use is a prime concern.
- A very rapid increase in use during the last ten to fifteen years has occurred in group activities. This is evident in youth and adult league sports such as softball and soccer but also true of group picnicking and camping.
- The total of all outdoor recreation uses by Californians is about 2.5 billion visitor days per year. With a state population growth of nearly 3 percent in 1990, the increased demand in that one year is 90 million visitor days of use, or the equivalent of thirty Yosemite National Parks in one year.
- Approximately 70 percent of all use occurs within one hour of home.

TABLE 15.1
OUTDOOR ACTIVITY PARTICIPATION (1987 SURVEY)

	Percent of Total Population Participating	Average Days Per participant/yr
Walking	76.6	52.5
Driving for pleasure	75.6	33.4
Visiting museums, zoos, etc.	72.0	10.1
Beach activities	67.9	24.5
Picnicking—developed sites	64.4	14.4
Use of open-turf areas	64.4	28.1
Swimming—lakes, rivers, ocean	59.0	18.8
Attending sports events	50.4	16.2
Attending cultural events	49.7	7.9
Bird watching, nature study	47.4	23.4
Camping—developed sites	46.1	12.5
Trail hiking/mountain climbing	37.7	10.0
Freshwater fishing	36.3	19.5
Play equipment/tot lots	34.0	24.7
Swimming—pools	31.1	31.5
Softball, baseball	25.6	21.0
Sledding, snow play, ice skating	25.0	7.6
Camping—primitive/backpacking	24.9	10.4
Bicycling	23.0	32.9
Power boating	19.8	16.6
Saltwater fishing	18.5	13.7
Tennis	17.6	21.4
Downhill skiing	17.5	8.4
Golf	16.4	30.7
Kayaking, rowboating, etc.	15.7	7.2
Water-skiing	14.6	12.0
Four-wheel driving	14.3	23.1
Target shooting	14.0	9.4
Off-road vehicles	13.0	22.4
Jogging/running	12.6	58.3
Horseback riding	12.5	16.3
Hunting	12.2	15.0
Basketball	11.5	23.1
Sailing, windsurfing	10.3	11.5
Cross-country skiing	9.5	6.3
Football	9.1	15.8
Soccer	7.4	43.8
Surfing	4.1	25.7

SOURCE: California Department of Parks and Recreation.

The survey also determined the public's relative preference for outdoor recreation activities, and seven major groupings emerged as high priorities.

Camping at developed sites ranked first in preference. People would have participated more if additional and better facilities had been provided, and they supported greater funding by state and local government. Camping in primitive areas also ranked high. It is interesting that the provision of developed camping areas does not seem to be a priority by either activist groups or most park providers.

Visiting museums, zoos, and other cultural/educational/ recreational facilities ranked second; another high-ranking activity was the attendance at outdoor cultural events. Here again, the high status is out of sync with park providers and activists, who are less involved with cultural events, perhaps because provision of these services is usually under a nonprofit agency. These local agencies, however, are receiving and reflecting strong citizen and group support, as is the state Department of Parks and Recreation.

The third-ranking activity was trail usage for walking and bicycling. People strongly support urban trails in quality environments such as waterfronts, stream corridors, and parks.

The next identified high priority was for picnic facilities. Two interesting changes have occurred in recent years: many of California's newcomers—Southeast Asians and Hispanics in particular— like to picnic in large extended family groups and frequently require different facilities than the traditional picnic unit. There has also been a dramatic increase in group and company picnics. These require companion facilities such as open turf areas, softball fields, or swimming areas.

Beach activities and swimming in lakes, rivers, and pools are a top priority of the public. The preferences between ocean, lake, river, or swimming pools most likely relates to proximity to home. Where available, however, people seem to prefer the natural beach, river, or lake settings rather than pools.

Bird watching and nature study ranked sixth, with 47 percent of the population participating. An interesting companion finding was that survey respondents felt that "increasing the protection of scenery and the natural environment" was the most important change that park agencies should accomplish and was supported by 90 percent of the population. The survey indicated that a vast majority of people support natural environment protection, even if they are not direct participants.

The final high-priority activity was the use of open turf areas, the primary feature of nearly all developed parks.

The significance of the experience to the individual can sometimes get lost when talking about 2.5 billion days of use per year by Californians. Park and recreation providers, however, have the obligation to make each recreation use as meaningful as possible.

For instance, the naturalist may get a real sense of renewal with every walk through a forest or meadow. Perhaps an early, life-directing wilderness experience shaped the entire career of some fortunate person. Another couple might be avid softball enthusiasts. They may have been part of the phenomenal growth in team sports, perhaps even met each other and their closest friends at a game. Such examples are endless. For providers, enhancing the quality of these experiences and providing a diversity to match the public's desires are important measures of success.

In addition to their importance to individuals, there are many ways that parks are vital to the community. Well-executed parks add to the assessed value of nearby property, to the local economy, to a sense of place, and to the perceived quality of life. Great value is also given to a community when its citizens work together to create a common asset.

Two basic types of parkland exist: developed areas where provision and encouragement of recreation use are paramount, and lands where resource protection comes first and use is restricted to compatible types and levels. Many gradations and blendings between these two concepts exist. Interesting observations can be made when the two basic types of parks are viewed in six categories.

1. Developed parks, including mini park/tot lots, neighborhood/community parks, community centers, sports complexes, zoos, botanic gardens, historic and cultural facilities. Most communities in California strive for a standard of five acres of developed parks for every 1,000 people. Some exceed this level, but most are below— some as low as one acre per 1,000. The average is probably close to four acres per 1,000, or 100,000 to 120,000 acres statewide. These parks probably average 100,000 visitor days of use per acre for a statewide total of more than 1 billion days of use per year.

2. Golf courses. The acreage of golf courses probably equals that of all developed parks in California, or a total of about 96,000 acres.

The use per acre is far less than developed parks and may total about 50 million days per year (estimates range from 50 million to 150 million).

3. Near-urban, resource-based parks, including regional parks, natural streams and rivers through urban areas, urban waterfronts, open space preserves, and beaches adjacent to urban areas. Usually these parks have a portion of their land developed and the remainder devoted to water or natural land resources. The total area is more than 200,000 acres, with a visitation of about 200 million days per year, more than one-half being ocean beach use.

4. State parks and wildlife areas, including state parks, historic parks, recreation areas and beaches, fish hatcheries, and state wildlife areas. The California state park system totals 1.25 million acres with a visitation of 75 million days per year.

5. National parks, including national parks, monuments, historic sites, and recreation areas. The national park system in California totals 4.5 million acres with a visitation of 30 million visitor days.[1]

6. Other federal lands, including U.S. Forest Service and Bureau of Land Management multiple use lands, wilderness areas, wildlife areas, U.S. Fish & Wildlife Service refuges, and Bureau of Reclamation and Army Corps of Engineers reservoir sites. The total in California is 38 million acres, and the use is 100 million visitor days, 85 percent in national forests.[2]

Nonfacility use includes most bicycling, walking, and driving for pleasure. More than one-third of all outdoor recreation use takes place on rights of way apart from public lands. The use is often related to the suitability of the neighborhood, city, or countryside.

Table 15.2 summarizes use and acreage of California parkland.

FACTORS INFLUENCING THE FUTURE

Rapid growth in population, fiscal crisis at all levels of government, increasing social ills, and rising expectations comprise the four major influences shaping our future park systems.

TABLE 15.2
USE AND ACREAGE OF CALIFORNIA PARKLAND

	Acres	Annual Days of Use
Developed Parks	100,000	1,000,000,000
Golf	100,000	50,000,000
Near-urban Resource Parks	200,000	200,000,000
State Parks	1,250,000	75,000,000
National Parks	4,500,000	30,000,000
Other Federal Lands	38,000,000	100,000,000
Nonfacility	Not known	1,000,000,000

SOURCE: California Department of Parks and Recreation.

Increasing Population

More and more people cause extreme stress on parks and recreation facilities.

- An increasing population results in new service demands. A 3 percent jump in population in 1990 brought nearly 1 million people to California, and if their recreation patterns matched those of the existing population, the result would be an increase of 90 million days of use per year. At least 5,000 acres of developed park and 25,000 acres of natural resource parks should have been added in one year just to keep pace.
- The net in-migration to California is primarily from other countries rather than other states, and these immigrants are settling in the urban cores. A result has been increased density of both people and children, primarily impacting existing developed urban parks.
- The new immigrants are to a measure displacing existing urban residents, who are primarily moving to inland southern California, the East Bay, and the Central Valley.
- The new inland growth areas have witnessed a rapid disappearance of important open spaces. Mass grading projects around the rim of the Los Angeles basin, the extinction of wildlife species in southern California, the loss of farmland in the Central Valley, and the sprawl of the Bay Area have all become realities in the last ten years.
- Pollsters find that the most common phrases used are "too

much," "too fast," "too many," and that growth control is both an important local and statewide issue.

Fiscal Crisis

For nearly ten years, federal, state, and local agencies have felt a financial squeeze, with tighter budgets, reduced discretionary funds, and forced cutbacks. The 1990–1992 recession moved tight budgets to the crisis point, with many ramifications:

- Most agencies have been cut back in their operating and capital improvement budgets. In some situations, entire recreation program staffs have been eliminated, parks closed, and departments merged into other agencies.
- Most agencies have looked for opportunities to increase revenues; in many cases these revenues have made up for budget cutbacks. Local agencies are using a multitude of funding, planning, and regulatory mechanisms to preserve open space, pay for operation and maintenance, and for other functions.
- Some agencies have seen increases in capital improvement dollars, particularly when improvements result in revenue generation or economic enhancement of a community.
- Local agencies are relying on fees from new urban growth for park acquisition and development.
- Nearly all federal grants to local governments have been eliminated and, although state grants have increased, their relationship to total need at the local level has decreased dramatically.
- The federal government is beginning to fund greater acquisition and capital improvements for the National Park Service, U.S. Fish and Wildlife Service, U.S. Forest Service, and the Bureau of Land Management.
- All California resource departments have struggled for capital and operations funds. The Department of Fish and Game has suffered the most operationally in the past, but the Department of Parks and Recreation is now facing massive cuts and layoffs.

Increasing Social Ills

The increasing degradation of our society is influencing parks and resources and the agencies that provide for them. Parks have never been islands, free from the litany of problems found within our cities or society. In certain instances, in fact, parks have become places where our social ills are magnified far beyond the average of the community. Unresolved, these problems have the potential to dramatically diminish the livability of our cities and jeopardize our parks.

Many communities that are deficient in usable park space also plunge into downward social spirals. Overcrowding magnifies cultural or ethnic differences among users and results in aggressive users displacing passive ones. The community at large becomes disenfranchised and withholds support for park expansion, maintenance, and programs. Without adequate supervision or control, parks become dangerous trouble spots for the community's social problems involving crime and drug use. In response, some cities have hired urban park rangers and some have started local youth employment programs patterned after the California Conservation Corps.

Rising Expectations

People want to improve the quality of their communities, and their vision is seen in urban waterfront projects from San Diego Bay to the south shore of Lake Tahoe, in trails around San Francisco Bay, in museums throughout California, in natural area preservation and restoration, and in urban beautification, such as landscaped medians, public art, and downtown renewal. After a sense of complacency in the early 1980s, support for improvement has grown in many areas, along with a growing sense of community pride. The success of the California Wildlife, Coastal, and Parklands Bond Act citizens' initiative of 1988 is a prime indicator of these shared statewide values.

FUTURE ACTIONS NEEDED

The problems and opportunities are clearly evident. How will California respond to this combination of influences? Will there be a collection of independent actions—some positive, others negative? What degree of leadership and direction will the state provide? What actions should be undertaken during this decade to prepare for the next century? The following five items examine the possibilities.

1. Greater empowerment of local agencies. The first building block in providing community assets comes from the community itself. Greater diversity, sense of place, and richness will surely result from each community creatively dealing with its own problems and opportunities. The following funding ideas would empower local agencies to address their park and open space needs.

The state legislature has arbitrarily limited the ability of communities to finance their needs by requiring a two-thirds majority to finance general obligation bonds. Voter authorization should be reduced to a simple majority.

Ever-increasing burdens have been placed upon local government (counties in particular) by the state without the financial means to pay for them. The result has been a continual drying up of discretionary spending for items such as parks and open space. This situation desperately needs to be rectified because it is affecting essential and discretionary services, and many counties are on the verge of bankruptcy.

Cities and counties have the authority to impose fees on new development to acquire parklands for open space and wildlife areas and to develop parks and trails (through development impact fees). Many agencies are now using these funds to keep pace with growth. The legislature rightly precluded use of such fees from solving existing community needs. A companion funding mechanism, however, is vital to solve this particular need. An equitable balance to the new development fees could be a real estate transfer tax on existing development.

Local agencies are required to take the lead in planning for the protection of endangered species. Some have found that the required habitat conservation plans can be an effective tool in preserving open spaces. Additional state and federal legislation is required to provide local agencies with the tools necessary to implement early multispecies preservation planning in advance of the species being listed as endangered.

2. Encouragement of volunteerism and citizen support. All levels of government should give greater support and encouragement to citizen involvement in park programs. Volunteers can accomplish much and define a community's sense of purpose and pride at the same time as providing valuable service.

The private and nonprofit sectors have grown to be major partners in recreation and resource preservation. The Nature Conservancy has preserved thousands of acres and stimulated the formation of dozens of land trusts. The Planning and Conservation League has spearheaded state legislation and initiatives creating funding for preservation. Likewise, recreation organizations and providers such as sports leagues, the YMCA, and Boys Clubs provide vital recreation enrichment services.

3. Greater state action on statewide issues and opportunities. The state needs to increase its level of commitment toward concerns and opportunities of statewide significance, including the following:

• Most state parks have either inholdings or adjacent private lands that threaten the integrity and quality of the parks.
• Many parks are in need of refurbishment or expansion, and in some cases initial improvements are necessary to make newly acquired areas accessible to the public.
• California's coastal parks (25 percent of California's shoreline) are nearly all in need of rehabilitation and provision of access and support facilities.
• Many state wildlife areas could provide wildlife and interpretive experiences but are inadequately developed and staffed.
• Funding is now available for acquisition of wildlife corridors and habitat areas, but statewide prioritization is necessary for the effective use of these funds.
• Resources such as San Francisco Bay's shorelines, the Delta, inland rivers, wetlands, deserts, Lake Tahoe, forests, and oak woodlands are inadequately protected, yet offer promise for meeting future needs.
• Protection of our biodiversity requires integrated planning with urban, park, and recreation needs.

4. Greater federal action with federal lands. With ownership of 46 percent of California's land base, the federal government has a major stake in our environmental quality. The mountains, deserts, and national park units are vital, and wildlife areas and military properties are gaining increasing importance.

The federal government is reactivating its land and water conservation program by budgeting for federal acquisition and development projects. This emphasis should continue until some of the tremendous federal needs are met.

Surplus military lands have the potential to meet important resource protection and recreation needs. Prime examples are Fort Ord's expanse of coastal dunes and beaches on Monterey Bay and the Presidio's historic, recreation, and open space resources within San Francisco. The potentials for preservation of resources and provision of services should be studied as a part of every base closure.

5. State leadership and partnerships. State leadership is needed to make things happen. Because it has related state responsibilities, the logical entity is The Resources Agency, in close policy and financial partnership with local, state, and federal providers. Leadership is needed in many areas.

Umbrella planning is needed regarding recreation use patterns, responding to preservation of wildlife habitat and corridors, and preservation of rivers and the coastline. Meeting the state's increasing water supply needs should be coordinated with recreation and wildlife protection.

Local agencies should be encouraged to utilize available tools for raising funds and accomplishing needs rather than becoming increasingly deficient. They should also be encouraged to focus on meeting priority needs.

Coordination and encouragement of federal actions are needed.

Partnerships should be established for river, coastal, and desert protection.

SUMMARY

In the past decade, dramatic growth in California's population was accompanied by growing economic problems for public parks and a drift in leadership by state and federal governments. Local governments and citizens took greater responsibility for solving problems and meeting rising expectations for the quality of life and the environment. New issues and solutions have emerged, not necessarily changing what people want for the future, but only how to achieve it.

A strong realization has dawned on the people of California that valued recreation opportunities are rapidly being overrun and resource values lost. In some rapid-growth communities, the next decade will be the last opportunity to preserve these important areas.

As we look forward to the next century we must focus on building quality communities. We must preserve the open spaces that shape them, the park and cultural places that become their focal points, and also the landscaped boulevards, streams, rivers, trails, and other linear spaces that knit the communities together.

We must also look at our greater park and open space areas as not just isolated museum pieces of the environment to be put on display. The long-term health of these natural places must be assured through adequate scale, proper boundaries, connections and corridors, and a dedication toward the preservation and primacy of natural processes.

We cannot forget our obligation to provide people with meaningful experiences to match their individual needs. We need to look for every opportunity to heal social ills and divert young people from becoming involved in criminal behavior.

We need to organize, coordinate, stimulate, cooperate, and be creative to get the job done. The future of California—hopefully the home of our children and children's children—depends on it.

CHAPTER 16

Wildlife and Endangered Species: In Precipitous Decline

SALLY W. SMITH

THE AMERICAN EPICENTER OF EXTINCTION

With the highest peak and the lowest valley in the continental United States, eleven biogeographic provinces, 396 habitat types,[1] and 101,563,500 acres, California is home to more plant and animal species than any other state. But while the variety of habitats and species in California is legendary, the natural heritage is uniquely at risk. Major processes affecting loss of biological diversity are usually due to human activity and include habitat conversion, degradation, and fragmentation, direct species mortality, and altered species interactions such as introduced species outcompeting native populations.

Sally W. Smith studied anthropology and mass communications at the University of California at Berkeley and has served as director of public information for The Nature Conservancy of California. She currently works with the Conservancy's Habitat Restoration Team, a volunteer group that plants trees and understory shrubs, herbs, and grasses throughout the state.

Human demand on resources is increasing: about 2,000 people are added to the state's population every day.[2] To accommodate that growth, between 1 million and 2 million acres will be developed in the next decade,[3] and millions of acres of native grasslands, tidal marshes, vernal pools, and oak and redwood forests have already been lost. Compared to historic levels, California has lost 99 percent of its native grasslands, 89 percent of its riparian woodlands, 80 percent of its coastal wetlands, and 94 percent of its interior wetlands (see Figure 16.1).[4] Of those wildlands that remain, few are in pristine condition.

As a result of habitat loss, California is the epicenter of extinction in the continental United States, with more than twice the number of federally listed endangered species as any other western state. Much of our natural heritage, developed over millennia, could be eradicated in a short time if native plants and animals lose their fight for survival. Many of these species exist nowhere else in the world; once lost, they are lost forever.

FIGURE 16.1
WETLAND LOSSES IN CALIFORNIA

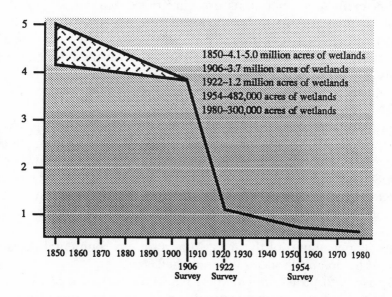

1850–4.1-5.0 million acres of wetlands
1906–3.7 million acres of wetlands
1922–1.2 million acres of wetlands
1954–482,000 acres of wetlands
1980–300,000 acres of wetlands

SOURCE: U.S. Fish and Wildlife Service, *Pacific Flyway Waterfowl in California's Sacramento Valley Wetlands*, 1983.

NOTE: Estimates prior to 1900 range from 4.1 to 5 million acres.

The word *wild* was historically used to mean those plants and animals that could survive without the aid or intervention of humans. Increasingly, more of our native species *cannot* survive without human protection and respect. *Wildlife* was often used in the past to refer exclusively to animals, principally vertebrates. In this chapter it is used to mean those species, both plant and animal, that are neither human nor domesticated. Habitat refers to the places where the plant or animal normally lives, and natural community refers to a group of interdependent organisms with common habitat. Ecosystem refers to a mosaic of related communities and their chemical and physical surroundings; an ecosystem is a functional unit of nature, including both organisms and their nonliving environment—climate, geography, and geology. Landscape refers to assemblages of ecosystems. Biological diversity (biodiversity) refers to the variety of life forms that comprise the natural world—from genes to species to natural communities.

WHY CARE ABOUT DISAPPEARING DIVERSITY?

While extinction is part of nature, current extinction rates are 40 to 400 times faster than during the era of the dinosaurs,[5] and rates are accelerating. If current trends continue, 5 percent to 10 percent of the world's species will be lost per decade over the next quarter-century,[6] greatly exceeding the natural attrition rate and far beyond the rate at which natural processes can replace them. Scientists and others agree that this loss of wildlife and natural communities is a very real threat to our economic, physical, and spiritual well-being.

Unfortunately, public perception of the problem does not match that of the scientific community. In ranking environmental threats, the Science Advisory Board of the U.S. Environmental Protection Agency rated habitat alteration and loss of species (along with global warming) at the top of the list because those losses are irreversible. But when a Roper poll asked the American public to rank its perception of the most important environmental threats, loss of habitat and species was not cited.[7]

Reasons to protect our natural world are as varied as they are complex, ranging from pragmatic to ethical. The most obvious values of natural diversity are the material resources organisms provide: food, drink, fuel, energy, fabrics, medicines, building materials, and industrial products. Equally important are the ecological services provided by healthy natural communities: creation of soil, maintenance of soil fertility, protection of watersheds and flood plains, transformation of solar energy to biomass through photosynthesis, maintenance and moderation of climate, abatement of water and air pollution, biological control of pests, and pollination of agricultural crops. Domesticated strains of food crops are hybridized with their wild cousins to reinvigorate the population and so enable them to better withstand disease, predators, and changes in climate.

On an individual level there are a multitude of reasons to conserve species. Wasp wings are studied for their aerodynamic qualities. The Madagascar periwinkle produces an ingredient critical to the manufacture of a medicine that gives patients a 95 percent chance of remission from lymphocytic leukemia. Barnacle byproducts led to a dental cement more powerful and less toxic than ones previously known. The Hawaiian gunnera plant produces its own fertilizer and as a result can exist on rugged terrain with poor soil. Chalcid wasps serve as a natural control for ticks carrying Lyme disease. Microbes are used to process sewage and oil spills. Polar bears are studied for their ability to collect solar energy. A fungus in China has anticlotting properties useful in treating human disease. These examples illustrate only a handful of uses we already know about. The only truly useless species are those that have become extinct.

Most of our natural world has not been fully explored. While almost half of all the pharmaceutical products humans depend on are derived from other species, it is estimated that, at most, 2 percent of the plants available to us have been fully investigated for medicinal value. The recent discovery of the Pacific yew tree's cancer-fighting properties underscores the worth of the seemingly unimportant. Considered a "weed" tree, the yew is scraggly, short, and yields no timber of value. As a result, it has been uprooted, burned, and cut down at every opportunity to make room for more desirable species. Recent studies indicate the Pacific yew holds promise for treating breast, ovarian, and lung cancers and leukemia. (Ironically, at this point, six 100-year-old trees must be harvested to treat one patient; 10,000 women die a year in the United States from ovarian cancer. The complex molecule is years away from being synthesized in the laboratory.[8])

From an aesthetic standpoint, any natural place that people call beautiful is almost certain to be a diversified, healthy ecosystem, whether it be a coastal wetland, a desert, or an alpine meadow.

But there are other values to wildlife beyond the ability to provide humans with oxygen, raw materials, recreation, or inspiration. All plants and animals have their own intrinsic value. Every living thing on earth is a storehouse of genetic information reaching back 3.8 billion years, and for that reason alone we should pay attention to species' survival.

WHAT DO WE HAVE?

There are an estimated 7,850 kinds of vascular plants (species, subspecies, and varieties) in California, more than in the entire central and northeastern United States and adjacent Canada combined.[9] (Vascular plants have vessels to carry the plants' fluids and include the seed producers, ferns, and fernlike plants.) The state's nonvascular flora include approximately 1,000 to 1,200 lichens, 4,000 to 5,000 gilled fungi, 300 to 400 slime molds, and 660 mosses and liverworts.[10] One-third of the vascular native plants are endemic—they are found nowhere else in the world[11]—and roughly 1,000 plant species in California have been introduced from elsewhere.

Of the 2,300 vertebrate species found in the United States, 748 are in California. Of these, 38 percent of the freshwater fish, 29 percent of the amphibians, and 9 percent of the mammals are endemic.[12] There are approximately 28,000 insect species.[13]

WHAT IS LOST OR THREATENED?

At least seventy-three plants and animals (including the California grizzly bear, symbolized on the state flag) are already extinct. Half of California's terrestrial communities and 40 percent of its aquatic communities are currently rare or threatened.[14]

In the spring of 1990, 524 animals were listed or proposed for listing as threatened or endangered under state and federal law, or were listed as "species of special concern" by the Natural Diversity Data Base run by the state Department of Fish and Game.

In the fall of 1991, 212 plants were listed as rare, threatened, or endangered under state and federal law. But according to the California Native Plant Society, 541 plants may merit status as threatened or endangered but are not yet listed.

WHAT IS PROTECTED?

California is roughly 824 miles long and 200 miles wide, spanning 158,693 square miles. State government holds 2.5 percent of the land area; the federal government, 46 percent; and private landowners, 51.5 percent. Up to 40 percent of the land area is used for grazing, 17 percent for logging, 12 percent for agriculture, 5 percent for urban or suburban use, 3 percent for defense, 12 percent for parks or reserves, and 11 percent for roads, water districts, or miscellaneous uses.[15]

Of the 12 million acres in some sort of reserve or protected status, half are managed primarily for the benefit of wildlife. Some habitat types are better represented in the reserve system than others. For example, two habitat types (alpine dwarf scrub and subalpine conifer forests) have more than 90 percent of their acreage included in reserves, while less than 1 percent of riparian habitat (the richest habitat for terrestrial vertebrates) is protected.

About 85 percent of the California land held in reserve is managed by the federal government. The U.S. Forest Service and Bureau of Land Management hold 38 percent of California's total area and are mandated to open portions of their landholdings to multiple use—grazing, logging, mining, and gas and oil exploration.

According to the California Department of Forestry's Forest and Rangeland Assessment Program, more than 17 million acres of California have been converted from natural habitat to urban or agricultural use, excluding grazing. More than 41 million acres in the state are available for grazing, with more than half of these acres owned by the federal government. Between 1950 and 1980, 3.8 million acres were converted to agricultural land and 1 million acres to urban uses.

Conifers cover 23 percent of the state; hardwoods, 9 percent; shrublands, 19 percent; grasslands and other herbaceous types, 9 percent; deserts, 21 percent; and alpine barrens or rock, 2 percent. One percent of the state's area is covered by water. Habitats associated with water (wetlands, vernal pools, riparian vegetation) have lost proportionally more acreage than other types.[16]

Aquatic species, less able to survive habitat loss or degradation, serve as indicator species reflecting the health of their ecosystems. A majority of the threatened and endangered animals in California are dependent on aquatic or riparian habitats, and more fish are officially listed as threatened or endangered than any other type of animal; about 20 percent of the sixty-six native fish species are endangered.[17] Inland native fish populations decline for several reasons: habitat loss and alteration, competition from introduced (nonnative) species, and overharvesting. Aquatic habitat loss and alteration in California is caused primarily by dam building, water diversion (irrigation), drainage of wetlands, channelization of streams, and changes in water temperature and nutrient availability due to loss of surrounding riparian vegetation. More than one-third of the freshwater fish fauna is made up of nonnative species.

There are numerous federal laws protecting wildlife, the foremost being the Endangered Species Act. Passed in 1973 and subject to periodic review, the act seeks to protect any species in danger of going extinct "throughout all or a significant portion of its range" (endangered classification) or likely to become endangered within the foreseeable future (threatened classification).

What does it take to list a species as endangered or threatened? A petition requesting listing is filed with the secretary of the interior (which can be done through the U.S. Fish and Wildlife Service), or, in the case of marine species, with the secretary of commerce (through the National Marine Fisheries Service). Anyone can file a petition for listing. After the petition is filed, the agency has ninety days to respond whether it deems the listing warranted. If agency biologists agree that listing should be considered, the species becomes a "candidate species" and a proposed rule is drafted within the first year after the petition is accepted (with a possible six-month extension). Once the draft proposal is published, there is a sixty-day period for public comment and additional information to be collected; then a final ruling is made.

Once the species is listed as threatened or endangered, the Fish and Wildlife Service or National Marine Fisheries Service issues regulations to protect it. The killing, capture, export, import, harm, harassment, and sale of a protected animal species are prohibited wherever they occur, regardless of land ownership. It is illegal to remove a protected plant species from lands under federal jurisdiction. All federal agencies are required to consult with the Fish and Wildlife Service or National Marine Fisheries Service before beginning a project that would impact wildlife. Violation of the law is a federal offense, punishable by both civil and criminal penalties of up to $100,000 in fines and/or one year in jail.

In case of conflicts when a development project is likely to harm an endangered species and where all other attempts at resolution have failed, the Endangered Species Committee (consisting of the secretaries of interior, agriculture, and army, the heads of the Council of Economic Advisors, the Environmental Protection Agency, the National Oceanic and Atmospheric Administration, and a representative from the state where the species is found) has the power to grant exemptions to the act where no "reasonable and prudent" alternative exists, provided the project is of national and regional significance, and when the benefits clearly outweigh the benefits of alternative choices.

California also has an Endangered Species Act, which provides important protections but only on state lands or for projects of which a state agency is the principal sponsor.

The endangered species acts are critical tools for use in wildlife protection—the best available—but they do have their limitations. The acts specify protection of single species meeting certain qualifications. Many scientists now believe that the single-species approach is too small a focus and usually comes too late—after the species is already in crisis. By focusing on individual species, the general public may lose sight of the larger picture. It is easy to miss the point that the spotted owl and marbled murrelet are representatives of an entire endangered ecosystem. The spotted owl is not the problem; the loss of old-growth forests is. Too often, nomination for listing can become some sort of popularity contest, with cute mammals or majestic birds given priority. Plants are not given priority under the law, and natural communities are given no standing. Designation as an endangered species does not guarantee survival. In California, 58 percent of the state-listed animal species and 75 percent of the state-listed plant species are still in decline despite listing.[18] Of the species listed as endangered by the federal government, nearly half lack any recovery plan, even though these plans are required by the act. Government wildlife personnel responsible for protecting imperiled species are making a superhuman effort but are too often hampered by insufficient funding and staff.

Responsibilities for wildlife protection have historically been divided among several agencies and organizations without common guidelines or review opportunities. Success of protection efforts can be undermined as a result of this diffused responsibility. With these limitations in mind, ten state and federal agencies have signed an agreement that will regionalize environmental and wildlife protection planning. Called the Executive Council on Biological Diversity, this interagency group includes representatives from the University of California's Agriculture and Natural Resources Division, California's Departments of Forestry and Fire Protection, Fish and Game, State Lands Commission, and Parks and Recreation, and the U.S. Bureau of Land Management, National Park Service, Forest Service, and Fish and Wildlife Service; the council is headed by the secretary of the state's Resources Agency. California is divided into eleven regions, with council members drawing up protection plans for each. The goal is to develop statewide strategies to protect biological diversity and transcend the traditional jurisdictional boundaries between federal, state, county, and local governments and agencies. The creation of this council is an important move toward consistent and thorough protection of our natural heritage.

PRESERVATION AND RESTORATION STRATEGIES FOR NATURAL AREAS

Identification

The first step in wildlife protection is to identify and monitor areas with the highest levels of biodiversity and with functioning ecosystems in place or restorable. The rarest of California's plants, animals, and natural communities are inventoried and monitored by the California Department of Fish and Game's Natural Diversity Data Base. In addition to tracking the threatened and endangered species already listed under state and federal endangered species acts, this computerized inventory tracks plants protected under the state native plant law (officially designated "rare") and those plants, animals, and natural communities not yet protected under law but still considered by Data Base biologists to be in trouble. ("Species of special concern" is a term used by the Data Base to characterize animals not yet legally protected but meriting attention.) The University of California at Santa Barbara, the California Department of Forestry and Fire Protection, and others are mapping the state's vegetation to better identify critical habitat.

Using new computer systems known as geographic information systems, it is possible to combine collected data to generate maps of plant, animal, and natural community distributions, threats, and more. This technique has been used to analyze gaps in the state's preserve system and so determine effectiveness of protection efforts. Gap analysis is extremely useful to conservation biologists and land use planners because, with increasing fragmentation of habitat, wildlife corridors and landscape linkages are essential to the survival of species, in particular the larger mammals, such as the black bear, mountain lion, and pronghorn. Additionally, with real estate, political, economic, and population pressures such as they are, new preserves are increasingly more difficult to create. Preservation efforts will, of necessity, be concentrated on adding selectively to those protected areas already established. Once wildlife needs are understood, creative solutions might be seen. For example, not all habitat needs are in remote areas; wildlife corridors can include sewer line rights of way, jogging and riding paths, and even abandoned railroad tracks.

Protection Techniques

To be effective, species protection must focus increasingly on "thinking big"—the multispecies approach, protection of natural communities, preventive care, and safeguarding not only the pieces but the processes.

To best manage for wildlife values, property acquisition by public and private agencies is still an obvious choice in land protection. But it is not feasible to buy all the land necessary to ensure adequate protection of the state's rich biological diversity. (Adequate protection, according to The Nature Conservancy's estimate, could be achieved if roughly 30 percent of California's total area was managed to enhance wildlife values, with proportionate representation of all eleven biogeographic provinces and major habitat types. The approach would not exclude all economic uses of that area but would rely on partnerships with existing property owners and compatible economic uses outside key wildlife preserves.)

Many conservation organizations work directly with landowners who voluntarily agree to manage their property to enhance wildlife values while retaining ownership. A typical landowner agreement might involve not mowing or grazing a particular portion of property while endangered plants are setting seed for the next generation.

Conservation easements are an approach to land protection wherein property owners agree contractually and usually in perpetuity not to develop or manage their land in particular, specified ways. Conservation easements have three parts: prohibited uses (which forbid specified activities), retained rights (allowing the landowner certain uses), and transferred rights (which delineate what the holder of the easement—typically a conservation organization, land trust, or governmental body—is allowed to do). For example, a conservation easement might prohibit anyone from developing home sites on the property, cutting timber, exploring for minerals, or intentionally changing streambeds. At the same time, the owner might retain the right to live on the property in an existing building. If the easement is given to a qualified organization in perpetuity, the property owner is allowed a charitable deduction for federal income tax purposes. In some cases, easements result in lower property taxes.

Habitat conservation plans (HCPs) are a product of the Endangered Species Act. These are management agreements made by property owners—often developers—to design and implement wildlife conservation strategies before or after an imperiled species is officially listed as rare, threatened, or endangered. This technique is innovative in that it is an attempt to stay ahead of the "extinction curve" by seeking to protect habitat and species at risk before they reach the crisis point.

Cooperative management agreements are agreements made between public and private agencies stipulating ways in which the signing parties will cooperate in the inventorying of species and in the design and implementation of wildlife management plans on a given piece of property. These agreements are a step in the right direction but are not legally binding.

Management Techniques

After species and natural communities have been identified and protected legally, they must be managed to ensure survival. Traditional management techniques have included fencing, controlled burns, weeding, and other practices. In addition to these more traditional approaches to stewardship, new approaches are constantly being considered and old ideas challenged.

Restoration ecology is a new science of restoring altered habitats by approximating their natural pattern of structure and function. Restoration can be a controversial subject because many people fear the concept will lead to a false sense of security, that conservation and prevention opportunities will not be vigorously pursued because of the perception that eventually restoration will make it "all better." There is no restorationist anywhere who will tell you restoration is as good as the original. Nonetheless, restoration is the only way to bring back wildlife habitat that has already been degraded or destroyed.

Zoos, botanical gardens, tissue cultures, seed storage banks, and captive breeding programs are attempts to preserve, independent of habitat, species that would otherwise go extinct. The California condor provides the most celebrated example of this approach. While each strategy has its uses, many people would argue that the important issue of habitat is overlooked. There is no point in returning captively bred species to an environment that can no longer support them.

Because 51.5 percent of the state is in private hands, local governments have primary decision-making responsibility for land use and management. Most lack comprehensive plans to protect biodiversity. Economic incentives (real estate values and property and sales taxes) too often encourage development of wildlands. The federal government owns 46 percent of the land and controls about 60 percent of the state's biodiversity, but agencies controlling most of this area are still operating under regulations put into place a long time ago—laws that were intended to support rural economies (for example, laws concerning grazing and water subsidies) but today encourage overuse and misuse of diminishing resources.

WHAT NEXT?

To protect the state's remaining biodiversity, we must continue to increase habitat acquisition and environmental review capabilities of agencies. We must accelerate the listing process for endangered species and concentrate on the needs of our natural world *before* species reach the crisis point. The state and federal endangered species acts should be broadened to recognize natural communities, to provide funding for habitat acquisition, and to better protect plant life. Additionally, the scope of California's endangered species act should be expanded to include private land. Water policy in the state must be revised to be more equitable, to encourage conservation, and to dedicate water rights to wildlife needs. Economic incentives must be created and strengthened to further promote habitat protection, restoration, and control of invasive nonnative species. Laws and policies that encourage and reward nonsustainable uses of the state's resources must be amended to discourage those practices. The status of California's natural heritage should be included in the governor's annual State of the State Report. Education (on every level) about the values of biodiversity is crucial to the future health of Californians—human and otherwise. Similarly, research on the state's ecosystems must be a top priority, including the establishment of baseline data for intact, functioning systems. People must come to realize that just as loss of habitat and species does not always happen on a large scale but rather can be incremental and cumulative, so too can protection efforts start small and still be effective. A degree of difference may not look like much at the beginning, but over time, with the participation of many individuals, that degree of difference is vast.

Increasingly, we have come to realize that fragmented pieces of protected habitat—more like wildlife museums than meaningful expanses of habitat—are not enough to ensure protection for plants and animals. The new focus of wildlife management strategies needs to encompass entire ecosystems, typically configured by natural boundaries—a watershed, for example. Protection strategies must include ways to meet both wildlife needs and human needs. Land use methods will necessarily be refined so that wilderness sanctuaries will coexist with reasonable economic activity. People do not generally embrace wildlife protection if they think those measures will hurt them economically. Farmers may think a nature preserve will threaten their ability to make decisions for their own land. Counties may feel the loss of tax revenues if a wildlife preserve is created instead of a shopping mall.

In a pluralistic society, many demands, often conflicting, will be made on resources. How best to meet fairly the needs of a complex society and at the same time protect the resource base is our challenge for the future—how to create and strengthen models of mutual coexistence of humans and nature that allow economic growth but at the same time protect nonrenewable resources. As the problems confronting our natural world become more complex and the solutions fewer and less obvious, cooperation between public and private sectors will become increasingly important.

Cooperation starts with the recognition that we, as a society, have more in common with one another than we have in opposition. To confirm this, we need only recognize that the basic systems of the planet—on which all life relies—are interdependent. For example, the atmosphere is not a permanent fixture but is continuously being consumed and recreated. Destruction and manipulation of those plants and animals responsible for helping to create the atmosphere can have lethal ramifications for all life on earth. Coastal marshes, as another example, serve as a freshwater barrier that prevents saltwater intrusion into the inland freshwater supply. By overpumping that resource, large pieces of coastal agricultural lands will be affected.

The American West has been world famous for its large landscapes, revered not only for their beauty but for their richness of life. Because there was so much of it, the land was taken for granted, overused, and underprotected. But that time has gone. We live in a world of limited resources, and our precarious balance with the natural world can only be maintained by conscientious use and management. The next few years must, of necessity, be a time of change in attitude, a turn toward enlightened self-interest, when humans recognize that just as we are a part of nature, nature is a part of us, to be cherished, understood, and above all respected.

FURTHER INFORMATION

Edna Bakker, *An Island Called California* (Berkeley: University of California Press, 1984).

Lester R. Brown et al., *State of the World: 1992* (New York: W.W. Norton, 1991).

Lester R. Brown et al., *Saving the Planet: How to Shape an Environmentally Sustainable Global Economy* (New York: W.W. Norton, 1991).

Walter Corson et. al., *Citizen's Guide to Sustainable Development* (Washington D.C.: Global Tomorrow Coalition, 1989).

Anne and Paul Ehrlich, *Extinction* (New York: Random House, 1981).

Deborah Jensen, Margaret Torn, and John Harte, *In Our Own Hands* (Berkeley: University of California Press, 1991).

Kathryn A. Kohm, *Balancing on the Brink of Extinction* (Washington, D.C.: Island Press, 1991).

Gay Mackintosh et al., *Preserving Communities and Corridors* (Washington, D.C.: Defenders of Wildlife, 1989).

Robert Ornduff, *Introduction to California Plant Life* (Berkeley: University of California Press, 1974).

Walter V. Reid et al., *Keeping Options Alive* (Washington, D.C.: World Resources Institute, 1989).

Peter Steinhart, *California's Wild Heritage* (San Francisco: Sierra Club Books, 1990).

E. O. Wilson et al., *Biodiversity* (Washington, D.C.: National Academy Press, 1988).

CHAPTER 17

The Native California Landscape

TIM PALMER

THE LAND AS IT ALWAYS WAS

In spite of a 200-year settlement by nonnative peoples that might more appropriately be called an onslaught, landscapes with stunning beauty and functioning ecosystems remain in California. They survive by neglect—many are remote, difficult places. And they survive by design—public policy tortuously arrived at but finally allowing some places to exist as they always have, even amidst the perpetual boom. Many survive on borrowed time that is surely running out.

Though none of California's native landscapes show much more than remnants of what once was, some are significant in quality or importance, such as the wilderness areas. The Sierra Nevada, from Tuolumne Meadows to the South Fork of the Kern River, is the longest protected wilderness outside Alaska. Except for that state, only five areas exist in the United States where a person can be ten miles from any road; two are in the Sierra. Designated public lands wilderness includes 5.9 million acres of such eclectic diversity as the Trinity Alps, the Farallon Islands, and Joshua Tree National Monument—more protected acreage than in any other state but Alaska. Roughly 10 million acres are wilderness but are not designated and not likely to remain wild without political intervention—the full-time pursuit of the California Wilderness Coalition.

California's national parks—Redwood, Lassen, Yosemite, Kings Canyon, Sequoia, and the Channel Islands—are also islands of native landscape, as are its seven national monuments and some state parks. Isolated pieces of the mountains, forests, wetlands, and coast also stand as living monuments to the original California.

To look with more depth at the native landscape, three areas were chosen for discussion in this chapter, each offering special promise but under special siege: the deserts, which stretch to the horizon in huge splendor; the oak woodlands, which cast shade and host vital habitat near the homes of so many Californians; and the rivers, which create ribbons of life running from mountaintop to seashore.

The Desert: A Landscape to Protect

Regarded as the archetypal wasteland since the first European discovery, the American deserts have had few champions through the years. The people most familiar with them—miners and Mormons—regarded these places as threats and obstacles to be overcome in order to make money or to carve out a homeland as close in green and agrarian appearance as possible to, say, Ohio. There have been, however, movements to protect deserts; the fight to protect Canyonlands National Park in Utah in the mid-1960s was the best example—until now. In the early 1990s, the campaign for California's deserts ranked as the largest effort ever to protect deserts and as the foremost land preservation battle in California.

The southern deserts alone—principally the Mojave but also the Colorado, which runs from Palm Springs to Mexico—blanket 25 million acres, or one-quarter of the state. Using the geographer's guideline—that rainfall of ten inches or less defines a desert—the southern Central Valley and parts of the Modoc Plateau in the northeast likewise qualify. Arid and semiarid lands together occupy two-thirds of the state.

A tapestry of mountains, canyons, dunes, alkali flats, Joshua tree groves, forests of piñon pine and juniper, perennial and intermittent streams, endangered plant communities, unusual wildlife habitat, and space upon space with silence upon silence compose the desert of southeastern California, regarded as a wasteland no longer. This is one of the most diverse deserts in the world. The land climbs 11,300 feet from Death Valley to Telescope Peak. In a span of ninety-two miles, the nation's lowest point, 282 feet below sea level in Death Valley, soars to the highest U.S. summit outside Alaska— Mount Whitney at 14,494 feet in the Sierra Nevada. The Eureka Dunes are the second-highest on the continent. With surveys completed for only 6 percent of 25 million acres, archaeologists found 14,000 prehistoric sites; some call this desert the richest archaeological region in the United States.[1] Creosote bushes, alive for 11,700 years, are the oldest living things on earth.[2] The desert tortoise stores enough water that it needs to drink only a few times a year. Besides being California's official state reptile, the tortoise is the desert's indicator species, dependent on native qualities and highly vulnerable to damage of many types. Since 1980, populations have plummeted by 80 percent in some places.

This remains one of the wildest, least affected regions of the United States. Next to "dry," "fragile" best describes the environment here. The tread marks of Patton's tanks can still be seen where they practiced for northern Africa during World War II. The tire track of a dirt bike laid down in 1992 might last as long. Plant communities that established their individual strongholds over a course of centuries can be wiped out by one contingent of off-road vehicles in a few minutes, and recovery, if it occurs, may take geologic time. If streams or springs would be polluted by mine waste, the effects could last forever, and the water supply may be the only one accessible to wildlife.

The California desert is an American Galapagos of evolution and adaptation. Mountain ranges are islands surrounded by land as intractable as a sea. Species of snails are unique to individual springs. Species of beetles are unique to individual sets of dunes.

This landscape is reasonably mild nine months of the year and dazzlingly colorful and inviting in the spring. It draws visitors with a wide appreciation for the place and offers a classroom, laboratory, museum, surrealistic view of the Golden State, and a splendidly silent escape from the urban life that hums and grinds only a mountain range away in the Los Angeles megalopolis, home of the great majority of the desert's recreational visitors.

The National Park Service manages 2.5 million acres of the desert, but most of the public domain, 12.1 million acres, is administered by the Bureau of Land Management (BLM), a Department of the Interior agency that inherited acreage not claimed by homesteaders and not reserved as national forest or under other designations.

Sections of desert as large as some states remain intact, but much of it faces problems and threats. For years, cattle have been turned loose to roam the drylands, eating to the dirt the tobosa grass, vital to the bighorn sheep, trampling what they don't eat of sparse, rare, and endangered plant communities, and taxing the life-giving riparian habitat to its literal death. The BLM permits 84,000 animal unit months (each AUM is enough for one cow and calf for a month) of grazing on its public lands in the desert. Cows requiring one acre in the East and twenty to forty acres in other parts of the West might require five hundred or more acres on desert lands, where foraging can ruin irreplaceable habitat to put a minuscule number of steaks on the table, each requiring enormous taxpayer subsidies because the ranchers pay only half the cost of administering the BLM program.[3] In one day a cow eats enough forage to last a desert tortoise for a year. The exceptional habitats that persist today generally do so only where cows have not been put out to pasture in this pasture-less setting.

The main threat is off-road vehicles. Responsible drivers are not the problem. Thousands, however, come to the desert to do what they are not allowed to do elsewhere. Aerial views of sensitive desert lands show a grated surface of tire tracks in thousands of gutterlike paths. Soil erodes, plants die, and 90 percent of small mammals disappear,[4] though by 1991 the BLM tightened its regulatory program and reduced intensive off-road vehicle use to half a million officially permitted acres. The 1976 Federal Land Policy and Management Act directed the agency to recognize a "California Desert Conservation Area" as a "total ecosystem that is extremely fragile, easily scarred, and slowly healed." The long-awaited plan identified only 2.1 million acres for potential wilderness—17 percent of the BLM desert land. This modest effort was undercut by Reagan administration officials, who allowed a whole new generation of abuses. The Las Vegas to Barstow off-road vehicle race, in which 3,000 bike riders had annually cut a scar a half-mile wide for 150 miles, was reopened even after the event had been discontinued by the BLM. (The agency was later successful in stopping all point-to-point races.)

Seeking permanent protection, Senator Alan Cranston introduced the California Desert Protection Act in 1986 to protect in wilderness and national parks an area two times the size of New Jersey (see Figure 17.1). A Mojave National Park would be created, and 4.5 million acres of BLM land would become newly designated wilderness. The bill would leave 13,000 miles of dirt roads and 20,000 miles of unimproved roads open to motorized use. It would affect five ranching operations. The cattlemen and off-road vehicle users were strong political forces against the bill.

The California Desert Protection Act, still under consideration in the early 1990s, is one of the last opportunities to save a truly large piece of the original American landscape; another Alaska lands bill or an Idaho wilderness bill are the only actions that might even come close. The desert now receives the attention it deserves for its life and intrinsic beauty—no less, in the eyes of some, than the sequoia trees or Big Sur. The protection of the best that remains of the desert could be a landmark toward a mature appreciation and stewardship for the fully represented native landscapes of California.

OAK WOODLANDS: THE HOME LANDSCAPE OF CALIFORNIA

More than redwoods, more than mountains, even more than the Pacific Coast, the oak woodlands are the native landscape where Californians live. Along with wetlands and riparian woodlands, of which some oaks form an integral part, oak woodlands stand at the top of the critical habitat types, vitally important to entire webs of life.

Hardwood habitats, principally oaks, house more species of wildlife than any other vegetation type in California. At least 331 vertebrates breed there, and 32 kinds of birds and 39 species of mammals feed regularly on acorns.[5] Additional species winter in the oaks and migrate through. The California condor, nearly extinct, foraged in oak woodlands extensively and will again if reintroduction succeeds. The troublesome and precipitous decline of California's black-tailed deer herds was preceded by a decline in oaks. California spotted owls nest in oaks in the Tehachapi Mountains and

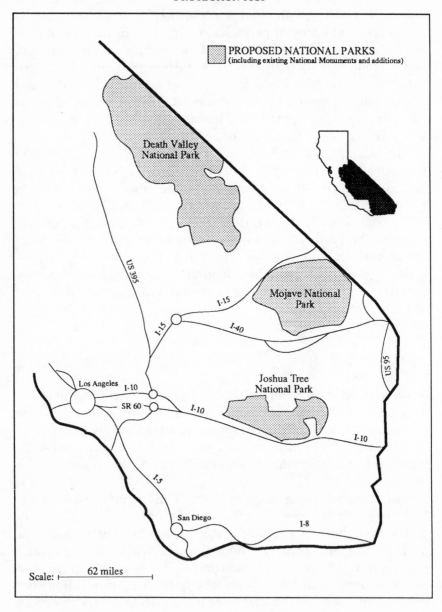

Sierra foothills.[6] Often growing on steep slopes, the blue oaks hold soil in place with fibrous root systems; massive erosion can be expected without them.

The valley oak (*Quercus lobata*), a photogenic and memorable giant of the interior flatlands, grows 150 feet tall with branches that span an arena; it is the largest oak in North America. Its open groves grew spacious and parklike, drawing the awe of early visitors, as the few remaining big trees do today. An indicator of deep soils and high water tables, these landmarks showed farmers where the most productive lands lay for clearing and plowing. Along with the blue oak (*Quercus douglasii*), the valley oak is endemic—it grows nowhere but in California. Likewise, the Engelmann oak lives only in a narrow niche in southern California.

Central to the California scene, the oaks serve up a cherished image, gracing the Coast Range, the savannah of the Central Valley, the Sierra foothills, and the dry slopes of the southlands. Their acorns were to the Indians what wheat and corn were to later settlers. *California Spring*, painted by Albert Bierstadt in 1875, displays a Sacramento Valley bathed in luxurious strips of oaks and cottonwoods. Highlighting the tawny waves of hills and valleys, the oaks, with muscular arms, richness of color, and a breadth of sculptural artistry, are what the eye settles upon.

Settlers named towns and crossroads after oaks: Oakland, Oakdale, Thousand Oaks, Oakhurst, Oak Run—more than 150 place names in all, not to mention uncounted campgrounds, schools, streets, and, of course, shopping centers.

The oaks that symbolize California have been cut down or choked out so that those places could become something else less worthy of being named after. Like the needless killing of an oak in the John Steinbeck novel *To a God Unknown*, the destruction of today's oak forest marks the loss of something irredeemable and irreplaceable in the quality of life in the Golden State.

More than a million acres of oaks have been cut since 1945 alone. That still leaves a lot of acres, and a family so ubiquitous has not attracted the attention that the last redwoods have received. But looking further, there are alarming reasons for concern. Three of California's fifteen oak species—the valley, blue, and Engelmann—stand only in isolated islands of their past range. Valley oaks live in only 1.5 percent of their original habitat. The great trees once shaded the banks of the Sacramento River in groves 300 feet wide, but their habitat is now irrigated for crops or lies dusty and brown in the absence of all but scattered oak landmarks here and there and in a few fabulous expanses of savannah, such as along the lower Feather and Bear rivers.

People cleared hundreds of thousands of acres of oaks for firewood, charcoal, crops, and orchards. Ranchers cleared 32,000 acres of oaks *per year* between 1945 and 1973, much of it paid for by the government (2,400 acres per year are now cleared for cattle).[7] Reservoirs flooded many groves, and much larger groves were killed by the reduced stream flows and groundwater depletion that resulted from irrigation diversions and flood control, including such apparently incidental effects as unexpected explosions of gophers, which had earlier been held in check by occasional floods before the dams were built. Gophers eat acorns and decimate young trees. With farmers encouraged to expand crops onto dam-controlled flood plain areas, riparian forests in the Sacramento Valley were reduced to less than 2 percent of their original extent.

Even more alarming than the gross losses, however, is the fact that many of the large oaks seen from the highway were seen by the Spanish and are nearing the end of their life span. Because some of the oaks last 200 to 300 years, their plight lacks the immediacy of the last blue whale, and if a good season came even once in perhaps thirty years, the legacy would be assured, but there has scarcely been a wide-scale, successful nursery crop for the last century.[8] Explanations repeatedly turn to cattle and their secondary effects.[9] Cows eat oak seedlings along with grass, they eat acorns, and they trample young trees. More important, annual grasses, introduced with the herds, have displaced native grasses entirely. The new grasses cover the ground uniformly, unlike the native bunchgrasses had done, and allow less room for oaks and other species. Water hogs compared to native grasses, the introduced species tap inordinate amounts of springtime moisture and preempt it from the oaks. With profuse yields of seeds, the exotic grasses have made explosions of gophers, field mice, and ground squirrels possible. Meanwhile, the nearly religious extermination of predators such as the coyote, fox, and badger has made inevitable the rampage of rodents, hungry for acorns and oak seedlings.

Filling narrow ecological niches, the valley and blue oaks are not being replaced by similar trees. ''When we allow a species to be taken away, not knowing how it will be replaced, that's not stewardship," said Dr. Norman Pillsbury, a forestry professor at California Polytechnic State University at San Luis Obispo and one of the preeminent oak experts. "That's a mining operation. By attrition, we're losing those woodlands and there's nothing on the horizon that will reverse the process. There isn't a single researcher who hasn't met incredible frustration trying to find a way to economically regenerate the valley and blue oaks out on the landscape." About 3 million acres of blue and valley oaks—the third most valuable habitat in the state—will likely degenerate to a monotony of grass and shrubs if current problems remain unsolvable.

Will the future of the oak woodlands depend on the rehabilitation of predator populations so that gophers are kept in check? Has the extermination of native grasses doomed the oaks with which they evolved through the eons? Must we reinstate floods to have a riparian forest? Should we turn to these ecological solutions to arrest the loss of these important species before it's too late? "I'd endorse that approach heartily," Pillsbury said in a 1991 interview. "We've tried the obvious approaches, such as screening off tree plots, and they haven't worked. The consequences of our failure are enormous. Eventually I think we may have to turn to an ecological solution if we want to be successful."

To protect oaks on public land is difficult enough, but the problems of protecting privately owned oaks are formidable. While only 30 percent of conifer forests are found on private land in California, 80 percent of the oaks are, and cattle graze on 75 percent of the oak areas where owners earn a livelihood and support a lifestyle from their use of the land. Most farmers and ranchers now work around the remaining large oaks, but that does nothing to encourage new offspring.

Suburbanization has resulted in the most conspicuous loss of oaks in the last forty years and hit the beleaguered valley, blue, and Engelmann oaks especially hard. Each year, 20,000 acres of oaks are cleared for urban use.

Even oaks that survive the subdividers' grid often die. The sprinklers that soak the vivid lawns so prized in the suburbs kill the oaks, well adapted to summer drought but intolerant to fungi thriving in the sprinklers' wake.

Until 1980, little interest in oak protection surfaced, except by enthusiasts such as members of the California Native Plant Society, but since then, government agencies have recognized the problem, and citizen groups have taken stands trying to protect groves from rampant urbanization.

Rejecting a proposal to regulate the cutting of oaks, even though its own Hardwood Task Force—which included broad representation and gathered widespread public input—recommended it, the California Board of Forestry established an "integrated hardwood range management program" in 1986 for research and public information. In 1989, the state senate passed a resolution ordering all state agencies to assess the effects of their decisions on oak woodlands and to adopt policies to protect oaks under their jurisdictions. The results are due, but nobody expects a revolution in management. The California Oak Foundation has encouraged replanting programs, acquisition of the most valuable sites, and experimental grazing reforms. More than 100 cities and counties have regulations of some type for the protection of oaks, though many of the ordinances have little effect. The Nature Conservancy has acquired several oak preserves, and a few showcase groves are protected in state parks. Oak restoration projects are under way at Yosemite Valley, Malibu Creek State Park, and the Nature Conservancy's Cosumnes River Preserve. The city of Visalia, active in oak protection since 1911, established linear parks for oaks where mowing is discontinued and acorns are allowed to fall on mulch beds and sprout.

Regarding the use of public bond money for acquisition of open space, Gerald H. Meral of the Planning and Conservation League said, "There is more interest in protecting oak woodlands than any other type of land." In 1990, the PCL sponsored Proposition 117, an initiative requiring the state to spend at least $10 million a year to acquire primarily oak woodlands. Acquisition may be the only way to preserve the rare remaining groves of valley oaks, but these efforts will at best safeguard only select sites from loss and do little to solve the regermination problem or halt the fragmentation of habitat throughout urbanizing California. The California Oak Foundation hopes to establish voluntary oak preserves on private lands where land management would favor the oaks.

It is not likely that the valley, blue, and Engelmann oaks will go extinct—they can be raised by hand. But the oak woodlands on any large scale or in an ecologically meaningful context could join the dark history of extermination in California unless we acquire the knowledge and desire to correct the ecological catastrophes of the past. The fate of the oaks may be tied to the fate of predators and native grasses. While the oaks that decorate the landscape from one end of California to the other have survived long after the ruin of their associated grasslands, their ultimate plight illustrates the forces we've unleashed on the ecosystems of California, and the oaks, too, may go the way of the bunchgrasses and the condor if the wide-reaching importance of ecological integrity is not recognized. Without the oaks, the landscape in which people live will become flat and dull, literally without shade and roots, unfortunately matching the communities that take the place of the groves.

"The way we got to where we are was ignorance," said Ginger Strong in a 1991 interview. As president of the California Oak Foundation and city arborist for Visalia, Strong added, "Now we are more aware. Dams have stopped flood waters needed for valley oak propagation, but a bill in Congress would seek to restore some of that balance of life. That's just one example. People are now looking at what we've done and saying, 'Maybe we *do* need some water and space for those trees.' I see some hope that we will quit fighting against the environment and start living *with* it."

RIVERS: FLOWING THROUGH THE HEART OF CALIFORNIA

It is perhaps the most magnificent system of rivers in America; certainly it is the most varied, most used, and most fought over. The rivers of California show the life of the state, from mossy coastal forests to flash floods in the Mojave, from ice-bound headwaters on Mount Lyell to brackish bay waters at the Delta. The 103 named rivers and hundreds of streams signify life, highlight the land, and tie it all together, from mountaintop to ocean. By seeing the rivers, you will see California, and a remarkable sight it is.

In the far north, the Smith River flows as a national gem, wealthy with green water to match green shores. The Klamath, second-largest river in the state, ranks as one of America's finest steelhead fisheries, with one of the longer free-flowing reaches on the West Coast—188 miles. The Trinity drains vast, wild forests, as does the Eel, winding through redwoods. The Mattole lies secretive and idyllic between ridges of the Coast Range. The Noyo snakes through lush greenery, and the Russian sees more fun-loving canoeists than nearly any other river in America. The Sacramento, California's longest and largest river, has one remaining reach of natural low-land habitat, a showcase of the riparian heritage that once ran throughout the valley. From the forested wilderness south of Mount Shasta, the McCloud River runs through shaded rapids and pools.

Fifteen major rivers burst brilliantly from the peaks of the Sierra Nevada. The largest—the Feather—is considered by some to be the most beautiful river in California. The Yuba returned from a brutal heritage of gold mining to be a superb recreational river, as did the American—the most popular whitewater in the American West. Boaters prize the Tuolumne—also an outstanding trout stream—as one of the finest difficult whitewater runs in the nation. The Merced is an elegant showcase of Yosemite Valley. The Kings displays the greatest undammed vertical drop of any river in North America and its deepest canyon; the Kern crashes wildly from the slopes of Mount Whitney. In the Coast Range, the Sespe drains the largest unprotected roadless area in the state and the heart of the endangered California condor's habitat. These are just some of the rivers, outstanding in appeal.

The other side of the California rivers picture is, unfortunately, as grim as the previously described side is bright. Only one major river system remains free of dams—the Smith. Even where the 1,336 large dams are not found,[10] their effects are; irrigation diversions at the dams or below them have reduced long sections of river to wreckage, and the near-elimination of floods has ruined many riverbeds and riparian zones. Pollution has claimed thousands of miles—much of the lower San Joaquin, for example, is poisoned, desiccated, and dead. Land development crowds other banks and preempts ever more acreage of the wildlife-rich riparian zone. The Trinity River has been shunted south, decimating 90 percent of its rich salmon run. The most popular whitewater and deepest limestone canyon in the West was flooded at the Stanislaus in 1982, though the river returned phoenixlike in 1990, when New Melones Dam was drawn down during the drought, once again exposing the magnificent, immortal river, to which Californians immediately flocked in rafts, kayaks, and on foot, feasting on the sight of the Stanislaus once again.

Even on national forest land, where at least half of the water in the state originates and where many of the quality rivers wind their way through the mountains, 1,200 dams have been built, and new ones go up without Forest Service objection in such extraordinary places as Gabbott Meadow in the North Fork Stanislaus basin. The agency in charge of husbanding the forests readily permits private developers and water districts to cash in the woodland, wildland, wildlife, and river values for a few more kilowatts of electricity, which could readily be provided by modest conservation efforts.[11]

The work to protect California rivers has been intensely waged in Congress and the state capital, in local communities, and in media of all kinds. As of 1991, national wild and scenic river status prohibiting dams or destructive water projects has been granted to eleven major rivers and a number of their tributaries (see Figure 17.2). Though older campaigns were waged for particular fishing reaches or to improve water quality, concentrated efforts to protect a broad range of river values began only in the late 1960s. Since then, only three major water projects have been built: the North Fork Stanislaus hydroelectric project, New Melones Dam on the Stanislaus, and Warm Springs Dam on Dry Creek, a tributary of the Russian River. The tightening economics of development, the exhaustion of practical dam sites, and the political mobilization of river enthusiasts with coalitions were all effective in bringing to a standstill the type of development that has left so little natural remaining.

Yet, as conservationists gain strength and more people see the need for natural places and free-flowing rivers, the population of California soars, the demand for water increases, the price of hydropower will escalate, the grip of agribusiness tightens, and the specter of drought worsens. With a new round of threats, there is new evidence of gross riparian losses, endangered species, the crash of anadromous fisheries, and the insidious effects of dams and diversions on downstream river reaches, with devastating riverbed modifications.[12] Evidence mounts that even ocean beaches are being ruined by the excess of dams on rivers: silt, trapped in reservoirs, flows no longer to the sea and cannot balance the natural erosion of sand by waves.

Groups such as Friends of the River, operating on lean resources but as imaginative as artists and tenacious as bulldogs, push their agenda for balance in the management of California water and try to overturn a history that has dammed rivers as a matter of principle, diverted 100 percent of the flow from waterways as significant as the Kings, Kern, and San Joaquin, and allowed creatures as

FIGURE 17.2

THE NATIONAL WILD AND SCENIC RIVERS OF CALIFORNIA, 1991

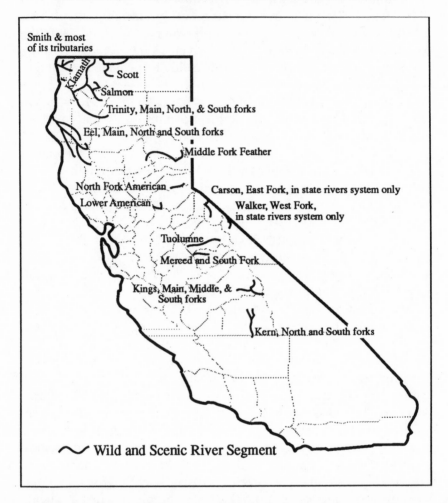

Smith & most
of its tributaries

Scott

Salmon

Trinity, Main, North, & South forks

Eel, Main, North and South forks

Middle Fork Feather

North Fork American

Lower American

Carson, East Fork, in state rivers system only

Walker, West Fork,
in state rivers system only

Tuolumne

Merced and South Fork

Kings, Main, Middle, &
South forks

Kern, North and South forks

∿ Wild and Scenic River Segment

emblematic of environmental quality as the chinook salmon to become species rapidly bound for extinction.[13]

Six major river protection themes are emerging for the coming years.

1. Auburn Dam. While the era of big dam construction died, the proposal for one particular big dam did not. Originally planned as a huge multipurpose reservoir above Sacramento on the American River, Auburn Dam became an anachronism from a bygone era. It would have cost too much, destroyed too much, and benefited too

few. But in 1991, for flood control, a new dam was proposed. Though alternatives, including levee improvements, flood plain management, and a smaller flood control dam, would provide protection,[14] the Army Corps of Engineers proposal would periodically flood forty miles of extraordinary canyons used by half a million people a year.[15]

2. Hydropower. New hydroelectric dams are proposed at several dozen sites, and a rise in energy costs could push them to a feasible level. Threatened are such streams as the trout fishery of Rock Creek in the eastern Sierra, the wilderness of the Clavey River, a popular recreation section of the Mokelumne, and the most used whitewater river in southern California, the lower Kern, each project yielding a pittance of power.

3. National forest and Bureau of Land Management rivers. Protection of public lands rivers has become a new focus as the Forest Service modifies plans criticized by citizens in the 1980s, as it responds to directives from the agency chief to recommend rivers for national wild and scenic protection, and as the BLM initiates a similar study process. Friends of the River launched a "100 rivers campaign" to designate the finest Forest Service streams. With two-thirds of its forest plans complete, the Forest Service recommended thirty-one segments for designation, though virtually all threatened rivers were bypassed to give developers free rein.

4. Anadromous fisheries. The protection of salmon, steelhead, and other species that live in the ocean but swim up the rivers to spawn is one of the most critical river issues in the West. With the Sacramento River winter-run chinook salmon listed as an endangered species, federal agencies are obligated to make the fish's survival a priority. Lawsuits such as the Natural Resources Defense Council's action against the Bureau of Reclamation over the total diversion of the San Joaquin will continue and will play increasing havoc on the one-sided use of rivers that still prevails, even after the times and public opinion have dramatically changed. New management to restore some of the anadromous runs is the only long-term answer.

5. Riparian habitat. The preservation and restoration of this supremely important habitat will be a central issue of the coming decades. Three-quarters of the state's wildlife species are dependent on riverfront or water-influenced habitat, while 90 percent of that habitat has been destroyed by water projects, agriculture, grazing,

and development. The solutions lie in improved releases from dams, restoration of shorelines destroyed by levees and agriculture, flood plain zoning, and grazing reform.

6. Urban rivers. River conservation will grow as a people's movement in areas accessible to the crowds. California's cities once had quality rivers flowing through them. Sacramento's parkway along the American River, used by 5.5 million people a year, constitutes one of the nation's finest examples of capitalizing on the open space of an urban river. Similar opportunities exist with the San Joaquin River in Fresno, the Sacramento River in Redding, and the Feather River in Marysville, where river parks could well become the highlight if not the salvation of the towns. River recreation is a common denominator across social, economic, racial, and ethnic lines; healthy rivers are a resource that all Californians can use.

To address these themes requires more than the site-specific campaigns of the past and more than the legal challenges to the agencies that serve up 80 percent of the state's usable water supplies to agriculture with only token amounts to all other users. Citizen organizations and government agencies, such as the General Accounting Office, have been saying for years that federal water projects, subsidized up to 92 percent, should not be so one-sidedly the domain of large agricultural interests.[16] That message finally seems to be taking hold, and a willingness to consider all uses of rivers is becoming more common with the government, the courts, and the public at large. One sign of changing times was the proposed Rogers Crossing Dam on the Kings River in 1987, defeated in Fresno—the heart of the agribusiness industry—even though big water users proposed and fought for the dam with virtually unlimited funds.

In a 1991 interview, David Bolling, the executive director of Friends of the River and a participant in unprecedented three-way talks between environmentalists and urban and agricultural water contractors who are seeking solutions to water supply problems, had this to say: "Rivers will remain at risk as long as outdated and destructive policies govern the management and allocation of water. If we can make the environment an equal partner in water policy decision making, we may be able to protect what is left of the river system and even restore some of what has been mindlessly destroyed."

The rivers will never really be protected, however, until their watersheds are protected. More than any other feature, California's rivers integrate the landscape and remind people that the fabric of the state is woven together in delicate patterns touching each other. The rivers are evidence that anything less than ecosystem management will mean an impoverished California for the future. Erosion from haphazard logging or illegal dumping of toxic wastes at the top of a river affects people far below. The quality of the entire environment could be symbolized by the spawning journey of salmon, which need pristine headwaters, clean water in a free-flowing river, and a nourishing ocean. The cycle of the rivers and the health of their flow could well be a measurement of all that we do to the environment of the Golden State.

CHAPTER 18

An Action Agenda for the Future

GERALD H. MERAL

PROTECTING AND RESTORING CALIFORNIA

While reading this book and this chapter, each Californian might keep in mind that a spectrum of environmental quality is available to us. At one end is the goal we all seek: a state with clean air, plentiful open space, abundant fish and wildlife, efficient transportation corridors, sparkling pure water, uncrowded parks, and beautiful urban landscapes.

We all know that such an environmental Eden is rarely achieved. The other end of the spectrum has become all too common throughout the world: skies heavily veiled from pollution, wildlife so depleted that a bird song is a rarity, roads so crowded that driving to a city center is tightly regulated, urbanization so dense that the

Gerald H. Meral received his doctorate in zoology from the University of California at Berkeley. He served four years as staff scientist at the Environmental Defense Fund and eight years as deputy director of the California Department of Water Resources. He is executive director of the Planning and Conservation League and the PCL Foundation. He created and ran the successful initiative campaigns for the 1988 Wildlife and Park Bond Act, the 1990 Rail Bond Act, and the 1990 Wildlife Protection Act.

sole open space is the land within freeway interchanges, and forests stripped so long ago that they remain only a distant memory.

Dismal scenes such as these are, in fact, typical in much of the rest of the world, and such a future is possible in California. The reaction of decision makers and citizens to the message that our environment must be protected and restored will determine which future California will have. The decisions will be made by the governor, the legislature, and the people in the coming decade, and they will largely be irreversible.

Some will argue that California cannot afford to restore and maintain anything approaching an ideal environment; they will say that the economic costs are far too high. In fact, in a resource-rich state such as this, the ability to sustain the productivity of the land, to keep money inside the state's borders rather than squandering it on imported oil and gas, and to create an environment attractive enough to retain existing businesses and to attract tourists is vital to our continued economic well-being and to prevent high unemployment.

Environmental protection should be a stimulus, not a drag, on the economy. Much of the technological knowledge needed to make the environment safe and productive can and should be developed by California industry, which has a history of technological innovation.

In many of the solutions proposed below, new taxes and revenue sources are called for. Some will argue that the state cannot afford these programs. But each new environmental improvement program should be examined in the hard light of economic effectiveness. If the new program passes that test, the legislature should not be afraid to approve it. One way to make these proposals economically viable is to remove the enormous subsidies to consumption and resource depletion that currently exist in local, state, and federal laws.

If the legislature is concerned that the measures proposed here might go beyond what the voters would support, then these proposals should be submitted directly to the voters, who in 1988 approved a large increase in the tobacco tax to fund health and environmental programs, and in 1990 voted to raise the gasoline tax for transportation purposes. Voters in nearly every urban county have approved sales tax increases for transportation, environmental, and criminal justice purposes. In each case, the key to approval was establishment of dedicated funds for specific purposes—a successful model used to develop the following program of environmental restoration.

AN AGENDA FOR POLITICAL ACTION

The problems described in this book could appear to be hopelessly confusing unless placed in a larger context. Ecologists often say that everything is tied to everything else, yet California's environmental problems can be viewed in several discrete categories:

- Population growth and urban water use.
- Urban problems, including energy, land use, air quality, and transportation.
- The resource base, including rural lands, forests, parks, wildlife, and rivers.
- Waste and recycling.

Population growth in California is due to internal growth coupled with continued heavy immigration. Since irrigation in California has been stable for years, the cause of increased water use is solely population growth in urban areas.

Urban problems are among our most serious environmental issues, resulting from the ways we have allowed our cities to grow. Urban growth after World War II has been mostly horizontal, with sprawling business parks, subdivisions, and light industry covering rapidly increasing amounts of the California landscape. Poorly planned growth has resulted in auto-dependent transportation systems. The vast increase in driving needed for people to get to work, shop, and recreate has resulted in an enormous increase in energy consumption and air pollution. There is still no statewide approach even under serious consideration by the legislature to remedy poor land use planning.

The resource base of California's land and water is fundamentally treated as disposable. Nowhere is this more evident than in our use of agricultural and forest lands. Forestry during the past two decades has consisted of a mining operation depleting trees, soils, wildlife habitat, and fisheries. The idea that forest soils should be kept in place for future generations has barely been considered, let alone implemented. With the loss of soils comes loss of forest productivity, fouling of streams, and destruction of forest landscapes.

Agricultural land use suffers from lack of concern regarding long-term productivity of the soil and from conversion of farmland to urban uses. The division of prime agricultural lands into unproductive "ranchettes," the transformation of farmlands to suburbia, and the treatment of farmworkers as if they are disposable resources who can be poisoned by agricultural chemicals reveals a completely inappropriate attitude about rural lands and peoples.

By treating fish and wildlife as disposable resources, we are losing our biological heritage. Little is done to restore endangered species, hundreds of which are not even officially listed as threatened. Loss of fisheries is blamed on sport and commercial anglers, but nothing is done about the tremendous damage done by water development and logging. Preference for short-term economic gain again results in long-term economic and environmental loss.

Waste management is the key to many of California's environmental problems. We do not treat our chemical and mineral resources as renewable, resulting in an enormous waste of resources and energy. Imposing high taxes to recycle while giving tax breaks to mine new minerals results in the creation and disposal of toxic and solid waste rather than recycling and waste prevention.

SOLVING THE PROBLEMS

A number of solutions to the problems discussed in the preceding chapters appear to be environmentally necessary, economically feasible, and politically possible.

Population

While there is no longer any serious debate about the problems associated with population growth, neither is there any serious debate about what should be done to reduce that growth. Poll after poll shows that voters want to reduce the rate of population growth, but not a single bill addressing the problem has been introduced in the legislature in the past twenty years.

Those willing to address the issue worry that they will be accused of racial or economic bias, even though population growth probably impacts disadvantaged residents even more than others. Job competition, low wages, and unemployment are results of runaway population increases. Water scarcity, habitat loss, and a host of other environmental problems result, especially in urban areas.

California should assist the federal government in enforcing existing immigration laws. Compared to other countries, our laws are very liberal in allowing new immigration. At least those limits should be strictly enforced at our borders, factories, and fields. California should also revise its tax, welfare, and other statutes and eliminate incentives that encourage or reward reproduction. The legislature should eliminate tax deductions beyond the second child; provide free contraception information, education, and devices; and undertake a major educational program to encourage smaller family size.

Urban Problems

California is the most urbanized state, with more than 90 percent of its people living in cities and towns. The quality of urban life ultimately will define our environmental quality as a whole.

Nothing will solve the problems of urban areas unless the land use and transportation complex is modified. There are several ways to do this—some with state assistance and some that must be implemented at the local level. The state must provide massive incentives and assistance to implement a "European" transportation system. We simply must put into place a public transportation system that makes it possible to commute and travel without a car and that makes transit more desirable than going by car.

Transit's share of the transportation market has not grown in the last decade. In areas of severe sprawl, such as Contra Costa and Orange counties, transportation "experts" argue that low densities make public transportation permanently impractical. But there are things that can be done to make transit workable.

We must level the field between cars and transit. Public dollars must be moved from parking structures and road building to transit. Appropriate sources of funds for transit are gasoline taxes, downtown redevelopment funds, and general funds. Highway advocates will argue that gas taxes are paid by motorists—what better way to spend them than reducing highway congestion and making the roads more usable? These measures will also promote ride-sharing among those who must drive to work.

The state should provide financial incentives to local agencies that create high-density zoning around transit corridors and stations; nothing will induce use of transit more than people living and working near it.

All the costs of sprawl must be borne by those who live and work in it. New development beyond the urban fringe should not be subsidized by those already living within urban limit lines. By simply requiring local jurisdictions to impose all the costs of extending water, sewer, energy, transportation, and other utilities on those seeking to build in prime agricultural and other lands beyond the urban fringe, governments could cause this sprawl to quickly come to an end. Once urban areas are built up to what zoning allows, expansion of urban limit lines could be considered.

Local government should be prohibited from approving any new development unless it can certify that the infrastructure needed to support it—electricity, gas, water, sewer, roads, schools, police, and fire protection—is already available, or will be provided by the developer. All new office and manufacturing development should have associated housing to allow for minimal commuting distances. The state must ensure that these rules are enforced.

To recognize California's responsibility in creating the greenhouse effect through pollution of the atmosphere by carbon dioxide and other chemicals, we should impose a fee on energy generated from fossil or biomass fuels and use the money (up to several hundred million dollars a year) to create the type of electrified transit infrastructure that would greatly reduce traffic congestion, air pollution, and continued carbon dioxide generation. This plan of electrification should include investing heavily in a California-based solar electric-generation industry. Such an efficient technology could eventually make possible a serious effort toward electrification of the automobile.

The Resource Base

California's vast natural resources are the envy of other states and countries and the foundation of our wealth. Tourism, heavily reliant on scenic quality and natural beauty, is the state's largest industry.

The watchword and guiding principle of California resource management must become "sustainability." This is not some far-reaching concept about taking care of the next ten generations; it is a practical necessity to prevent the state from sliding into ruin in the coming few decades.

If there is a single, horrible example that California can learn from, it is how forests have been managed over the past twenty years. Because of the nonsustainable clear-cutting of our private forest lands, local economies have been devastated, commercial and sport fisheries demolished, wildlife depleted, and much of the scenic attractiveness of the North Coast and Sierra lost for decades or forever.

This type of resource plundering is the antithesis of sustainability. A steady, sustained flow of forest products, including healthy fish and wildlife populations, could make the North Coast one of California's most attractive places to live. Changes were recently proposed to improve state law to require sustained-yield forestry. The Board of Forestry should enact regulations that require monitoring of forest soils to ensure they are not lost on steep, erosion prone slopes.

Covering much of the mountain regions of the state, our national forests must be managed to provide a steady stream of wood, wildlife, water, and fisheries. This will guarantee stable local mountain economies.

Agriculture suffers from schizophrenia regarding preservation of California farmland. Farmers know their economic and political power is derived from the giant farm economy, but a farmer's greatest asset is the ability to convert farmland to urban uses. Some have argued that saving irrigated California farmland is futile, since, historically, all irrigated land salts up. However, modern irrigation technology can keep most farmland in production for a century or more—long enough to make preservation worthwhile.

Should all farmland be saved? No. A great deal of water was imported into coastal southern California for urban development. While waiting for that development to occur, some of the water was temporarily put into agricultural use. Now the water is needed for urbanization, and only the highest-value crops will remain. Even water that was originally dedicated to agriculture, as in the Imperial Valley, will slowly be converted to urban use as southern California's population grows, because it is the cheapest available water source for the urban areas.

Likewise, irrigation that uses a disproportionate share of water for low-value crops anywhere in our dry state should be gradually discontinued. Some examples of irrationally wasteful water use include growing federally subsidized rice and irrigation of mountain pastures to grow increasingly marginal livestock. Likewise, irrigating in areas where toxic drainage water is created should be discontinued. State and federal subsidies for these crops and irrigation systems should be immediately discontinued, and strict water conservation and pollution-control regulations should be imposed. If irrigation of these lands and crops were discontinued, it would be possible to use the water to restore much of California's lost fisheries and wetlands.

But the vast majority of productive farmland and highly productive coastal grasslands should be preserved in perpetuity. The easiest way would be to zone them for agriculture permanently at the state level. While most Californians would agree that this is the highest and best use of these lands, organized agriculture virulently opposes the loss of a farmer's ability to sell out to developers.

Given that political reality, farmers should at least endorse the following system. Part of the huge profit developers make by converting farmland to development would be taxed by the state. The revenue would be used to acquire development rights in other endangered farmlands. The acquisition of a development right means that in the future the land can be used only for farming. Thus the development of a small fraction of the state's productive farmland could finance the preservation of much of the rest of it.

Sustaining agriculture on the urban fringe may also require state support for marketing, irrigation drainage, and other farm systems. Farms can help define the urban boundary, and state and local assistance to overcome the stresses of urban neighbors may be worthwhile. The use of agricultural chemicals seriously reduces biodiversity, causes cancer and birth defects, and causes tremendous health problems among farmers and farmworkers. The state should provide special emphasis and funding for programs to develop methods of chemical-free farming.

Sustainability must also become the management plan for the native plants and animals of California. While much has already been lost, we need to stabilize and restore native plant, fish, and wildlife populations. Large areas of the state must be managed for biological diversity. The cost of such a system of preserves and managed lands will be tens of billions of dollars, and there is great urgency since much continues to be lost today.

The only way we can afford such a system of preserves is through local, state, and federal funding, and by requiring those who would develop habitat to save some and pay for the preservation and restoration of additional habitat. Funds such as the tobacco tax approved by the state's voters in 1988 and 1990 need to be established to remove from the legislature the temptation to raid the funds when economic crises arrive.

The most logical funds would be taxes on water and land use, since these uses are what cause habitat loss. Billions of dollars a year can be generated. A 10 percent property tax increase would generate 2 billion dollars a year. Taxing just urban water consumers four dollars a month would raise more than 600 million dollars a year. These are the amounts needed for aggressive restoration of biological diversity and maintenance of environmental quality.

These large new funds can be shared with other social programs. Vermont uses a real estate transfer tax to fund both land preservation and housing programs. Building necessary housing for lower-income people within urban limit lines would be a worthy use of such funds in California.

Waste and Recycling

As so eloquently pointed out in chapters 12 and 13 of this book, waste generation by people and industry is a serious problem. It is a familiar problem to microbiologists: as a mass of organisms generate waste, they eventually make life in their test tube impossible because of the waste poisons they create.

California is not so large as to escape the same fate. Overflowing and leaking landfills, pollutants flowing with insufficient treatment to the ocean, hundreds of thousands of tons of industrial waste shipped to poorly regulated landfills in other western states, more than a ton of solid waste generated from each Californian, tumbling prices for recycled materials—these are all signs of a system seriously out of balance.

To bring the system back into balance, the state must adopt the principle of sustainability described above. The guiding principle of our tax and fee system must be preference to reuse over creation (and disposal) of new materials. This principle can be applied in the following ways.

- Apply stiff extraction fees on mining (including minerals and oil) and use the revenue to create incentives to purchase and recycle materials that have already been produced.
- Require a high level of recycled material content in certain products, such as paper, packaging, glass, and steel.
- Heavily tax or prohibit outright the use of wasteful materials in packaging and other forms of consumption.
- Require all governments to give preference to purchase of recycled materials, even when up to 20 percent more expensive than materials made from virgin stock; this will partially neutralize nationwide subsidies for the use of virgin materials.
- Apply fees to generators of toxic and hazardous materials that will create incentives to reuse the materials on site instead of disposing of them in water, air, or on land. These fees could replace existing high disposal fees.
- To avoid dumping our waste problem on other states and nations, require that California dispose of its waste within our borders.

With the guiding principle of a closed planetary system, the idea of sustainability can help create a more robust California economy and greatly improve the quality of our environment.

A Personal Action Agenda

The condition of California as described in this book could inspire one of two personal reactions. The first is that the Golden State will become a hopeless environmental basket case with fouled air and water, devoid of beauty and biological diversity, and crowded beyond tolerance and comprehension. The second is that while environmental conditions are bad and growing worse, decisive citizen action can correct many of our problems, and California can restore its tarnished environmental amenities.

We hope you will finish these pages with the second reaction. To make that hope become a reality, we urge you to adopt a personal agenda that will help make California's environmental restoration possible.

Population growth stymies even moderate environmental progress. More than half our growth comes from an excess of births over deaths. As pointed out in this book, preserving land and cleaning up pollution cannot solve the problem if California is inflicted with additional millions of even clean cars and well-designed subdivisions covering the landscape. Do your part: limit your family to two children.

Land use is decided at the local level, and the accumulation of unwise land use decisions is destroying our state. Challenge decisions that do not recognize the impact of development on transportation, air quality, and wildlife. Make sure that new development pays its fair share of the costs of new infrastructure, including housing for all Californians, not just the wealthy.

Seek reform of our political system. The fact that we allow the environmental decision makers—our city council members, county supervisors, and legislators—to take large contributions from special interests and still vote on their projects and programs makes it difficult to achieve real environmental reforms. Challenge the vote of an elected official who takes money from the economic interest group affected by the official's vote.

You are not alone. Join a local or state conservation group and become active. If no group is doing what needs to be done, start your own.

Be bold in your vision of California's future. When is the last time you heard a politician talk about what is needed to make this state livable a hundred years from now? Or even in twenty years? We have a right to a better environment today, and future Californians have a right to what we have today. If we do not plan for a sustainable future, we may as well give up the fight.

We must plan for the preservation of what we have and the replenishment of what we once had. The goal must be restoration, since what we have today is too polluted, defaced, and developed to provide the quality of life all Californians deserve.

We must involve all Californians in the effort to provide a good quality of life, including ethnically diverse people who are rapidly becoming the majority. Every Californian must benefit from environmental restoration.

California has been the cradle of much of the world's most advanced technology, which should be called on to clean up difficult pollution problems, provide energy efficiency, find agricultural chemicals that have the minimum impact on health and wildlife, and develop vehicles that produce far less pollution than those of today. In creating these technologies, environmentally sound industries and jobs will also be created.

The conservation community of California has never been stronger. Membership is at record levels, and people in poll after poll say that they consider themselves environmentalists. This public support must be translated into real results through action by the legislature and the governor.

The political leadership in California needs to put this desire of Californians for a better environment to work. In light of an awesome growth rate, voters are desperate for some way to improve their quality of life. Politicians who respond to that desire will be those who are most successful in the coming years.

We cannot make progress without a vision of what we seek. We will never restore the California that many of us still remember. But we can have clean air and water, we can restore much of the biological diversity that makes California unique, and we can preserve and repair much of our remaining beautiful landscape.

The only way to achieve these goals is the involvement of every concerned citizen. Without that, continued and even accelerated degradation will be our fate. As you put down this book, think about the kind of California you want, and act on your beliefs. The future of our state is in your hands.

Notes

CHAPTER 1

1. Bob Hall and Mary Lee Kerr, *The 1991–1992 Green Index* (Washington, D.C.: Island Press, 1991), 3, 11.
2. Jones and Stokes Associates, *Sliding toward Extinction: The State of California's Natural Heritage* (Sacramento: The Nature Conservancy, 1987). Available from The Nature Conservancy, 785 Market Street, San Francisco, Calif. 94103.

CHAPTER 2

1. Ramon G. McLeod, "The Challenge Posed by State's Ethnic Mix," *San Francisco Chronicle*, February 26, 1991.
2. Dan Walters, *The New California* (Sacramento: California Journal Press, 1986), 15.
3. California Department of Finance, computer printouts, 1991.
4. California Department of Finance, *Projected Total Population for California* (Sacramento: Department of Finance, February 1988), unpublished paper.
5. California Department of Finance, computer printouts, 1991.
6. Walters, *The New California*, 14.
7. Nancy Vogel, "Is California Bursting at the Seams?" *California Journal*, July 1991.
8. Ibid.
9. Judith Kunofsky, "Why Limiting Population Growth Is So Difficult to Talk About in California," *The Social Contract*, Spring 1991.
10. The Roper Organization Inc, commissioned by the Federation for American Immigration Reform, *American Attitudes toward Immigration* (Washington, D.C.: Federation for American Immigration Reform, 1990), unpublished paper.

CHAPTER 3

1. Jane Hall et al., "Valuing the Health Benefits of Clean Air," *Science*, February 14, 1992, 812.
2. South Coast Air Quality Management District, *Draft Air Quality Management Plan*, (El Monte, Calif.: December 1990).
3. Dalia M. Spektor et al., "Effects of Ambient Ozone on Vigorously Exercising Children to 0.12 ppm Ozone Exposure," *American Review of Respiratory Diseases* (1988): 133.
4. Morton Lippman, "Health Effects of Ozone: A Critical Review," *Journal of the Air Pollution Control Association* (1989): 672.
5. Russell Sherwin, "Centriacinar Region (CAR) Disease in the Lungs of Young Adults: A Preliminary Report," in *Tropospheric Ozone and the Environment*, eds. Ronald L. Berglund et al. (Pittsburgh: Air and Waste Management Association, 1991), 178.
6. California Air Resources Board, *The Atmospheric Acidity Protection Program: Annual Report to the Governor and the Legislature, 1990* (Sacramento: California Air Resources Board, 1990).
7. Tom Knudson, "Smog Fouls Crystal-Clear Mountain Air: The Sierra in Peril," *Sacramento Bee*, June 10, 1991, 1.
8. California Air Resources Board, *Air Quality and Growth in the San Joaquin Valley* (Sacramento: California Air Resources Board, January 1989).
9. Judy Pasternak, "Pollution Is Choking Farm Belt," *Los Angeles Times*, April 22, 1991, 1.
10. California Air Resources Board, *Air Quality and Growth in the San Joaquin Valley*.
11. Pasternak, "Pollution Is Choking Farm Belt."
12. Knudson, "Smog Fouls Crystal-Clear Mountain Air."
13. California Air Resources Board, *California Air Quality Data: Summary of 1988 Air Quality Data Gaseous and Particulate Pollutants* (Sacramento: California Air Resources Board, 1989).
14. South Coast Air Quality Management District, *Draft Air Quality Management Plan*.
15. Lloyd G. Connelly, "A Proposal to Gradually Halt Burning of Rice Straw," *Sacramento Bee*, April 25, 1991.
16. California Air Resources Board, *California Air Quality: A Status Report*, (Sacramento: California Air Resources Board, 1990).

CHAPTER 4

1. R. Doctor et al., *California's Electricity Quandary III: Slowing the Growth Rate* (Santa Monica: Rand Corporation, September 1972).
2. Thousand Springs, a large, coal-fired plant proposed for northeastern Nevada, recently met its demise due to a lack of potential buyers for its power from the nation's fastest-growing region. In spite of such seemingly clear market signals, the Bush administration continues its strong support for the coal industry in the National Energy Strategy. After an introduction replete with glowing references to "the free market" and "government nonintervention," the Strategy goes on to note proudly the federal government's intention to be a "financial partner" with the coal industry in its new Clean Coal Technologies program.
3. Nancy Rader, *The Power of the States: A Fifty-State Survey of Renewable Energy* (Washington, D.C.: Public Citizen, June 1990).
4. Coalition for Energy Efficiency and Renewable Technologies, *A Vision for California* (Sacramento: Coalition for Energy Efficiency and Renewable Technologies, 1991).
5. California Energy Commmission, *Energy Efficiency Report* (Sacramento: California Energy Commission, October 1990), 1, 19, 20, 89.
6. All air pollution and automotive statistics in this section are taken from California Energy Commission, *Energy Efficiency Report*, chapters 2 and 7.
7. In 1988, the federal government predicted, at most, a 0.127 percent increase in oil spills as a result of its decision to reduce the average fuel economy of 1989 and 1990 cars. In those two years alone, the *Exxon Valdez* spilled 11 million gallons in Alaska, the *American Trader* (running over its own anchor) spilled 390,000 gallons in Los Angeles Harbor, and more than 700,000 gallons leaked into New York Harbor between January and February 1990 from three separate pipeline and barge accidents. Natural Resources Defense Council, "No Safe Harbor: Tanker Safety in America's Ports" (San Francisco: Natural Resources Defense Council, 1990).
8. John Javna, Seth Zuckerman, and Chris Calwell, *30 Simple Energy Things You Can Do to Save the Earth* (Berkeley: Earthworks Press & Southern California Edison, 1991), 9.
9. John Harte and Erika Hoffman, "Possible Effects of Acidic Deposition on a Rocky Mountain Population of the Tiger Salamander *Ambystoma tigrinum*," *Conservation Biology*, June 1989, 149–58.
10. D. Lashof and D. Tirpak, eds., *Policy Options for Stabilizing Global*

Climate, draft report to Congress (Washington, D.C.: U.S. Environmental Protection Agency, February 1989).

11. The National Academy of Sciences offers the following reassurance: "While adaptation [for a coastal city] might be costly, the costs would in most cases be lower than the cost of moving the city." National Academy of Sciences, *Policy Implications of Greenhouse Warming* (Washington, D.C.: National Academy Press, 1991), 46.

12. California Energy Commission, *Global Climate Change: Potential Impacts and Policy Recommendations*, draft (Sacramento: California Energy Commission, March 1991), 6-2.

13. California Energy Commission, *The Impacts of Global Warming on California*, interim report (Sacramento: California Energy Commission, June 1989), 84.

14. Many of the most powerful greenhouse gases have atmospheric lifetimes of 50 to 200 years. Thus, even if we reduced emissions to zero today, the gases emitted yesterday would continue warming the planet for generations to come.

15. National Academy of Sciences, *Policy Implications of Greenhouse Warming*, 62 (approximated from Figure 6.4).

16. Chris Calwell, Allen Edwards, Cliff Gladstein, and Lily Lee, *Clearing the Air: The Dollars and Sense of Proposition 128's Atmospheric Protection Provisions* (San Francisco: Natural Resources Defense Council, September 1990).

17. Calwell, Edwards, Gladstein and Lee, *Clearing the Air*, 38–44.

18. Chris Calwell and Ralph Cavanagh, *The Decline of Conservation at California Utilities: Causes, Costs and Remedies* (San Francisco: Natural Resources Defense Council, July 1989).

19. Marc Ledbetter and Marc Ross, *Supply Curves of Conserved Energy for Automobiles* (Berkeley: Lawrence Berkeley Laboratories, March 1990).

20. California Energy Commission, *Conservation Report* (Sacramento: California Energy Commission, October 1988), 9.

CHAPTER 5

1. Southern California Association of Governments, *Regional Mobility Plan, 1989* (Los Angeles: Southern California Association of Governments, 1989), I-2.

2. Jennifer Coverdale, "League Wins Transit Funding Suit," *Tahoe Daily Tribune*, May 7, 1991, 2A.

3. Assembly Transportation Committee, *Hearing on Gas Tax Apportionments: Counties* (Sacramento: California Legislature, 1985).

4. Natural Resources Defense Council, *Clearing the Air* (San Francisco: Natural Resources Defense Council, September 1990), 20.

5. Department of the California Highway Patrol, *1989 Annual Report of Fatal and Injury Motor Vehicle Traffic Accidents* (Sacramento: Department of the California Highway Patrol, 1989).

6. Gray Davis, *Financial Transactions Concerning Transit Operators and Non-Transit Claimants under the Transportation Development Act, Annual Report 1989–90* (Sacramento: State Controller, 1990), Table 4.

7. Federal Highway Administration, *Highway Statistics 1989* (Washington, D.C.: Federal Highway Administration, 1989), 39.

8. Environmental Defense Fund and Regional Institute of Southern California, *Transportation Efficiency: Tackling Southern California's Air Pollution and Congestion* (Berkeley: Environmental Defense Fund, March 1991), 21.

9. Campaign for New Transportation Priorities, *Transportation and Tax Policy* (Washington, D.C.: Campaign for New Transportation Policies, 1991), 2.

10. Gray Davis, *Financial Transactions Concerning Streets and Roads of Cities and Counties of California, Annual Report 1988–89* (Sacramento: State Controller, 1989), xii, xvii.

11. Senate Advisory Committee on Cost Control in State Government, *Getting the Most Out of California's Transportation Dollar* (Sacramento: California Legislature, October 1990), 39.

12. Applied Management and Planning Group, *Traffic Congestion and Capacity Increases* (San Francisco: Sierra Club Legal Defense Fund and Citizens for a Better Environment, August 1990). See also R. Remak and S. Rosenbloom, *Peak Period Traffic Congestion*, Transportation Research Board Special Report 169 (Washington, D.C.: Transportation Research Board, 1976), 62.

13. Environmental Defense Fund and Regional Institute of Southern California, *Transportation Efficiency: Tackling Southern California's Air Pollution and Congestion*, 20.

14. Ibid., 11.

15. Ibid., 4.

16. American Public Transit Association, *Mass Transit: The Clean Air Alternative* (Washington, D.C.: American Public Transit Association, 1990). Brochure.

17. Applied Management and Planning Group, *Traffic Congestion and Capacity Increases*.

18. California Transportation Commission, *Seventh Annual Report to California Legislature* (Sacramento: California Transportation Commission, December 1990), i-62.

19. Peter Newman and Jeffrey Kenworthy, "Gasoline Consumption

and Cities," *Journal of the American Planning Association*, Winter 1989.

20. Senate Advisory Committee on Cost Control in State Government, *Getting the Most Out of California's Transportation Dollar*, 17.

21. Campaign for New Transportation Priorities, *Urban and Suburban Transportation* (Washington, D.C.: Campaign for New Transportation Priorities, 1991), 5.

22. Ibid.

23. Richard W. Willson and Donald C. Shoup, *The Effects of Employer-paid Parking in Downtown Los Angeles: A Study of Office Workers and Their Employers* (Los Angeles: Southern California Association of Governments, 1990).

24. Senate Advisory Committee on Cost Control in State Government, *Getting the Most Out of California's Transportation Dollar*, 13.

25. John Pucher, "Urban Travel Behavior as the Outcome of Public Policy," *Journal of the American Planning Association*, Autumn 1988.

26. Paul Bloom, *Rail and County Transportation Sales Taxes* (Sacramento: Planning and Conservation League Foundation, June 1990).

27. Department of Transportation, *California Rail Passenger Development Plan, 1991 Through 1996 Fiscal Years* (Sacramento: Department of Transportation, July 1991), 27.

CHAPTER 6

1. California Department of Water Resources, *California Water: Looking to the Future, Statistical Appendix* (Sacramento: California Department of Water Resources, January 1988), 7.

2. Ibid.

3. California Department of Water Resources, *The California Water Plan: Projected Use and Available Water Supplies to 2010* (Sacramento: California Department of Water Resources, December 1983), 29.

4. *California Water*, 7 (derived from).

5. Assembly Office of Research, *Restoring Hetch Hetchy* (Sacramento: Joint Publications, California Legislature, June 1988), 40.

CHAPTER 7

1. State Water Resources Control Board, *Nonpoint Source Assessment Report* (Sacramento: State Water Resources Control Board, 1988).

2. Alvin J. Greenberg and Gordon Hart, *The State of the State's Rivers and Bays* (Sacramento: Planning and Conservation League, 1986).
3. State Water Resources Control Board, *Toxic Substance Monitoring Program for 1983* (Sacramento: State Water Resources Control Board, 1985).
4. Harte et al., *California Policy Seminar Final Report Number 6; Trace Metals in California's Inland Surface Waters* (Berkeley: Institute of Governmental Studies, June 1985).
5. State Water Resources Control Board, *California State Mussel Watch 1983–84* (Sacramento: State Water Resources Control Board, 1985).
6. Harte et al., *California Policy Seminar Final Report Number 6.*
7. State Water Resources Control Board, *Polychlorinated Biphenyls (PCBs)* (Sacramento: State Water Resources Control Board, 1983) and SWRCB, *Toxic Substance Monitoring Program for 1983.*
8. California Central Valley Regional Water Quality Control Board, *Draft Amendment of the Water Quality Control Plan Report for Sacramento River Basin (5A)—Sacramento–San Joaquin Delta Basin (5B)—San Joaquin Basin (5C)* (Sacramento: Central Valley Regional Water Quality Control Board, 1990).
9. State Water Resources Control Board, *Selenium and Other Trace Element Studies in California* (Sacramento: State Water Resources Control Board, 1986); Bay Institute of San Francisco, *Selenium and Agricultural Drainage; Implications for San Francisco Bay and the California Environment* (Tiburon: Bay Institute of San Francisco, 1986); SWRCB, *Toxic Substances Monitoring Program for 1983*; and Harte et al.
10. Alvin J. Greenberg and Dianne Kopec, "Decline of Bay-Delta Fisheries and Increased Selenium Loading: Possible Correlation?" in *Selenium and Agricultural Drainage: Implications for San Francisco Bay and the California Environment.*
11. State Water Resources Control Board, *1990 Water Quality Assessment (WQA)* (Sacramento: State Water Resources Control Board, 1990).
12. Ibid.
13. State Water Resources Control Board, *Final Draft Pollutant Policy Document, San Francisco Bay Sacramento-San Joaquin Delta Estuary* (Sacramento: State Water Resources Control Board, 1990).
14. Greenberg and Kopec, "Decline of Bay-Delta Fisheries."
15. California Department of Health Services, *Final Report on a Monitoring Program for Organic Chemical Contamination of Large and Small Public Water Systems in California* (Sacramento: Department of Health Services, April 1986 and June 1990).
16. State Water Resources Control Board, *Water Quality Control Plan for Salinity* (Sacramento: State Water Resources Control Board, 1991).
17. State Water Resources Control Board, *Development of Water Quality*

Control Plans for Inland Surface Waters of California and Enclosed Bays and Estuaries of California (Sacramento: State Water Resources Control Board, 1990).

18. State Water Resources Control Board, *Nonpoint Source Assessment Report*.

CHAPTER 8

1. Alan Lufkin, ed., *California's Salmon and Steelhead* (Berkeley: University of California Press, 1991).
2. Andrew Neal Cohen, *An Introduction to the Ecology of the San Francisco Estuary* (Oakland: San Francisco Estuary Project, 1990).
3. National Audubon Society, *Endangered Habitat: A Report on the Status of Seasonal Wetlands in San Francisco Bay and a Recommended Plan for Their Protection* (National Audubon Society, 1989), 1. Available from National Audubon Society, Washington, D.C.
4. Citizens for a Better Environment,, *Toxic Hot Spots in San Francisco Bay* (San Francisco: Citizens for a Better Environment, 1987).
5. Cohen, *An Introduction to the Ecology of the San Francisco Estuary*, 24.
6. Ibid., 17.
7. U.S. Department of Commerce, *Gulf of the Farallones National Marine Sanctuary Management Plan* (San Francisco: U.S. Department of Commerce, 1987), 11.
8. Gregory Silber and Rasa Gustaitis, "Disaster Insurance for a Favorite Species," *California Coast and Ocean*, Winter/Spring 1991, 17.
9. Malcolm Margolin, *The Ohlone Way* (Berkeley: Heyday Books, 1978), 8.
10. Jill Kauffman, *Cleaning North America's Beaches: 1990 Beach Cleanup Results* (San Francisco: Center for Marine Conservation, 1991).
11. Louanne W. Murray, "The Toll of a Routine Oil Spill," *California Coast and Ocean*, Summer 1990, 46.
12. Peter Steinhart, *California's Wild Heritage: Threatened and Endangered Animals in the Golden State* (San Francisco: California Department of Fish and Game, California Academy of Sciences and Sierra Club Books, 1990), 69.
13. Ibid., 68, 70.
14. Natural Resources Defense Council, *Ebb Tide for Pollution: Actions for Cleaning Up Coastal Waters* (San Francisco: Natural Resources Defense Council, 1989), 6.
15. Henry Schafer et al., "Chlorinated Hydrocarbons in Marine Mammals," Southern California Coastal Research Project, Biennial Report (Long Beach, Calif.: Southern California Coastal Research Project, 1984), 111.

16. San Diego Interagency Water Quality Panel, *San Diego Bay Report 1989–1990* (San Diego: San Diego Water Quality Panel, 1990), I-15.
17. "San Diego Fined $3 Million for Clean Water Act Violation," *California Environmental News*, May 1991, 5.
18. Katherine E. Stone and Benjamin Kaufman, "A Legal System to Protect the Shores of the Sea," *California Waterfront Age*, Winter 1989, 16.
19. Richard Townsend, *Shipping Safety and America's Coasts* (San Francisco: Center for Marine Conservation, 1990), 5.
20. Regional Response Team, "Fact Sheet on Shell Oil Spill" (Regional Response Team, September 1988), 2. Available from EPA, San Francisco.
21. Regine McGrath, "Ocean as Dispose-all," *California Coast and Ocean*, Winter/Spring 1991, 21.
22. Jennifer Kassalow, *Testing the Waters: A Study of Beach Closings in Ten States* (San Francisco: Natural Resources Defense Council, 1991), 6.
23. Greg Karras, *Hidden Polluters of California's Coast* (San Francisco: Citizens for a Better Environment, 1990). Available from Citizens for a Better Environment.
24. James G. Titus, ed., *Greenhouse Effect, Sea Level Rise and Coastal Wetlands* (San Francisco: Environmental Protection Agency, 1988), 9.
25. Steinhart, *California's Wild Heritage*, 75.

CHAPTER 9

1. Woody Guthrie, "Do-Re-Mi," *Library of Congress Recordings* (New York: Elektra Records, 1964).
2. Richard Sybert, speech before annual meeting of the Planning and Conservation League, Sacramento, February 16, 1991.
3. California State Office of Planning and Research, *The Growth Revolt: Aftershock of Proposition 13?* (Sacramento: California State Office of Planning and Research, 1980).
4. California Association of Realtors, *Matrix of Land Use Planning Measures, 1971–1988* (Los Angeles: California Association of Realtors, 1987); Madelyn Glickfeld, Leroy Graymer, and Kerry Morrison, *Trends in Local Growth Control Ballot Measures in California*, UCLA Journal of Environmental Law and Policy, 1987.
5. Andrew Schiffrin, *The Story of Measure J: Santa Cruz County's Growth Management Program* (San Francisco: People for Open Space Regional Exchange, 1984).
6. Elizabeth Deakin, *State Programs for Managing Land Use, Growth, and Fiscal Impact, A Report to the Senate Office of Research* (Sacramento: Senate Office of Research, 1990).

7. California Office of Tourism, *"The Californias"* Map (Sacramento: California Office of Tourism, 1990).

8. Bay Vision 2020 Commission, *Bay Vision 2020/The Commission Report* (San Francisco: Bay Vision 2020 Commission, 1990); People for Open Space, *Endangered Harvest, The Future of Bay Area Farmland* (San Francisco: People for Open Space, 1980); and People for Open Space, *Room Enough: Housing and Open Space in the Bay Area* (San Francisco: People for Open Space, 1983).

9. Sierra Club, San Gorgonio Chapter, *Environmental Impacts of Population Growth in California's Inland Empire* (San Bernardino: Sierra Club, 1989); also Los Angeles 2000 Committee, *LA 2000* (Los Angeles: Los Angeles 2000 Committee, 1988).

10. American Farmland Trust, *Risks, Challenges and Opportunities* (San Francisco: American Farmland Trust, 1989).

11. California Assembly Office of Research, *California 2000: Getting Ahead of the Growth Curve* (Sacramento: California Assembly Office of Research, 1989).

12. California Council for Environmental and Economic Balance, *California's Urban Renaissance* ((San Francisco: California Council for Environmental and Economic Balance, 1991).

13. Sierra Club, *Policy Before Planning: Solving California's Growth Problems, Sierra Club California's 1991 Green State of the State Report* (San Francisco: Sierra Club, 1991).

14. Adam Smith, *An Inquiry into the Nature and Causes of the Wealth of Nations* (New York: Modern Library, 1937).

15. James Longtin, *Longtin's California Land Use* (Malibu, Calif.: Local Government Publications, 1987).

16. League for Coastal Protection, *Ten Years of Coastal Zone Management* (San Francisco: League for Coastal Protection, 1986).

17. Greenbelt Alliance/People for Open Space, *Endangered Harvest—The Future of Bay Area Farmland* (San Francisco: Greenbelt Alliance, 1980).

18. Michael Cameron, *Transportation Efficiency: Tackling Southern California's Air Pollution and Congestion* (Los Angeles: Environmental Defense Fund and Regional Institute of Southern California, 1991).

CHAPTER 10

1. California Department of Food and Agriculture, *California Agriculture: Statistical Review 1989* (Sacramento: California Agricultural Statistics Service, 1990).

2. Ibid.

3. Ibid.
4. Harold O. Carter and Carol F. Nuckton, eds., *Agriculture in California: On the Brink of a New Millennium 1990–2010* (Davis, Calif.: Agricultural Issues Center, University of California, 1990), 55.
5. California Department of Conservation, Office of Land Conservation, *Farmland Conversion Report 1986–1988* (Sacramento: State of California, September 1990), 16.
6. Ibid., 17.
7. California Department of Water Resources, *California Water: Looking to the Future*, Bulletin 160-87 (Sacramento: State of California, November 1987).
8. Ibid.
9. Ibid., 33.
10. California crops, on average, use three acre-feet of water per year, or enough to flood an acre of land three feet deep. An acre-foot of water is about equal to the yearly water use of a family of five.
11. American Farmland Trust, *Risks, Challenges and Opportunities: Agriculture, Resources and Growth in a Changing Central Valley* (San Francisco: American Farmland Trust, 1989), 29.
12. Ibid., 35.
13. Ibid., 25.
14. Wells Fargo Bank, "Economic Monitor" newsletter, April 15, 1991.
15. American Farmland Trust, *Eroding Choices, Emerging Issues* (San Francisco: American Farmland Trust, 1986), 13.
16. American Farmland Trust, *Risks, Challenges and Opportunities*, 17.
17. California Department of Conservation, *Farmland Conversion Report 1986–1988*.
18. American Farmland Trust, *Risks, Challenges and Opportunities*, 17.
19. Ibid., 18.
20. Alvin D. Sokolow, *The Williamson Act: 25 Years of Land Conservation* (Davis, Calif.: Agricultural Issues Center, University of California, 1989), 48–49.
21. American Farmland Trust, "Williamson Act Contract Nonrenewals in Yolo County, 1991," unpublished data.

CHAPTER 11

1. California Department of Forestry and Fire Protection, *Forest and Rangeland Resources Assessment Program (FRRAP), California's Forest and Rangelands: Growing Conflict Over Changing Uses* (Sacramento: California Department of Forestry and Fire Protection, 1988), 59–63, 111. Most of the data cited in this chapter were obtained from this

source, commonly known as the FRRAP Report. The report is the first comprehensive assessment of forest, range, and other wild lands in California, required reading for anyone interested in forest conditions and policy in California.

2. Ibid., 313.
3. Proposition 130 (1990) and SB 854 (Keene), 1991.
4. California Department of Forestry and Fire Protection, FRRAP Report, 35, 190.
5. Ibid., 296.
6. Public Resources Code, Sec. 4513 et seq.; 14 California Code of Regulations, Sec. 895 et seq.; Public Resources Code, Sec. 4513.
7. California Board of Forestry, *Annual Report* (Sacramento: California Board of Forestry, 1990), 8.
8. Ken Delfino, deputy director for Forest Management, California Department of Forestry and Fire Protection, Memorandum to Regional Chiefs, May 11, 1991.
9. James F. Morrison, "The National Forest Management Act and Below Cost Timber Sales: Determining the Economic Suitability of Land for Timber Production," *Environmental Law* 17 (no. 3, 1987): 557, 562.
10. Federal Register, vol. 56 (May 6, 1991), 20816.
11. California Board of Forestry, *Annual Report* (Sacramento: California Board of Forestry, 1990).
12. California Department of Forestry and Fire Protection, FRRAP Report, 313.
13. Ibid., 119.

CHAPTER 12

1. Tellus Institute, *Disposal Cost Fee Study* (Boston: Tellus Institute, February 1991).
2. Ibid., ES-6.
3. John E. Young, "Discarding the Throwaway Society" (Washington, D.C.: Worldwatch Institute, January 1991), 16.
4. R. W. Beck and Associates, *Achieving Optimal Waste Recycling and Source Reduction: Methods to Reach Your County's Recycling Goal* (Sacramento: R. W. Beck and Associates, May 1989), 1–10.
5. Young, "Discarding the Throwaway Society," 9–10.
6. William K. Shireman, *Can and Bottle Bills* (Stanford, Calif.: Stanford Environmental Law Society/California Public Interest Research Group, 1982), 28, 36.
7. Robert Cowles Letcher and Mary T. Sheil, "Source Separation and

Citizens Recycling," in *The Solid Waste Handbook*, ed. William D. Robinson (New York: John Wiley and Sons, 1986).

8. R. W. Beck and Associates, *Achieving Optimal Waste Recycling and Source Reduction*, also Tellus Institute, *Disposal Cost Fee Study*,

9. Tellus Institute, *Disposal Cost Fee Study*, ES-6.

10. Young, "Discarding the Throwaway Society," 31; also U.S. Department of the Interior, Bureau of Mines, *Mineral Commodity Summaries 1990* (Washington, D.C.: Department of the Interior, 1990).

11. Ernst & Young and R. W. Beck and Associates, *Convenience Zone Effectiveness Study* (Sacramento: Ernst & Young et al., 1991), v-13–v-17.

12. Ibid., iii-3.

13. Ibid., v-13–v-17.

14. Ibid., iii-9.

15. R. W. Beck and Associates, *Achieving Optimal Waste Recycling and Source Reduction*, 1–10.

16. Diana Gale, Seattle Solid Waste Authority, interview, October 1990.

17. William K. Shireman, "A State 'Green Tax' Polluters Would Have to Pay," *Sacramento Bee*, June 6, 1991, B9.

CHAPTER 13

1. California Department of Health Services, Toxic Substances Control Program, *Fact Sheet #3, Westminster Tract #2633* (Long Beach, Calif.: California Department of Health Services, June 1990). Brochure.

2. California Department of Health Services, Toxic Substances Control Program, Alternative Technology Division, *Draft Status Report on Hazardous Waste Management in California* (Sacramento: State of California, September 15, 1989).

3. California Office of Emergency Services, *Toxics Release Inventory Database* (Sacramento: California Office of Emergency Services, 1991).

4. Environmental Research Foundation, *What Chemicals Each Industry Uses: A Sourcebook for Citizens* (Princeton: Environmental Research Foundation, December 1, 1988).

5. Sheridan V. Merritt, *Waste Minimization for Hazardous Materials Inspectors: Module 1* (Riverside, Calif.: University Extension, University of California, Riverside, January 1991), 9–10. Prepared for California Department of Health Services, Toxic Substances Control Program, and U.S. Environmental Protection Agency.

6. California Department of Health Services, *Draft Status Report*, 47.

7. Toxics Assessment Group, *Nowhere To Go: The Universal Failure of Class 1 Hazardous Waste Dump Sites in California* (Sacramento: Environmental Defense Fund, June 1985), ii.

8. U.S. General Accounting Office, *Hazardous Waste Sites: State Cleanup Status and Its Implications for Federal Policy* (Washington, D.C.: GAO/RCED-89-164, August 1989), 12.

9. Ibid., 25.

10. California Department of Health Services, Toxic Substances Control Program, *Hazardous Waste Management in California, Biennial Report 1988–1990* (Sacramento: California Department of Health Services, 1991), 72–73.

11. Kenneth M. Mead, *Improvements Needed in FRA's Hazardous Materials Inspection and Safety Reporting Programs*, statement before the Subcommittee on Government Activities and Transportation, Committee on Government Operations, House of Representatives (Washington, D.C.: Subcommittee on Government Activities and Transportation, February 28, 1990), 1–3.

12. Jane Kay, "Minorities Bear Brunt of Pollution," *San Francisco Examiner*, April 9, 1991 (part 3 of an *Examiner* special report).

13. California Department of Health Services, *Biennial Report 1988–1990*, 58–60.

14. Diana M. Peebler and José A. Robledo, *California's Exports and Imports of Hazardous Waste 1986–1988* (Sacramento: California Department of Health Services, Toxic Substances Control Program, Alternative Technology Division, July 1990), 14.

15. Ibid., 17.

16. Ibid., 32.

17. Ibid., 37.

18. Ibid., 34.

19. *California Environment Reporter*, vol. 1, no. 16, June 10, 1991.

20. Lester R. Brown et al., *State of the World: 1991* (New York: W. W. Norton, 1991), 143.

21. Ibid.

22. Ibid.

23. California Department of Health Services, *Draft Status Report*, 25.

24. Ibid.

25. California Department of Health Services, *Biennial Report 1988–1990*.

26. Kathryn Barwick, ed., *Economic Implications of Waste Reduction, Recycling, Treatment and Disposal of Hazardous Wastes* (Sacramento: California Department of Health Services, Toxic Substances Control Program, Alternative Technology Division, July 1988).

CHAPTER 14

1. California Department of Food and Agriculture, *Pesticide Usage in California and the United States—Report HS-1071* (Sacramento: K. T. Maddy, 1983), 3. Comparisons of pesticide sales and use information is difficult and controversial because the pesticide companies generally assert that these data are trade secrets and because various agencies include different chemicals as pesticides. Exclusion of disinfectants, water treatment chemicals, and wood treatment chemicals would retain the same ratio but roughly halve the total reported pounds.
2. David Pimentel and Lois Levitan, "Pesticides: Where Do They Go?" *The Journal of Pesticide Reform*, Fall 1987, 2.
3. E. Smith and D. Pimentel, eds., *Pest Control Strategies* (New York: Academic Press, 1978), 56.
4. Richard Paddock, "Chemical OKd for Farms Despite Safety Questions," *Los Angeles Times*, May 31, 1991, 1.
5. Federal Register, vol. 53 (October 19, 1980), 41126.
6. National Research Council, *Regulating Pesticides in Food—The Delaney Paradox* (Washington, D.C.: National Academy Press, 1987), 25–27.
7. California Department of Health Services, *Epidemiologic Study of Adverse Health Effects in Children in McFarland, California, Phase II Report* (Berkeley: California Department of Health Services, 1988), 1–4.
8. California Department of Health Services Environmental Epidemiology and Toxicology Branch, *McFarland Child Health Screening Project* (Emeryville: California Department of Health Services, 1989), 1–2.
9. Sheila Hoar et al., "Agricultural Herbicide Use and Risk of Lymphoma and Soft-Tissue Sarcoma," *Journal of the American Medical Association*, September 5, 1986, 1141.
10. U.S. Environmental Protection Agency, *Suspended, Cancelled, and Restricted Pesticides* (Washington, D.C.: Environmental Protection Agency, February 1990). Karen Klinger, "Pesticide Tied to Birth Defects," *San Jose Mercury News*, September 28, 1980, 1.
11. Larry Parsons, "Poisoned Farm Workers File Federal Suit," *Salinas Californian*, September 16, 1983, 1.
12. *Ferebee v. Chevron Chemical Co.*, 736 F.2d 1529 (D.C. Cir. 1984).
13. Keith Schneider, "Faking It: The Case Against Industrial Bio-Test Laboratories," *Amicus Journal*, Spring 1983, 14.
14. U.S. Environmental Protection Agency, *Pesticide Reregistration Progress Report* (Washington, D.C.: Environmental Protection Agency, July 1991).

15. L. Duncan Saunders et al., "Outbreak of Omite-CR-induced Dermatitis Among Orange Pickers in Tulare County, California," *Journal of Occupational Medicine*, May 1987, 409.

16. Ibid., 413.

17. U.S. Environmental Protection Agency, *Guidance for the Reregistration of Pesticide Products Containing Parathion*. (Washington, D.C.: Environmental Protection Agency, 1986), 20.

18. California Department of Food and Agriculture, *Summary of Illnesses and Injuries Reported by California Physicians as Potentially Related to Pesticides*, annual reports (Sacramento: California Department of Food and Agriculture, 1973, 1974, 1987, 1988). The author has used total physician reports for this comparison. The Food and Agricultural Department uses lower numbers as confirmed cases.

19. California Department of Food and Agriculture, *1988–89 Report 5 Summary* (Sacramento: California Department of Food and Agriculture, 1989).

20. California Department of Health Services, Hazard Evaluation Section, *Pesticides: Health Aspects of Exposure and Issues Surrounding Their Use* (Berkeley: California Department of Health Services, June 1988), 97.

21. Lawrie Mott and Karen Snyder, *Pesticide Alert* (San Francisco: Sierra Club Books, 1987), 127.

22. California Department of Food and Agriculture, *A Field Study of Fog and Dry Deposition as Sources of Inadvertent Pesticide Residues on Row Crops* (Sacramento: California Department of Food and Agriculture, 1989).

23. James N. Seiber et al., "Airborne Concentrations of Selected Pesticide Chemicals in Three Communities in Kern County, California, from Sampling Done in June–July 1987" (Department of Environmental Toxicology, University of California Davis, 1988). Unpublished report.

24. California Department of Health Services, Office of Environmental Health Hazard Assessment, Hazard Evaluation Section, *Acute Health Effects of Community Exposure to Cotton Defoliants* (Berkeley: California Department of Health Services, March 1989).

25. California Department of Food and Agriculture, Division of Pest Management, *Report HS-894* (Sacramento: California Department of Food and Agriculture, 1982).

CHAPTER 15

1. The Resources Agency, California Department of Parks and Recreation, *California Outdoor Recreation Plan* (Sacramento: California Department of Parks and Recreation, 1984), 44.

2. U.S. Department of the Interior, Bureau of Land Management, California State Office, *Recreation 2000, A Strategic Plan for California Recreation* (Sacramento: Bureau of Land Management, 1990).

CHAPTER 16

1. Two hundred seventy-three terrestrial and wetland habitats and 123 aquatic habitats according to the California Department of Fish and Game's Natural Diversity Data Bank (NDDB), a computerized inventory of the state's rare, threatened, and endangered wildlife and natural communities.
2. Tim Schreiner, "50 Million in State by 2010, Expert Says," *San Francisco Chronicle*, August 19, 1991, A1.
3. Deborah B. Jensen, Margaret Torn, and John Harte, *In Our Own Hands: A Strategy for Conserving Biological Diversity in California* (Berkeley: University of California, 1990), 66. Available from California Policy Seminar, University of California, 109 Moses Hall, Berkeley, CA 94720.
4. Jones and Stokes Associates, *Sliding Toward Extinction: The State of California's Natural Heritage* (Sacramento: The Nature Conservancy, 1987). Available from The Nature Conservancy, 785 Market Street, San Francisco, CA 94103.
5. Paul and Anne Ehrlich, *Extinction* (New York: Ballantine, 1981), 8.
6. Walter V. Reid and Kenton R. Miller, *Keeping Options Alive* (Washington, D.C.: World Resources Institute, 1989).
7. William K. Stevens, "What Really Threatens the Environment?" *New York Times*, January 29, 1991, B7.
8. Gina Kolata, "Tree Yields a Cancer Treatment, But Ecological Costs May Be High," *New York Times*, May 13, 1991, A1, A9.
9. Jensen, Torn, and Harte, *In Our Own Hands.*
10. Jones and Stokes Associates, *Sliding Toward Extinction.*
11. P. H. Raven and D. I. Axelrod, "Origin and Relationship of the California Flora," *University of California Publications in Botany* (1978) 72:1–134.
12. Jones and Stokes Associates, *Sliding Toward Extinction.*
13. J. Powell and C. Hogue, *California Insects* (Berkeley: University of California Press, 1979).
14. Jones and Stokes Associates, *Sliding Toward Extinction.*
15. California Department of Forestry and Fire Protection, Forest and Rangelands Resource Assessment Program, *California's Forest and Rangelands: Growing Conflict Over Changing Uses* (Sacramento: Califor-

nia Department of Forestry and Fire Protection, 1988); California Department of Finance, *California Statistical Abstract* (Sacramento: Department of Finance, 1988); American Farmland Trust, *Eroding Choices, Emerging Issues: The Condition of California Agricultural Land Resources* (San Francisco: American Farmland Trust, 1986).

16. Jones and Stokes Associates, *Sliding Toward Extinction*.
17. Harold Mooney, "The Invasion of Plants and Animals in California," *Ecology of Biological Invasions of North America and Hawaii*, eds. H. A. Mooney and J. A. Drake (New York: Springer-Verlag, 1986), 250–72.
18. 1990 annual report on threatened and endangered species prepared by the California Department of Fish and Game for the Fish and Game Commission.

CHAPTER 17

1. Marc Reisner, "A Decision for the Desert," *Wilderness*, Winter 1986, 49.
2. Richard Conniff, "Once the Secret Domain of Miners and Ranchers, the BLM Is Going Public," *Smithsonian*, September 1990, 40.
3. Conniff, "Once the Secret Domain," 42.
4. Peter Steinhart, "Driving Out the Desert," *Audubon*, November 1980, 83–86.
5. University of California, Department of Forestry and Resource Management, *Integrated Hardwood Range Management Program* (Berkeley: Department of Forestry and Resource Management, 1990).
6. Tom Griggs, "Valley Oaks: Can They Be Saved?" *Fremontia*, July 1990, 44–47.
7. Lynn Huntsinger and Richard B. Standiford, "Saving Someone Else's Oaks," *Fremontia*, July 1990.
8. Sharon G. Johnson, *California Oaks, Their Status and Conservation Needs* (Sacramento: California Oak Foundation, about 1980), 9.
9. Douglas D. McCreary, "Native Oaks: The Next Generation," *Fremontia*, July 1990.
10. Bern Kreissman, *California, An Environmental Atlas and Guide* (Davis: Bear Klaw Press, 1991).
11. Tim Palmer, *Endangered Rivers and the Conservation Movement* (Berkeley: University of California Press, 1984), 258.
12. Steve Evans, "River Ecosystems on the Brink of Extinction," *Headwaters* (newsletter of Friends of the River), May 1991.
13. Jim Mayer, "Winter-run Chinook Appear Fast on Way to Extinction," *Sacramento Bee*, May 25, 1991, 1.

14. U.S. Department of the Interior, Fish and Wildlife Service, *Draft, American River Watershed Investigation, Auburn Area* (Sacramento: Fish and Wildlife Service, February 1991). Unpublished report.

15. Planning and Conservation League Foundation, *Protecting Our Heritage: A Proposal for an Upper American River National Recreation Area* (Sacramento: Planning and Conservation League Foundation, 1984). Booklet.

16. U.S. Comptroller General, *Federal Charges for Irrigation Projects Reviewed Do Not Cover Costs* (Washington, D.C.: General Accounting Office, March 13, 1981).

Selected Environmental Organizations in California

American Farmland Trust,
Western Office
1949 Fifth Street, Suite 101
Davis, CA 95616

California League of
Conservation Voters
965 Mission Street, Suite 705
San Francisco, CA 94103

California Native Plant Society
909 12th Street, Suite 116
Sacramento, CA 95814

Californians Against Waste
926 J Street, Suite 608
Sacramento, CA 95814

California Oak Foundation
909 12th Street, Suite 125
Sacramento, CA 95814

California Trout
926 J Street, Suite 617
Sacramento, CA 95814

California Waterfowl Association
3840 Rosin Court, Suite 200
Sacramento, CA 95834

California Wilderness Coalition
2655 Portage Bay East, Suite 5
Davis, CA 95616

Central Valley Safe Environment
Network
958 East 22nd Street
Merced, CA 95340

Citizens for a Better Environment
501 Second Street, Suite 305
San Francisco, CA 94107
and
122 Lincoln Boulevard,
Suite 201
Venice, CA 90291

Coalition for Clean Air
122 Lincoln Boulevard, Room
201
Venice, Ca 90291

Defenders of Wildlife
1228 N Street, Suite 6
Sacramento, CA 95814

Ducks Unlimited
9823 Old Winery Place, Suite 16
Sacramento, CA 95827

Earth Island Institute
300 Broadway, Suite 28
San Francisco, CA 94133

Environmental Defense Fund
5655 College Avenue, Suite 304
Oakland, CA 94618

Friends of the River
909 12th Street, Suite 207
Sacramento, CA 95814

Greenbelt Alliance
116 New Montgomery, Suite 640
San Francisco, CA 94105

Greenpeace Pacific Southwest
139 Townsend Street
San Francisco, CA 94107

Heal the Bay
1640 Fifth Street, Suite 112
Santa Monica, CA 90401

League to Save Lake Tahoe
989 Tahoe Keys Boulevard,
Suite 6
South Lake Tahoe, CA 96150

Mono Lake Committee
1207 Magnolia Boulevard
Suite D
Burbank, CA 90024

Mountain Lion Preservation
Foundation
614 Tenth Street
Sacramento, CA 95814

National Audubon Society
555 Audubon Place
Sacramento, CA 95825

National Toxics Campaign
1330 21st Street, Suite 102
Sacramento, CA 95814

Natural Resources Defense
Council
71 Stevenson Place, Suite 128
San Francisco, CA 94105
and
617 South Oliver Street
Los Angeles, CA 90014

The Nature Conservancy
785 Market Street, Third Floor
San Francisco, CA 94103

Planning and Conservation
League
926 J Street, Suite 612
Sacramento, CA 95814

Save San Francisco Bay
Association
1736 Franklin Street, Third Floor
Oakland, CA 94612

Sierra Club
1024 Tenth Street
Sacramento, CA 95814

Toxic Coordinating Project
942 Market Street, Suite 502
San Francisco, CA 94102

Train Riders Association of
  California
926 J Street, Suite 612
Sacramento, CA 95814

Trust for Public Land
116 New Montgomery, Fourth
  Floor
San Francisco, CA 94105

The Wilderness Society
116 New Montgomery, Suite 526
San Francisco, CA 94105

Acknowledgments

California's Threatened Environment was a cooperative endeavor of many people, principally the chapter authors, who gave of their time, knowledge, and insight. The idea for the book owes to the foresight of Francesca Gardner and Dennis Collins of the James Irvine Foundation, who were inspired by the Worldwatch Institute's *State of the World*; also to Jerry Meral of the Planning and Conservation League and Charles Savitt of Island Press, both among the foremost visionaries in the environmental field today.

Barbara Dean provided fine editorial assistance, and the entire Island Press and Planning and Conservation League staffs were important participants. Janie McGuin and Frank Esposito at Drawing Board Studio are responsible for the graphics. Nancy Jacques' thoughtful and perceptive comments were appreciated.

A draft of each chapter was read by several reviewers for accuracy and content. The time and thoughtfulness of all the following were important: Jerry Meral, who read the entire manuscript; Robert Berner, Marin Agricultural Trust; Nancy D. Campbell, University of California, Santa Cruz; Janet Cobb, East Bay Regional Parks District; Peter Detwiler, State Senate Local Government Committee staff; Jim Eaton, California Wilderness Coalition; Michael Eaton, energy consultant; Steve Evans, Friends of the River; Bob Fredenburg, State Senate Toxics Committee staff; Sandy Jarabek, Californians Against Waste; Jennifer Jennings, Planning and Conservation League; Deborah Jensen, University of California, Berkeley; Jim Knox, Planning and Conservation League; Sally Magnani, former legislative consultant; Taylor Miller, attorney, Sacramento; Larry Orman, Greenbelt Alliance; Norman Pillsbury, California Polytechnic State University at San Luis Obispo; Andy

Sawyer, State Water Resources Control Board staff; Ron Stork, Friends of the River; and Ginger Strong, California Oak Foundation.

Many of the chapter authors had additional outside experts review their chapters.

Tim Palmer

INDEX

Acid deposition, 36, 53–54
Acid fog, 39, 53
Acid rain, 39, 53
Advanced disposal fees, 180
Agenda for the future, 258–69
  categories of environmental problems, 260–61
  personal action agenda, 267–69
  population growth, 260, 261–62
  resource base, 263–66
  urban problems, 260, 262–63
  waste and recycling, 266–67
Agent Orange (2,4,5t), 211
Agriculture, 10, 139–53, 261, 264
  air pollution's effects on, 37, 139, 145–46
  Central Valley as core of, 140–41
  diversity of crops grown, 140
  global warming's effects on, 54
  insider's view of, 152–53
  irrigation, 142–43, 264, 265
  pesticide use, see Pesticides
  reducing negative effects on the environment from, 152–53
  soil erosion, 145
  soil salinity, 144–45
  water use for, 81, 84–85, 90, 142–44, 264–65
  see also Farmland
Air pollution, 5, 9, 26, 33–46
  from automobiles, 10, 12, 24–25, 34, 39–40, 42, 65, 70–72
  in Central Valley, 43
  challenges for the future, 42–43
  criteria pollutants, 35–36
  crops affected by, 37, 139
  ecosystem impacts of, 36–37
  health effects of, 35–36
  in Los Angeles area, 33–34, 41
  pesticides, 208–10
  programs to manage, 42
  progress in reducing, 44–45
  prospects for, 41
  scope of the problem, 37–39
  sources of, 39–40
  state of the air, 34–35
  summary, 45–46
  technology, future, 44
  unique conditions fostering, 34
  visual enjoyment impeded by, 37
    see also individual pollutants, e.g. Carbon monoxide; Ozone
Air Resources Board (ARB), 35, 36, 41, 42, 184, 209
Air Toxic "Hot Spots" Information Assessment Act, 189
Air travel, 68
Alamo River, 103–104
Alar, 211
Alaska, 26
Aldicarb, 198–99, 205
American Farmland Trust, 131
American River, 101, 256
Amtrak, 67–68, 77
Ancient forests, 164–65
Arizona, 26, 54, 82
Army Corps of Engineers, 119, 123, 255
Assembly Office of Research, 133
Association of American Railroads, 187
Auburn Dam, 91, 254–55
Automobiles:
  air pollution from, 10, 12, 24–25, 34, 39–40, 42, 65, 70–72
  congestion, 43, 65, 69–70, 71
  energy consumption, 52–53
  fuel efficiency, 60, 74
  fuel, improvements in, 60, 71
  future usage of, 78–79
  injuries and deaths, 67
  land use policies and, 75–76
  parking, subsidized, 74–75, 78
  population growth and, 24–25, 39, 64–65
  reduction of miles traveled per vehicle, 60–61, 71
  zero-emission, 44
    see also Highways and freeways

Bakersfield, California, 34–35
Banos Grandes, Los (reservoir), 91
Bay Area Rapid Transit (BART), 67
Bays, see Oceans, bays, and estuaries
Bay Vision 2020 Commission, 132
Beaches, sand loss from Southern California, 119–20
Berry, Wendell, 27
Bicycling, 69, 76
Biological diversity, 226
  reasons to care about, 228–31
    see also Endangered species
Biomass, 50

Birth Defect Prevention Act, 202
Birth rate, 20, 22
Black Congressional Caucus, 12
Bolling, David, 256
Bottle Bill, 175–78
Boxer, Barbara, 121
Brandt's cormorant, 115
British Columbia, 26
Brown pelican, 225–26
Bureau of Land Management, 165, 218,
    231, 244–45, 255
Bureau of Reclamation, 85, 86
Buses, 67, 68, 77
Bush, George, 116

California Aqueduct, 86
California Board of Forestry, 250
California Certified Organic Farmers, 206
California clapper rail, 113
California Clean Air Act, 41
California condor, 237, 245
California Conservation Corps, 221
California Council for Environmental and
    Economic Balance (CEEB), 133
California Department of Conservation,
    146, 178
California Department of Food and
    Agriculture, 200
California Department of Forestry, 157–58,
    231
California Department of Forestry and Fire
    Protection (CDF), 159, 160, 162, 235
California Department of Health Services,
    102, 106, 200, 207, 209
California Department of Parks and
    Recreation, 214
California Department of Transportation,
    68, 69
California Desert Protection Act, 245, 246
California Endangered Species Act, 233, 238
California Energy Commission, 48, 49, 53,
    61
    global warming and, 55, 57
California Environmental Protection
    Agency, 210–11
    Department of Toxic Substances Control
    (DTSC), 184, 186, 188, 190, 192
California Environmental Quality Act, 10–
    11, 27, 88, 151, 160, 184
California Expenditure Plan for Hazardous
    Waste Cleanup, 185
California Forest Practices Act, 165
California Futures, 179
California Hazardous Waste Management
    Act, 188
California Hazardous Waste Reduction and
    Management Act, 186, 188

California Labor Federation, 161
California Land Conservation Act
    (Williamson Act), 149, 150–51
Californians for Population Stabilization,
    28
California Oak Foundation, 250
California Public Utilities Commission, 61
California quail, 8
California Tomorrow, 14
California Transportation Commission, 61
California 2000 (Reinhardt et al.), 14
California Waste Exchange, 188
California Wilderness Coalition, 242
California Wildlife, Coastal, and Parklands
    Bond Act, 221
CalTrans, 61
Calwell, Chris, 47–63
Cancer:
    Pacific yew tree's pharmaceutical effect
    on, 229
    pesticides as carcinogens, 199, 200, 202,
    205, 209
Carbon dioxide, 25
    for burning fossil fuels, 48, 50
    environmental costs of new power plants,
    59–60, 62
    options for reduction of emissions from,
    57–61
Carbon monoxide, 35, 72
    harmful effects of, 36
    sources of, 39
    violation of standards for, 34
Carcinogens, pesticides as, 199, 200, 202,
    205, 209
Central Valley, 6, 114
    as agricultural core, 140–41
    air pollution in, 43
    desert, 242
    population growth in, 20, 32, 131
    wetlands, 8
Central Valley Project, 7–8, 85, 86–87
Century Freeway, 68
Children, air pollution's effects on, 42
Chinese clam, 114
Chloroform, 107
Chlorpyrifos, 208
Clean Air Act of 1990, 41
Clean Water Act, 95, 96, 108, 119
    Section 404, 123
Clear-cutting of forests, 163–64, 264
Coastal Act, 135–36
Coastal Commission, 117, 123
Coastal Conservancy, 116–17
Coastal Zone Management Act, 123
Coastline waters, *see* Ocean, bays, and
    estuaries
Cogeneration plants, 50, 57–59

Colorado, 25
Concerned Citizens of South Central, 187
Congested road conditions, 53
Conifer forests, 7, 9
Conservation easements, 236
Cooperative management agreements, 236
Cosumnes River, 101
Cosumnes River Preserve, 250
Cottonwoods, 156
Cranston, Alan, 245
Crime, 24, 213, 220–21
Criteria pollutants, 35–36
Crops, *see* Agriculture

Dams, *see* Water projects; *names of specific dams*
Dangermond, Pete, 212–25
Dasmann, Raymond, 16, 17
DBCP (dibromochloropropane), 105, 107, 199–200, 206, 207
Death Valley, 8
DeBonis, Jeff, 160
Def, 209
Delaney Clause, 200
Delta, the, 7, 10, 113–14
    fisheries, 87
    water quality of, 100, 101–103, 107
    water supply affected by sinking of, 82–83, 91
Delta smelt, 113
Demographics, 19–20
    birth rate, 20, 22
    ethnic breakdown, 19–20
    population growth, *see* Population growth
Department of Energy, U.S., 107
Department of Toxic Substances Control (DTSC), 184, 186, 188, 190, 192
Desalinization of water, 89, 91
Desert areas, 6, 242–45, 246
Desert tortoise, 8, 243
Destruction of California, The (Dasmann), 16, 17
Diablo, Mount
Diazinon, 208
Dolphins, 115, 118
Drought, 45
Dwyer, William, 162

Economy:
    growth of the, 128
    population growth's effects on the, 24
EDB, 211
Education, population growth's effects on, 23, 24, 30
Eel River, 98
Endangered species, 102, 113, 114, 227
    future protection of, 238–39

global warming's effects on, 54–55
identification and monitoring of, 234–35
management techniques, 237
Northern spotted owl, 162–63
protective measures, 231–34
techniques for protecting, 235–36
see also Wildlife
Endangered Species Act, 88, 162, 232, 236, 238
Endangered Species Committee, 233
Energy consumption, 51–52
    from automobiles, 52–53
Energy efficiency investments, 59
Energy sources, 48–51
    coal, 49–50
    natural, 49
    nuclear power, 50
    oil, 48–49
    renewables, 50–51
"Environmental Goals and Policy Report," 14
Environmental Protection Agency (EPA), 35, 37, 42, 45, 54, 118–19, 122, 125
    biological diversity and, 228
    drinking water standards, 83, 103, 107
    pesticides and, 199, 201, 202, 203, 204
    toxic wastes and, 183, 184, 185, 188, 190, 191, 192
Environmental Quality Act, 88
Estuaries, *see* Ocean, bays, and estuaries
Ethnic breakdown of California's population, 19–20
Executive Council on Biological Diversity, 234

Farallon Islands, 115
Farmland, 131, 134, 135–36
    acquisition of development rights on, 151
    conservation of, 149–51, 153
    conversion of, 25, 139, 142, 146–48, 153
    new prescriptions for protecting, 151–52
    statistics on, 141–42
    valuation of, 149
    see also Agriculture
Feather River, 101, 256
Federal Aviation Administration, 68
Federal land and water conservation programs, 223–24
Federal Land Policy and Management Act, 244
Federal Railroad Administration, 187
Federal Water Pollution Control Act, 95
Ferries, 67

Fish:
  heavy metals found in, 113
  see also specific types of fish
Fish and Wildlife Service, U.S., 113, 118,
    162, 218, 232, 233
Fisheries, 251, 255
  San Francisco estuary, 111
  water projects' effects on, 87
Folex, 209
Food and Agriculture Department, 100
Food and Drug Administration (FDA), 102,
    118
Food, pesticides in, 205–206
Forests, 154–68, 260–61
  ancient forests, 164–65
  California politics and, 161
  changing view of, 155–56
  clear-cutting of, 163–64, 264
  conclusions, 167–68
  federal government's role, 160–61
  jobs provided by timber industry, 158–
    59
  Northern spotted owl, 155, 162–63
  ozone's effects on, 159
  significance of, 154–55
  socioeconomic changes in forest-
    dependent communities, 166–67
  state regulation of, 159–60
  sustained yield, 165–66
  timber harvesting and, 156–58, 161–68
Forest Service, U.S., 160–61, 162, 165, 166,
    218, 231
Fossil fuels:
  as energy source, 48–50
  global warming from burning, 48
Friant Dam, 85, 87
Friends of Ballona, 117
Friends of the River, 253, 255, 256
Future agenda, *see* Agenda for the future

Garbage, *see* Solid wastes
Garbage collection fees, 175, 180
Gasoline:
  prices, 73
  taxes, 73–74, 78
General Dynamics, 193
Geothermal power, 50, 51
Gill nets, 116
Global warming, 54–62
  agriculture and, 54
  conclusions, 61–62
  endangered and threatened species
    affected by, 54–55
  fossil fuels as energy source and, 48
  impacts of, 54–55
  options for carbon emissions reduction,
    57–61

rationale for action, 55–57
sea level rise due to, 54, 125
smog and, 55
water resources and, 55
Golden trout, 8
Gophers, 8–9
Grand Canyon, 26
Grasses, native, 8–9
Greenberg, Alvin, 94–108
Greenhouse gases, *see* Global warming
Green Index, 1991–1992, 4
Greyhound, 68
Grizzly bear, 8
Groundwater quality, 105–107
  pesticides and, *see* Pesticides
Growth management, *see* Land use policies
    and growth management
Gulf of the Farallon National Marine
    Sanctuary, 115

Habitat conservation plans (HCPs), 236
Hall, Jane V., 33–46
Hazardous and Solid Waste Amendments of
    1984, 186
Hazardous Waste Reduction Award for
    Innovative Technology, 193
Hazardous wastes, *see* Toxic wastes
Health:
  air pollution's effects on, 35–36
  cancer, *see* Cancer
Hewlett-Packard, 188–89, 193
Highways and freeways, 64
  construction of, 10, 13, 66, 67, 68–69
  efforts to reduce congestion with new
    capacity, 70, 71
  user fees, 68
Hydrocarbons, 39, 72
Hydropower, 50

Idaho, 25–26
Illegal residents, 22
Immigration, 20, 22, 29
  limiting, 28, 30, 31
  out-migration, 20
Incinerators, 178–79
Industrial sources of air pollution, 39, 40,
    122
Integrated Waste Management Act, 178–79
Irrigation, 142–43, 264, 265

Jobs:
  availability of, 24
  timber industry, 158–59

Kesterton River and Wildlife Refuge, 101
Klamath River, 98
Kunofsky, Judith, 30

Landfills, 170–72, 178
  hazardous waste disposal at, 185, 186
  surcharges, 180
Landscape, *see* Native California landscape
Land use policies and growth management,
    127–38
  amount and rate of population and
      economic growth, 128
  automobile usage and, 75–76
  Coastal Act as success story, 135–36
  problems posed by growth, 129
  problems with current system, 132–35
  strategies for growth management,
      136–37
  survey of statewide growth patterns,
      129–32
  time for action, 138
  transportation planning, 76
Lange, Leif Erik, 64–79
Leaching Fields: A Nonpoint Threat to
    Groundwater, The, 206
Lead, 35, 36, 39
Least tern, 118
Light-footed clapper rail, 117–18
Lightstone, Ralph, 195–211
Logging, *see* Timber harvesting
Los Angeles, California, 5–6
  air pollution in, 33–34, 41
  "Big Green" environmental measure, 12
  economic growth in, 130
  garbage collection in, 175
  Metro Rail, 69, 77
  Mono Lake Basin diversion, 82, 86
  ozone level in, 41
  population growth in, 22, 32
  support for mass transit, 77
  water supply, 82
  water treatment, 118–19
Los Angeles County:
  discharge of sewage sludge, 119
  population growth in, 20–21, 22, 23, 32,
      128
Los Angeles Department of Water and
    Power, 59, 62
Los Angeles 2000 Committee, 132–33
Luz Solar, 51

Macdonald, Clyde, 80–93
Mad River, 98
Malibu Creek State Park, 250
Marbled murrelets, 110–11
Margolin, Burt, 176
Marin Agricultural Land Trust, 151
Mass transit, 60, 69, 263
  flexible funding policies, 77–78
  gasoline taxes directed toward, 74
  inventory of, 67–68, 69

  public investment in, 66–67
  public support for, 76–77
  safety record of, 67
  see also specific forms of mass transit
Matthews, Jessica, 55
Maxxam Corporation, 157
Meral, Gerald H., 250, 258–69
Methanol, 71
Methidathion, 208
Metropolitan Water District of Southern
    California, 81–82, 84
Mevinphos, 198–99
Mexico, 190
Military and hazardous wastes, 191–92
Mining wastes, 172
Modoc Plateau, 242
Mojave Desert, 242, 245
Mokelumne River, 101
Molinate, 200
Mono Lake, 82, 86, 88
Monterey Bay National Marine Sanctuary,
    116
Morro Bay, 116
Mothers of East L.A., 187
Motor vehicles, *see* Automobiles
Muir, John, 7
Multiple Use and Sustained Yield Act, 160,
    165
Mumma, John, 161

National Academy of Sciences, 55, 56
  water contaminant limits, 98, 99–100,
      101, 103, 104
National Forest Management Act, 160, 162
National Marine Fisheries Service, 232, 233
National parks, *see* Parks and recreation
National Park Service, 244
National Pollutant Discharge Elimination
    System (NPDES), 96
Native California landscape, 241–57
  the desert, 242–45, 246
  oak woodlands, 245–51
  the rivers, 251–57
Native Plant Society, 231
Natural Diversity Data Base, 230, 234, 235
Natural gas, 49, 71
Natural Resources Defense Council (NRDC),
    57, 255
The Nature Conservancy, 223, 235, 250
Nelson, Barry, 109–26
Nevada, 190
New Melones Dam, 85, 87, 253
New River, 103–104
Nisbet, Briggs, 139–53
Nitrogen dioxide, 35
  harmful effects of, 36
  sources of, 39

Nitrogen oxides, 39, 72
Nonpoint sources of water pollution, 87, 108
Norse, Elliott, 156
Northern spotted owl, 155, 162
North Fork Stanislaus project, 253
Nuclear power, 50

Oak trees, 9, 156
Oak woodlands, 25, 245–51
Ocean, bays, and estuaries, 109–26
  Central Coast, 115–17
  future of coastal protection, 126
  greenhouse effect and rise in sea level, 125
  Gulf of the Farallon, 115
  hopeful signs, 125–26
  North Coast, 110–11
  oil spills, 115, 117, 120–22
  planning efforts to protect, 125
  San Francisco Bay, 111–15, 122
  Southern California, 117–20
  wetlands protection, 123
Oceanside, California, 119–20
Off-road vehicles, 244–45
Offshore drilling, 120, 121
Oil, 48–49
Oil spills, 115, 117, 120–22
  sea otter threatened by, 116
Old Salinas River, 99
Open space land, 134
Orange County, economic growth in, 130
Oregon, 25–26
Oroville Dam, 86
O'Shaughnessy Dam, 86
Owen Valley water project, 88
Ozone, 9, 35
  forests affected by, 159
  harmful effects of, 35–37, 145–46
  in Los Angeles, 41
  sources of, 39
  violation of standard for, 34–35, 37–39

Pacific Fishery Management Council, 116
Pacific Gas & Electric, 50, 61–62
Pacific Lumber Company, 157
Pacific yew tree, 229
Palmer, Tim, 3–32, 154–69, 241–57
Paraquat, 201
Parathion, 203, 204, 208, 209
Parking, subsidized, 74–75, 78
Parks and recreation, 212–25
  categories, 217–18
  extent of, 212–13
  fiscal crisis, 213, 220
  future actions needed for, 221–24

population growth and, 213, 219–20
  rising expectations for, 213, 221
  social ills and, 213, 220–21
  summary, 224–25
  survey of usage, 214–17, 219
Particulate (PM$_{10}$), 35, 36, 39, 40
PCBs (polychlorinated biphenyls), 183–84, 186
PCE (perchloroethylene), 107
Peripheral Canal, 83, 84, 86, 88, 92
Personal action plan, 267–69
Pesticide Contamination Prevention Act, 207
Pesticides, 125–26, 152, 195–211
  acute toxicity of, 198–99
  in the air, 208–10
  application methods, 197
  carcinogens, 199, 200, 202, 205, 209
  chronic toxic effects of, 199–201
  extensive use of, in California, 195–96
  in food, 205–206
  in the home, 210
  systemic, 197–98
  testing of, data gaps in, 201–202
  toxicity of, 197, 198–99
  transitions away from, 210–11
  in water, 94, 95, 100–101, 103, 118, 206–208
  in the workplace, 202–205
"Pesticide Use Report," 100
Pillsbury, Dr. Norman, 248–49
Pinnipeds, 115
Planning and Conservation League, 29, 223, 250
Policy Implications of Greenhouse Warming, 55
Population growth, 4–5, 14, 19–32, 152, 260, 261–62
  areas of fastest, 20–21
  automobile use and, 24–25, 39, 64–65
  through births, 20
  economic limits on, 28
  effects of unlimited, 23–26
  growth management, 28–32
  through immigration, 20, 30
  limiting, 28–32
  parks and recreation and, 213, 219–20
  population distribution, 5, 7
  projected, 21–22
  rate of, 19, 27–28, 59, 128
  wildlife threatened by, 227
Population stabilization, 28–32
Porpoises, 115
Porter-Cologne Water Quality Control Act, 95, 96
Procurement policy and recycling, 181
Propargate, 203
Proposition 65, 189
Proposition 117, 250

Public lands, 6
Public transit, *see* Mass transit

Rail service, 67–68, 69, 77
  public support for, 76
Rand Corporation, 48
Reclamation of water resources, 89, 91
Recreation, *see* Parks and recreation
Recycling, 170, 175–81, 266–67
  Bottle Bill, 175–78
  challenges of the 1990s, 179–81
  content standards, 181
  environmental benefits of, 172, 173
  Integrated Waste Management Act, 178–79
  percentage of waste stream handled by, 179
  of toxic wastes, 191
Red Bluff Diversion Dam, 87
Redwood National Park, 110
Redwoods, 7, 8, 156, 164
Regional water quality control boards
  (RWQCBs), 95, 107
Reinhardt, Richard, 13–14
Renewable energy sources, 50–51
Resource Agency, 224
Resource Conservation and Recovery Act
  (RCRA), 184
Resources Planning Act, 160
Restoration ecology, 237
Richmond, California, 187
Right-to-know laws, 189
Riparian habitat, 25, 255–56
Rivers, 251–57
  protection of, 253–57
  see also individual rivers
Riverside County, population growth in, 20, 128
Rogers Crossing Dam, 256
Rominger, Richard, 152–53
Russian River, 98–99

Sacramento, California:
  population growth in, 22
  rail service, 69, 77
Sacramento County, population growth in, 131
Sacramento Municipal Utility District, 59
Sacramento River, 100, 113–14, 208, 255, 256
Safe Drinking Water and Toxics
  Enforcement Act, 96, 108, 189
Salinas River, 99–100
Salmon, 9, 13, 87, 102, 111, 112, 255
Salt accumulation in soil and water, 84, 91, 144–45
Salt marsh harvest mouse, 113

San Bernardino County, population growth
  in, 20, 128
San Diego, California, 119
  population growth in, 131
  rail service, 69, 77
San Diego Association of Governments, 24
San Diego Bay, 119
San Diego County, 187
  population growth in, 128, 130–31
San Francisco Bay, 6, 111–15, 122
San Francisco Bay Area, 6, 187
  air pollution in, 44
  automobile travel in, 25
  land use and growth management in, 130
  population growth in, 20, 22, 25, 32
San Francisco Bay Conservation and
  Development Commission (BCDC),
  123, 136
San Francisco Bay Guardian, 61
San Francisco Chronicle, 31
San Joaquin River, 113–14, 255, 256
  water quality of, 95
San Joaquin Valley:
  air pollution in, 44
  groundwater overdraft problem in, 24,
  91–92
  population growth in, 44
  salt accumulation in soil and water of, 84,
  91, 145
San Jose, California rail service, 77
San Luis Obispo County, population growth
  in, 131
Santa Monica Bay, 122
Savannah sparrow, 118
Seabirds, 115
Seal Beach National Wildlife Refuge, 118
Sea level rise from global warming, 54, 125
Sea otter, 115–16
Sequoia National Forest, 164
Shad, 102
Shasta, Mount, 7
Shasta Dam, 85, 87
Sher, Bryon, 178
Shireman, William K., 170–81
Sierra Club, 133
Sierra Nevada, 6, 7, 241
  acid levels of surface waters in, 36
  population growth in foothills of, 20
Sinkyone Wilderness State Park, 110
Smith, Adam, 133–34
Smith, Sally W., 226–40
Smith River, 98
Smog, 34, 52
  global warming and, 55
Social equity, 11–13
  population growth and, 28
Soil erosion, 145

Solar power, 50, 51, 263
Solid wastes, 170–81, 266–67
  creation of original materials, implications
    of, 172, 173
  incineration of, 178–79
  landfill disposal of, 170–72, 178
  legislation, 175–79
  reasons for generation of so much, 174–
    75
  recycling of, *see* Recycling
  source reduction of, 179–81
  statistics, 170
  waste stream, 173–74
Southern California Edison, 62
Sparks, Jody, 182–94
Stanislaus River, 101
State Board of Forestry, 162
State Food and Agriculture Department,
    207, 208, 209
State Forest Practices Act, 159–60
State Water Project, 85–86, 87
State Water Resources Control Board
    (SWRCB), 95, 96, 102, 103, 107,
    108, 122, 184
Steelhead, 111, 255
Striped bass, 87, 88, 102, 111, 112, 114
Strong, Ginger, 251
Subsidized water, 10, 12–13
Suburban sprawl, land use policies
    encouraging, 75–76
Suisun song sparrow, 114
Sulfur dioxide, 35, 36, 39
Superfund Amendments and
    Reauthorization Act, 189
Superfund program, 185
Supreme Court, U.S., 81–82
Surface water quality, 97–104
Surfrider Foundation, 111
Sustainability, 264–67
Sustained yield forest policy, 165–66
Sybert, Richard, 29, 128

Tahoe, Lake, 7
  air pollution's effects on, 37
  water quality, 100
Tahoe Regional Planning Agency, 136
Talbot Marsh, 117
Taxes on gasoline, 73–74, 78
Telone, 209
Through-Delta Canal, 86, 88, 92
Timber harvesting, 156–58, 161–68
Time, 30, 31
Tourism, 263
Toxic wastes, 182–94
  accidental spills of, 186–87
  disposal of, 185–86
  exemptions to regulations, 191–92

exportation of, 189–90
future handling of, 192–94
generation of, 183–84
military exemption from regulations,
    191–92
minimization of, 187–88
regulation of, 184–85
right-to-know laws, 189
waste reduction efforts, 188–89
at Westminster Tract, 182–83
Trains, electric, 66, 67, 71, 263
Transportation, 64–79
  by automobile, *see* Automobiles
  bicycling, 69, 76
  as environmental issue, 65–66
  flexible funding policies, 77–78
  inventory of, 67–68
  land use policies and, 75–76
  mass transit, *see* Mass transit
  public investment policy, 66
  water quality and, 122
Trihalomethanes (THMs), 83
Trinity Dam, 87
Truck weight fees, 68
Tuolumne River, 101

Unemployment, 24
United Farm Workers Union, 206
U.S. Navy, 193
University of California at Santa Barbara,
    235
Urban problems, agenda for, 260, 262–63
Utah, 26

Vaqueros, Los (reservoir), 91
Ventura County, population growth in,
    131

Warm Springs Dam, 253
Washington, 25–26
Waterfowl, 8, 9, 102, 111
Water pollution, 5
Water projects, 9, 10, 253
  environmental impact of, 86–87
  fisheries affected by, 87
  forces creating policy changes, 87–88
  in the future, 91
  see also individual projects
Water quality, 83–84, 93, 94–108
  of Central Coast waters, 99–100
  of Central Valley waters, 100–101
  the future, 107–108
  groundwater, 105–107
  of Lake Tahoe, 100
  of North Coast waters, 98–99
  pesticides and, 94, 95, 100–101, 103,
    118, 206–208

Water quality (*continued*)
  public health and groundwater quality,
    106–107
  regulation of, 95–97, 107
  of Sacramento-San Joaquin Delta, 101–
    103
  of Southern California waters, 103–104
  of surface water, 97–104
  transportation industry and, 122
Water resources, 80–92
  agricultural usage, 81, 84–85, 90, 142–
    44, 264–65
  cheapness of, 80
  conclusion, 92
  conservation programs, 89, 90, 91
  current water supply problems, 81–84
  current water use, 81
  desalinization programs, 89, 91
  federal subsidies for agricultural water
    projects, 85
  forces creating policy changes, 87–88
  the future, 90–92
  global warming and, 55
  history of water policy, 84–86
  politics affecting, 89
  population growth and, 25, 31
  reclamation programs, 89, 91
  water projects, *see* Water projects
  water transfers, 90, 91
Water transfers, 90, 91
Welfare system, 24, 30
West County Toxics Coalition, 187

Western gull, 115
Westminster Tract, toxic wastes at, 182–
  83
Wetlands, 7, 9, 25
  Central Valley, 8
  protection of, 123
  San Francisco estuary, 111, 112
  Southern California, 117–18
Whales, 115
Wheeler, Douglas, 29
Whitney, Mount, 7–8
Wildlife, 226–39, 261, 265–66
  biological diversity, 226, 228–31
  definitions, 228
  endangered species, *see* Endangered
    species
  future protection of, 238–39
  population growth and threats to, 227
  protective measures, 231–34
  reasons to care about biological diversity,
    228–31
Williamson Act (California Land
  Conservation Act), 149, 150–51
Wilson, Pete, 29, 30, 161
Wind power, 50
Worker exposure to pesticides, 202–205

Yolo Land Conservation Trust, 153
Yosemite National Park, air pollution's
  effects on, 36–37
Yosemite Valley, 86, 250
  groundwater, 105

Also Available from Island Press

Balancing on the Brink of Extinction: The Endangered Species Act and Lessons for the Future
Edited by Kathryn A. Kohm

Better Trout Habitat: A Guide to Stream Restoration and Management
By Christopher J. Hunter

Beyond 40 Percent: Record-Setting Recycling and Composting Programs
By The Institute for Local Self-Reliance

Coastal Alert: Ecosystems, Energy, and Offshore Oil Drilling
By Dwight Holing

The Complete Guide to Environmental Careers
By The CEIP Fund

Crossing the Next Meridian: Land, Water, and the Future of the West
By Charles F. Wilkinson

Death in the Marsh
By Tom Harris

The Energy-Environment Connection
Edited by Jack M. Hollander

Farming in Nature's Image
By Judith Soule and Jon Piper

Ghost Bears: Exploring the Biodiversity Crisis
By R. Edward Grumbine

The Global Citizen
By Donella Meadows

Green at Work: Making Your Business Career Work for the Environment
By Susan Cohn

Healthy Homes, Healthy Kids
By Joyce Schoemaker and Charity Vitale

Holistic Resource Management
By Allan Savory

The Island Press Bibliography of Environmental Literature
By The Yale School of Forestry and Environmental Literature

Last Animals at the Zoo: How Mass Extinction Can Be Stopped
By Colin Tudge

Learning to Listen to the Land
Edited by Bill Willers

Lessons from Nature: Learning to Live Sustainably on the Earth
By Daniel D. Chiras

The Living Ocean: Understanding and Protecting Marine Biodiversity
By Boyce Thorne-Miller and John G. Catena

Making Things Happen
By Joan Wolfe

Media and the Environment
Edited by Craig LeMay and Everette E. Dennis

Nature Tourism: Managing for the Environment
Edited by Tensie Whelan

The New York Environment Book
By Eric A. Goldstein and Mark A. Izeman

Our Country, The Planet: Forging a Partnership for Survival
By Shridath Ramphal

Overtapped Oasis: Reform or Revolution for Western Water
By Marc Reisner and Sarah Bates

Population, Technology, and Lifestyle: The Transition to Sustainability
Edited by Robert Goodland, Herman E. Daly, and Salah El Serafy

Rain Forest in Your Kitchen: The Hidden Connection Between Extinction and Your Supermarket
By Martin Teitel

Rivers at Risk: The Concerned Citizen's Guide to Hydropower
By John D. Echeverria, Pope Barrow, and Richard Roos-Collins

The Snake River: Window to the West
By Tim Palmer

The Sierra Nevada: A Mountain Journey
By Tim Palmer

The Wild and Scenic Rivers of America
By Tim Palmer

Taking Out the Trash: A No-Nonsense Guide to Recycling
By Jennifer Carless

Turning the Tide: Saving the Chesapeake Bay
By Tom Horton and William M. Eichbaum

Visions upon the Land: Man and Nature on the Western Range
By Karl Hess, Jr.

For a complete catalog of Island Press publications, please write:
Island Press, Box 7, Covelo, CA 95428, or call: 1-800-828-1302.

Island Press Board of Directors